John De Witt

Sermons on the Christian Life

John De Witt

Sermons on the Christian Life

ISBN/EAN: 9783337160715

Printed in Europe, USA, Canada, Australia, Japan

Cover: Foto ©Lupo / pixelio.de

More available books at **www.hansebooks.com**

SERMONS

ON THE

CHRISTIAN LIFE

BY

JOHN DE WITT, D.D

PROFESSOR OF CHURCH HISTORY, LANE THEOLOGICAL
SEMINARY

NEW YORK
CHARLES SCRIBNER'S SONS
1885

PREFACE.

The following sermons were written and preached when the author was a Pastor. They are not discussions of doctrine; they are sermons on various aspects and elements of human life. These are treated in their relations to Christianity. But the doctrines of Christianity, though not expounded, are implied. They underlie and support each discourse.

As the sermons were prepared, not for publication, but for delivery before the writer's congregation, their style and language often approach those of familiar conversation. In addressing his parishioners, a preacher feels that he is at liberty to indulge in abrupt turns of speech, in sentences rhetorically incomplete and in repetitions, which, in an essay, would be out of place. The form of the sermon is determined by the relations of the preacher to his audience, quite as much as it is by his theme.

LANE THEOLOGICAL SEMINARY.

CONTENTS.

PAGE.

I. MAN'S DANGER IN SUDDEN AND DISAPPOINTING TRANSITIONS 3

And when they had lifted up their eyes, they saw no man, save Jesus only.—MATTHEW xvii, 8.

II. THE PERSISTENCE OF THE CHRISTIAN CHARACTER 17

All the saints salute you, chiefly they that are of Cæsar's household.—PHILIPPIANS iv, 22.

III. THE COMPLETION OF MAN IN CHRIST . . . 31

And ye are complete in Him, which is the head of all principality and power.—COLOSSIANS ii, 10.

IV. THE UNIVERSALITY OF THE CHRISTIAN BENEVOLENCE 48

And let us not be weary in well-doing; for in due season, we shall reap, if we faint not. As we have therefore opportunity, let us do good unto all men. —GALATIANS vi, 9, 10.

V. THE CHRISTIAN CASUISTRY 62

I, therefore, the prisoner of the Lord, beseech you that ye walk worthy of the vocation wherewith ye are called.—EPHESIANS iv, 1.

		PAGE.
VI.	THE GAIN OF THE CHRISTIAN IN CHRIST'S DEPARTURE	83

Nevertheless, I tell you the truth; it is expedient for you, that I go away.—JOHN xvi, 7.

| VII. | THE SANCTIFICATION OF THE SECULAR LIFE. | 101 |

Whether therefore ye eat, or drink, or whatsoever ye do, do all to the glory of God.—I. CORINTHIANS x, 31.

| VIII. | THE GOSPEL A HOPE | 117 |

Blessed be the God and Father of our Lord Jesus Christ, which, according to his abundant mercy, hath begotten us again unto a lively hope, by the resurrection of Jesus Christ from the dead, to an inheritance incorruptible, and undefiled, and that fadeth not away, reserved in heaven for you, who are kept by the power of God, through faith unto salvation, ready to be revealed in the last time.—I. Peter i, 3, 4, 5.

| IX. | THE BURDEN OF THE BODY | 131 |

For we that are in this tabernacle do groan, being burdened.—II. CORINTHIANS v, 4.

| X. | THE RELATIONS OF RELIGION AND BUSINESS. | 150 |

Not slothful in business; fervent in spirit; serving the Lord.—ROMANS xii, 11.

| XI. | THE VALUE OF A RELIGIOUS ATMOSPHERE. | 166 |

And Saul went thither to Naioth in Ramah; and the spirit of the Lord was on him also, and he went on, and prophesied, until he came to Naioth in Ramah.—I. SAMUEL xix, 23.

| XII. | THE COST OF DISCIPLESHIP | 182 |

For which of you, intending to build a tower, sitteth not down first, and counteth the cost, whether he have sufficient to finish it? Lest haply, after he hath laid the foundation, and is not able to finish it, all that behold it begin to mock him, saying, This man began to build, and was not able to finish.—LUKE xiv, 28, 29, 30.

XIII. THE CHRISTIAN CONTENTMENT . . . 199

I have learned in whatsoever state I am, therewith to be content. I know both how to be abased and how to abound; everywhere and in all things I am instructed both to be full and to be hungry, both to abound and to suffer need. I can do all things through Christ, which strengtheneth me.—PHILIPPIANS iv, 11, 12, 13.

XIV. THE EARTHLY LIFE VIEWED FROM HEAVEN 215

Thy prayers and thine alms are come up for a memorial before God.—ACTS x, 4.

XV. THE HEAVENLY LIFE VIEWED FROM EARTH 230

Giving thanks unto the Father, which hath made us meet to be partakers of the inheritance of the saints in light.—COLOSSIANS i, 12.

XVI. THE TRANSFORMATION OF THE OUTWARD LIFE 244

Be ye transformed by the renewing of your mind.—ROMANS xii, 2.

XVII. THE CHRISTIAN NAME 259

And the disciples were called Christians, first at Antioch.—ACTS xi, 26.

XVIII. CHRISTIANITY A RELIGION OF JOY . . 275

These things have I spoken unto you, that my joy might remain in you and that your joy might be full.—JOHN xv, 11.

XIX. KEEPING IN THE LOVE OF GOD . . . 289

But ye, beloved, building up yourselves on your most holy faith, praying in the Holy Ghost, keep yourselves in the love of God, looking for the mercy of our Lord Jesus Christ unto eternal life.—Jude, 20, 21.

XX. THE LIGHT GRANTED IN DARKNESS . . . 307

But all the children of Israel had light in their dwellings.—Exodus x, 23.

XXI. PRAYING THE MORE BECAUSE DOUBTING. 321

And the multitude rebuked them that they should hold their peace; but they cried the more, saying, Have mercy on us, O Lord, thou son of David.—Matthew xx, 31.

XXII. CASTING ANXIETY ON GOD 336

Casting all your care upon Him; for He careth for you.—I. Peter v, 7.

XXIII. THE FOUNDATION AND THE BUILDING . 350

For other foundation can no man lay than that is laid, which is Jesus Christ. Now if any man build upon this foundation gold, silver, precious stones, wood, hay, stubble; every man's work shall be made manifest: for the day shall declare it, because it shall be revealed by fire; and the fire shall try every man's work of what sort it is. If any man's work abide which he hath built thereupon, he shall receive a reward. If any man's work shall be burned, he shall suffer loss: but he himself shall be saved; yet so as by fire.—I. Corinthians iii, 11-15.

XXIV. THE REWARD OF LOVE 364

She hath done what she could.
—Mark xiv, 8.

XXV. THE JUDGMENT OF THE SPIRITUAL MAN . 380

But he that is spiritual judgeth all things.— I. Corinthians ii, 15.

		PAGE.
XXVI.	THE RELATIONS OF HOPE AND PURITY	393

And every man that hath this hope in him purifieth himself even as he is pure.
—I. JOHN iii, 3.

XXVII.	CHRIST A GIFT, NOT A DEBT	405

Thanks be unto God for his unspeakable gift.—II. CORINTHIANS ix, 15.

SERMONS ON THE CHRISTIAN LIFE.

I.
MAN'S DANGER IN SUDDEN AND DISAPPOINTING TRANSITIONS.

And when they had lifted up their eyes, they saw no man, save Jesus only.—MATTHEW xvii, 8.

We shall not discern the meaning of the Transfiguration, unless we view it, not merely as an event in the life of Christ, but as an experience, also, of the apostles who beheld it. Not for him chiefly, but for them, was the Transfiguration ordained. He was never without a sense of the presence and approval of God. His habitual communion with his Father sustained Him throughout his ministry. Not for Him then, but for his weak and sinful disciples, did the heavens open, and celestial light fall upon the Son of Man, and Moses and Elias talk of the decease which He should accomplish, and the Father again acknowledge his well-beloved Son.

I shall not attempt to describe the influence which the entire experience exerted on the three apostles. I confine myself to a single point of time. Let us fix our attention upon them just at the moment, when, lifting up their eyes, "they saw no man." They had been raised to heaven. Suddenly, they found themselves on the earth. Instead of Moses and Elias, they saw only the hard outline of the mountain. Instead of the voice of God, they heard only earthly sounds that rose from the plain below. In this sudden and disappointing transition, in this violent exchange of the contemplation of celestial glories, for the contemplation of their prosaic life of labor and sacrifice, there was great danger to character. It would not have been strange, had their faith in Christ been destroyed; or, escaping this, had the vision unfitted them for the labors of discipleship. From each of these dangers, they were released only by the sight of their Lord after the fading of the vision. Beholding Him, they were assured of the reality of the Transfiguration; and they were prepared for the return to their earthly work. Here, then, behold their danger and their safety! "And when they had lifted up their eyes, they saw no man, save Jesus only."

The subject, which the text thus suggests, is one of the most important that can engage our attention;—*the dangers arising from sudden and disappointing transitions in life: and our only safety when character is menaced by them.*—The experience of the apostles at this point both illustrates and exemplifies a common experience of us all. Their danger was just what ours is, and the source of their safety then is the source of our safety now.

I. That you may see how practical our subject is, I ask you to notice first, *that such transition is a frequent human experience.* One of the most commonplace of remarks is the remark, that change is characteristic of the world and of human life. Nothing seems stable. The solid earth is moving through space with almost incredible speed, and the form of its surface is forever changing. The histories of no two days are precisely similar. Every hour brings something new, and almost every hour something unsuspected. Any one of a hundred events may occur at any moment, which, if it shall occur, will utterly destroy our present happiness. We can not predict the time of its occurrence; and often, even could we predict it, we could neither avert it, nor prepare ourselves for its shock. It is not too much to say, that every change, which shall exert a disastrous influence on our happiness, will occur violently, like the dissipation of the celestial vision to the entranced apostles. We live in the enjoyment of some object; when, suddenly, it is removed, and the whole world is dark to us. From youth to latest age, and in every relation of life, we are the prey of these violent mutations.

There comes, for example, a time in the life of every ingenuous youth, when, by a single act or event, the spell of youth is dissipated; and the world in all its hardness stands before the opened eyes of manhood. There are cases, no doubt, in which this disenchantment is gradual and expected; but oftener, perhaps, it is violent and unheralded. To a family, whose members are living in the enjoyment of each other, comes the hand of God, sundering those who compose it. The father falls suddenly in death, and the boy sees no one between him and the world. Life, which before seemed one long play, now reveals itself as a severe and long continued task, demanding labor and courage and vigilance. By as much as the world was transfigured in the light of his father's household life, by so much is he unprepared for the world in which he is now called to fight his way alone. The transition from the home life of youth—where every thing is transformed in the light of a father's or a mother's love, where the only prophecy of the world's friendliness is a brother's or a sister's affection, where rough paths are made smooth, and hard tasks made easy—the transition, I say, from such a life to the life of toil and combat, is often as sudden and disappointing as that in the minds of the apostles, when, lifting up their eyes, they saw no man. And the point of time at which the vision vanishes is one of great and special peril.

Or think of another experience more nearly universal;—the experience of bereavement. We are never prepared for it. However frequently and distinctly we may have been warned, the departure of one whom we have loved is at the last sudden and violent. We bear ourselves up until the latest moment. We summon all our powers to aid us in holding by the illusive hopes we cherish, but dare not utter for their wildness. We take refuge in our imagination. We compose ourselves to dream of what might be, if the destroyer's hand could be averted; when, suddenly, our reverie is broken by the return to God of the spirit that had transfigured our lives, and our whole being is shocked by the violence of the experience. Who, that has been subjected to such a trial, does not know, how hard it is to realize the approach of Death, until suddenly and rudely his presence is made known? Such a moment is one of great spiritual peril, and may easily become the crisis which shall determine spiritual destiny.

Or take another case; and all of us know how common such cases are. Year after year a man gives himself thoroughly to business. Every thing contributes to his success. Whatever he touches turns to gold. His success transfigures the world. He rejoices that he lives, and, like Peter on the mount, would make a tabernacle to abide here indefinitely. But suddenly, the storm of financial disaster darkens his firmament and bursts upon him unprepared. You, who have known men so overtaken, know, too well for me to describe it, what danger to character, to faith, to hope, to love of God and man, impends over the soul in such an hour. The transfiguration is passed; and he lifts up his eyes like the apostles, in darkness and the chill of night, on the hard and rocky mountain.

That I may not fail to appeal to the experience of all before me, I turn to the religious life. There are many, whose consciousness of the possibility of their spiritual destruction slumbers for years. For the spiritual world, because invisible, is by most men thought of as a distant, and, to them, largely an unrelated world. And so it is, that many live as though this world were all; as though God had not asserted that we shall see Him face to face; as though life and immortality had not been brought to light in the gospel of his Son. But, suddenly, a sermon, the voice of a friend, some one or other feeble human instrument is mighty with divine power, and seems, as to such a man it is indeed, the voice of God. He awakes to the reality of a spiritual world, as near to him as the Omnipresent God; eternal in its relations; and far more commanding in its behests than even the present world before appeared to him. The earth, which an hour ago was magnified and transfigured, now shrinks to its true proportions and loses all its splendor. He is aroused and convicted. And though it is true, that such arousal is a prerequisite to his redemption; it is also true, that because of the violence of the arousal, his soul is in great danger; and not salvation only, but destruction, is at hand. It was when Judas was thus aroused, that he went out from the presence of the priests and hanged himself.

Let me refer to but one other example. And here I address professing Christians. There are those in the Church of Christ, whose Christianity expends itself in enraptured contemplation of the spiritual privileges, which God has conferred on them through his Son. This is no uncommon perversion of religion. Nor is the perversion unnatural. It is one which the pulpit has at times promoted. It has never been absent from the Church. On the mount of Transfiguration itself, the apostle Peter, overjoyed before the glorified Christ and the vision of prophets, cried: "Lord, it is good to abide here;" *not knowing what he said.* Like him, there are men and women to-day, disposed to revel in religious joys. The glory, which they discern on the mount of spiritual privilege, hides the wretchedness of the world below them. But suddenly the vision fades. And, just as the apostles were made to see and hear once more the world beneath them, so these are made to hear their fellows' cry for help;—a cry calling them from religious enjoyment to service and sacrifice. I need not stop to tell you, with how severe a strain on the distinctively religious feelings, this summons must be attended; or how perilous the strain may be to religious faith itself. I must believe, that many a man has first learned to doubt the reality of all communion with God; when called to leave the mount on which the Lord displays his glory, and to engage in work and burden-bearing for his fellow men.

II. I gather these examples of sudden and disappointing transition, from widely differing circumstances; that you may the better see, that I am speaking of no strange experience. In attempting, therefore, to describe the *spiritual perils* of the experience—which I now proceed to do,—I shall be referring to evils, from whose menace no one of us is exempt.

There are two of these perils. Both do not attack the same person. But if one's temperament is such that he escapes the first, he will not escape the second.

The first, that I mention, is *the danger of skepticism:* using that term in a wider sense, than the technical sense in which we so often employ it. These sudden disenchantments are often followed by a denial of God's love, or of human happiness, or of the possibility of human goodness. Man, when rudely awakened from a long dream of perpetual bliss, is prone to doubt all goodness and happiness. Had Christ vanished with Moses and Elias, who does not know, that Peter, at least, would have become at once, skeptical of his Lord's Messianic claims; and would have become at last, a bitter and hopeless Sadducee?

To make my meaning clear, let me refer briefly to two of the illustrations already used. I will take the case of the boy, around whom have been thrown all the safeguards of a Christian home. Goodness and truth are embodied in his father, as he beholds him. Quite naturally, he looks upon his father, as a representative of the men whom he will meet in the world. Suddenly, he is thrown into it; and this vision of his young life is destroyed. What is the danger that besets him, but that he will become utterly skeptical of all manly honor and human goodness? I am sure, that young men are often dwarfed and embittered by this very process. When a man has thus become skeptical of human goodness, he has moved no slight distance from the point to which he must return, if he is ever to know what growth into the stature of the perfect man means. Believe me, friends, you do well to be anxious, as you think of this transition, which, one day, must be the lot of those whom God has given you. There is a point in every man's life, at which his greatest peril attacks him. And I know no peril, at once more insidious and more terrible, than this peril of a skepticism of the possibility of lofty character, which so often encounters one as he stands on the threshold of manhood.

Let us turn to another case. How many events within the past three years,* have made us feel the truth of the words of Israel's wise king: "Riches certainly make to themselves wings, they fly away as an eagle toward heaven!" Every one, experiencing this violent sweep from affluence to comparative want, is in great danger. No one, who has observed the influence of such a transition on personal character, can have failed to notice the strong tendency to this skepticism both of divine and of human goodness of which I have spoken. As their wealth is swept away, men are prone to grow unbelieving, uncharitable, and bitter. Their first impulse is to return, for adversity, disbelief and cynical contempt and scorn. And so spring up the fearful brood of spiritual vices—envy, malice, and all uncharitableness—which have destroyed how many souls, we shall learn only at the consummation of all things.

Did time permit, I could go through the whole catalogue of these violent disenchantments: and show how mighty in each case is the temptation to give one's self up to this terrible unbelief: than which,

---

* Preached, Central Church, Boston, 1874. In 1871 occurred the Chicago fire; in 1872 the Boston fire; in 1873 the financial panic.

it is not possible to conceive a more powerful enemy of whatever of the godlike remains in man. I wish that I knew the words, best suited to create a profound conviction of the peril of this evil. I fear that many regard the evil as for the most part imaginary. For we are so constituted, as to be more easily excited by the danger of palpable physical sins, than by the danger of those spiritual evils, which attack character directly. But if there is one truth, that the great Teacher taught distinctly; it is the truth, that the peril from these inner vices is greater, and more to be dreaded, than slavery to physical passions. For the publicans and the sinners, there was more hope, in Christ's view, than for those, who were blinded, by any cause, to the possibility of a lofty spiritual life. There may be little need of declaiming, from the pulpit, against open and flagrant crimes, which society, for its protection, denounces in its statute-books. But here is a peril of a far greater evil, which human laws can not mention: and yet a peril from which we can never be free, while in this world of disappointing change:—the peril of losing our spiritual life through unbelief in the divine love or human holiness. Again and again it happens, that the world is transfigured to our vision, and seems to glow with celestial radiance; and we could live forever rejoicing in its glory. But, suddenly, we lift up our eyes, and see only that the vision has faded. Then comes the terrible temptation to unbelief in all happiness and goodness alike; to doubt the love of the Father; to deny his Son; to live without God and without hope in the world; and so to wreck all hope of higher lives than those we live. I tremble for myself, I tremble for all of us, when I think of the many methods, in which this temptation assails us. For I see in our yielding to it, the beginning of that awful end, which the Bible calls the second death.

There are those, undoubtedly, whom this evil does not seriously threaten. But if they escape it, they are menaced by another; less terrible, indeed, at first sight; but not less fatal, when unsuccessfully resisted, to the development of lofty spiritual character. This is the danger of *despair*. To understand this second peril, let us turn to the narrative again. Suppose that the Lord had faded from their view with Moses and Elias. Peter would have gone down into the world, believing that Jesus had deceived him. He would have turned back to Judaism, hardened in heart and a Sadducee in faith. But on John, it seems to me, the effect would have been different. The beloved disciple would have become no skeptic; but, losing Christ, he would have been in despair; and the remainder of his life would have been lost in useless retrospect. He would have lived forever in the past. The blessing, which he enjoyed on the mount, would have unfitted him for a life of labor among men. And, thus, he becomes an illustration of the other peril, attendant on these sudden and violent transitions. If one's faith is so deeply rooted, that they do not harden his heart and destroy his faith in goodness and in God, they imperil hope; they tend to unfit the soul for activity; to compel a life of musing on the past, and of discouragement for the future. Have we not seen men and women, who, though not embittered by a sudden visitation of God, have still been undone by it; have lost all hope, all spiritual ambition, and have given over all struggle after better things, in despair? God has come into a household and taken from a mother's arms a little one whose presence had transfigured her life. That child had made the world more beautiful and life more blessed. But suddenly God called it to himself. Do I describe an unusual case when I say, that though the affliction has not embittered her, or made her skeptical, the light of her life has gone, and she lives henceforth in the past alone. She is fitted for no service; she is a burden to herself; she finds no joy in relief of others; she strives no longer after a higher life. All is gone, in the sudden and downward sweep from happiness to grief which God appointed.

But I will not add examples. The subject is one of which every day and every condition of life is full of illustration. My one endeavor has been to place clearly before you the dangers to character in these violent but frequent changes. Believe me, when I say again, that whichever danger attacks you, it is a peril threatening every thing that is best in you. Because it is distinctively a spiritual peril, and so not easily described, it is not less to be feared. Rather, on this account, you ought to be the more vigilant. The evil, whose danger besets you in the circumstances I have described, is subtle, and therefore deceitful. It is to be dreaded the more, because it imperils, not the body directly, but that which is of infinitely higher value, the immortal spirit.

III. And thus we are brought, finally to consider, *the soul's safety in the midst of these dangers.* "And when they had lifted up their eyes, they saw no man, *save Jesus only.*"

The danger, which for an instant beset Peter, was that he would become skeptical; and would go down from the mountain to the world, hardened and unbelieving; thinking the Messiahship of his Lord a delusion. What saved him; but that the Christ, who was the central figure in the celestial vision, remained when the vision had passed? Moses and Elias vanished. The light of heaven faded. The voice of the Father was no longer heard. *But the Lord remained.* And, the Lord remaining, the new kingdom of God was, thenceforth, to the apostle a reality. With the Lord remaining, it was possible even for Peter to go down from the mount of glory to the hard, dull life of labor in the world below. John, too, having the Lord with him, did not live thereafter simply in regretful recollection of the heavenly vision; but, strengthened by the glory he had beheld, engaged with new ardor in the work of his Lord's disciple.

And so, friends, will it be with us. There must be changes in our several lives. In the world we shall have tribulation. To-day all may be bright in our several households. To-morrow all may be darkness. As you view it now, the world may be so transfigured, that it seems cruel that God has appointed all men to die. But to-morrow, the world may be so full of gloom, that it will appear cruel, that God does not send death as a relief to your soul. We place our affections upon an object, and, in our enjoyment of it, the world becomes almost heaven. Then comes the hand of the hidden God and takes it from us. We lift up our eyes: and lo! our night has come. What do we need, but One, who will be central in the vision, while the world is radiant with celestial light; and who will abide still, when, lifting up our eyes, we can discern only that the light has gone? This is man's only safety. The Lord was the central personage in this wondrous vision on the mountain. And the same Lord remained to the disciples when the light was withdrawn, and Moses and Elias were caught up into heaven.

Behold, then, the only security for the immortal spirit. In this fickle, changing, disappointing life, in which we are ever the victims of new illusions; in which grief always follows fast after joy; and prosperity and adversity alternate as swiftly almost as sunshine and rain on an April day; in this life, in which all objects are now bathed and transfigured in celestial light, and are now enshrouded with unearthly gloom;—our hearts demand One, who will worthily call forth our supreme devotion; and who will remain the same amid all alternations. There must be a divine object of faith, when human objects of confidence have been shaken: else faith will die. The spirit must possess an all-including and eternal hope, that will flourish when special and temporal hopes have decayed: else hope will die. An object of supreme love must remain to man, when objects of lower affection have been wrested from him by death: else love will die. And in the death of faith and hope and love is involved the spiritual destruction of man.

Therefore, as announcing the complete provision, which God has made for your eternal safety, do I proclaim Jesus Christ: the same yesterday, to-day, and forever: abiding amid all losses, and unchanging amid all changes. The joy that is in Christ, is the only joy which time and disaster neither destroy nor impair. The divine Friend alone is present with power to the trusting soul, when earthly friends have vanished from our sight; as Moses and Elias vanished from the sight of the apostles. Wealth and honor and power,—all the positions and possessions for which men strive, because they have the power to transfigure the world,—who does not know, how easily and suddenly they escape us, like the vision on the mountain, and leave us in the darkness of skepticism or despair?

Your peril is imminent. Its sources are legion. It is a peril of destruction. We call you, therefore, to look to Him, and live in Him, and make Him central in every vision of joy or faith or hope, who will abide, when the vision shall have passed away. This is the meaning of faith in Christ. Let us learn its divine power by its exercise. Let the life, that we live in the flesh, be lived by the faith of the Son of God. Let every power be given to Him, who is the source of all power. Let every blessing be associated with Him, in whom all blessings meet and from whom all flow. These blessings will come like heavenly visitors. Like them, also, they will often vanish suddenly from our sight; and leave us in darkness, and desolate. And yet not desolate. For when these have gone, He who is all in all will still abide. Lifting up our eyes, if we see Him only, we shall still see Him. And beholding Him, in whom are all the riches of the love of God, we shall neither disbelieve nor be dismayed.

II.
THE PERSISTENCE OF THE CHRISTIAN CHARACTER

All the saints salute you, chiefly they that are of Cæsar's household.—PHILIPPIANS iv, 22.

These words are found at the close of the most affectionate and familiar letter of the Apostle Paul:—the letter written from Rome to the Church at Philippi. This friendly message fills a place in the letter so appropriately, that I need take no time to explain its presence. I have selected it as my text because it contains a theme of the deepest interest. This theme is *the persistence of Christianity: in life, in labor, and in love.*

Scarcely less interesting than the theme itself, are the completeness and vividness of its presentation in the text. For the text presents it in three beautiful and encouraging pictures, each one of which contains a striking contrast. The *first* is a picture of the Christian *life*, persisting in its development in the most unfavorable environment. "Saints of God in the household of Cæsar." The *second* is a picture of Christian *labor*, persisting in its successes against the greatest discouragements. Paul winning converts in "the household of Cæsar," though Paul was a prisoner, chained to a Roman soldier. And the *third* is a picture of Christian *love*, persisting in its outflow against the obstacles of absence and distance. The saints in Cæsar's household at Rome saluting saints, across the Mediterranean and Ægean seas, in Philippi of Macedonia. We shall best unfold the theme, by studying the pictures in which it is presented. And, better still, we shall thus, I trust, encourage our own spirits in Christian living, toil, and charity.

I. First, therefore, let us study this picture of the Christian *life*, persisting in the most unfavorable surroundings. "Saints of God in the household of Cæsar."

It must not be forgotten, that the Cæsar of the text was the most cruel and the most abandoned of the tyrants, who wore the imperial purple, as entitled to that mighty but dishonored name. "The criminal weakness of Claudius, the dark misanthropy, the tiger-like cruelty, the wild voluptuousness of Tiberius, and the horrible madness of Caligula were all repeated, in," what an historian, not given to superlative expressions, calls, "the bottomless vileness of the arch-tyrant Nero: who practiced unnatural vices with the most shocking shamelessness; who, in sheer wantonness, set fire to Rome and then burnt innocent Christians for it as torches in his gardens; who either poisoned with his own hand, or murdered by the hands of accomplices, his preceptors Burrus and Seneca, his mistress, his mother, and his wife; and finally, supported by a servant, stabbed himself, exclaiming: 'What an artist dies in me.'"

It would be difficult to find expressions strong enough, adequately to describe the debasement of the

Roman populace during his reign. No later historian has said worse things of any age and people than has Tacitus of his own people during Nero's reign. And no moralist has portrayed vice in darker lines, than those, in which the Stoic Seneca, portrays the condition of the capital and the empire during the life of this monarch. "All is full of outrage and vice. A monstrous prize contest of wickedness is being enacted. The desire to sin increases, and shame decreases every day. Crime is no longer practiced secretly, but in open view. Vileness gains on all the streets and in every breast; so that innocence has become, not only rare, but altogether extinct." We shudder—and well we may—as we read the description of mankind, in the first chapter of this Apostle's epistle to the Romans. But none knew better than those to whom it was addressed, the correctness of the description; for they were compelled to see its confirmation in the daily life of their great and wicked city. And to appreciate the details of this dark picture of the capital, we must remember, that the vice of the populace was not more the cause, than it was the effect of the vice at the imperial palace. It was not more the case, that Nero and his attendants were vitiated by the degradation of the populace; than it was, that the populace were vitiated by the degradation of the emperor. The "household of Cæsar" was the horrid fountain, from which issued the streams, which justified the mournful description of the Stoic philosopher, and the darker picture painted by the Christian Apostle.

Nothing more need be said, to bring vividly before us the contrast, contained in the first picture suggested by the text. "All the saints salute you, chiefly they that are of Cæsar's household." In this "household of Cæsar," there were saints of the living God. At the very center of this corrupt life of imperial Rome, lived examples of a life, whose pattern and inspiration were the Man who was holy, harmless, undefiled and separate from sinners. What a contrast is here! A bright star, sending golden light through a single rift in a clouded and angry firmament; a fountain of living and refreshing water, springing up in the midst of an arid desert;—these are its appropriate symbols.

The great truth, which this picture at once recalls to our attention, is the truth, that the Christian life is not dependent on any particular circumstances for its being or for its development. Deriving its power to be and to grow from a source superior to circumstance, it can flourish as well in the household of Cæsar, as in the church at Philippi. I do not assert that its surroundings will not determine its expression. That would be to deny what is obvious to every observer of the development of human character. It must be, that the type of Christian life, molded in the presence of vice and crime so open and so flagrant, as those which made the palace of Nero a hell on earth, will differ widely from the type of Christian life, formed within the walls of a Christian home. But I do say, that the life itself—and this is the teaching of the text—can exist, and increase in both vigor and beauty, whatever its surroundings, however full of temptation or of crime.

And to bring this truth into practical relation to our own lives, let me refer to a tendency, often observed by us in others, and doubtless often felt by us all: the tendency to charge our lack of growth in goodness, not to our own indisposition, but to the character of the life which encompasses us. It is too often the case, that we refer our imperfect, dwarfed and unlovely Christian character, to the business or the daily duties to which the providence of God has assigned us. It is true, that Christian living is a hard and continuous struggle, in whatever station a man is placed. Each station has its peculiar trials and temptations: and these no doubt will give form to Christian development. But each of us, seeing the troubles that surround his own life, and that tend to hinder his own growth in goodness, and, forgetting that every other man has troubles to hinder his, is prone to say, "If only the circumstances of my life had been other than they are, I might have been a better, more devoted man."

This tendency is not confined to Christian living. It is one of the evidences of a dissatisfaction that is as universal as humanity. Every man is convinced, that he would have been better or happier in different circumstances. A Latin poet most happily hits off this conviction in his most familiar satire. "How happens it," he writes, "that no one can live contented with the lot which either reason has assigned him, or chance has thrown in his way; but must extol those following other pursuits? 'Oh, fortunate merchants!' says the soldier, oppressed with years and broken by the labor of many a hard-fought battle. 'Oh, happy soldiers!' cries the merchant, as the south-west winds are tossing about his laden ships; 'for in their case an engagement is begun, and in one short hour comes relief of death or a joyful victory.' The lawyer, vexed with the cares of his many clients, praises the quiet of the farmer's life; and the farmer, called by his business to the town, proclaims only those happy who dwell within the bustling city's walls." And Horace's picture is exactly true. So it is in all life. So it is in the Christian life. "If my home life were only different; or if my business were not so filled with temptations; or if more opportunities for Christian culture were given me; or if I had more time for prayer, or more money for benevolence, or more talent for religious work, or more influence to be exerted for God and his Church; the light of my life would shine more and more unto the perfect day." With these and like excuses, do we seek to relieve ourselves, from living, as Christ calls us, in the lots in which we stand. God will not and can not accept them. He has promised us a strength, mightier than any foes that can assail us. He offers us a grace, sufficient against any temptations that He permits to allure us. And now, wherever we live, even though it be in "the household of Cæsar," He commands us to live as becomes the saints of the holy God.

If, to-morrow, burdened with the duties of your daily life, you shall be tempted to excuse your conformity to the world, by the reflection, that another business or another set of circumstances would find you a more nearly consistent Christian;—think of these saints in the household of Cæsar: and remember that the grace which upheld them in their conflict with surrounding sin, is yours as well; and that, as your allurements to live inconsistent lives can not be greater than were theirs, you may not charge your inconsistencies to temptations around you, but to that sin within you, but for which, all temptation would be powerless.

II. But Christianity is labor as well as life. Let us turn, therefore, to the *second* picture suggested by the text; a picture of Christian *labor*, persisting in the most discouraging circumstances. Paul gaining converts in the imperial household, while a prisoner chained to a Roman soldier.

Regarded from any point of view except his own, it is doubtful whether any situation could have been more unsuited to successful Christian labor, than was that of the great Apostle at this time. He was an old man; broken in body, we may well believe, by his repeated journeys, his labors, and his persecutions. Certainly, if it had been possible to discourage him in the work to which he had given his life, his position as a prisoner,—chained to a Roman guard, compelled to wait for a trial already long deferred, and to live in the presence of revolting iniquity,—would long before this have impelled him to yield to despair. It would not have been strange, had his touching farewell to Timothy, written just before his martyrdom, been written at the beginning of this confinement, while awaiting the trial, which, he must have feared, would terminate in his execution. Almost any other man would at least have sought rest from active labor, during this long imprisonment. At all events, we should scarcely expect to find this period of his career, marked by any but the most casual labor.

But how different was his actual life. It is hardly too much to say, that no other equal portion of his apostolic life is so crowded with successful work. Of the very small degree of liberty, that could be permitted him, consistently with "the military custody under which he was placed;" he was quick to take advantage. And he so declared the Gospel of Christ, that, to use his own words, "he begot many children in his chains." So, in this epistle, he writes to the Philippian Church: "I would ye should understand, brethren, that the things, which happened unto me, have fallen out rather unto the furtherance of the Gospel; so that my bonds in Christ are manifest in all the palace, and in all other places; and many of the brethren in the Lord, waxing confident by my bonds, are much more bold to speak the word without fear." Thus, what would have discouraged a less devoted disciple than was Paul, became in his case a means of greater usefulness. His very bonds gave forcefulness to his speech. That, which at first appeared to impede, must, as has been well said: "have deepened the impression of his eloquence. For who could see, without feeling, that venerable form subjected by iron links to the coarse control of the soldier who stood beside him? And how often must the emotions of the assembly have been called forth, by the upraising of that fettered hand, and the clanking of the chain which checked its energetic action?" Moreover, it was during this season of imprisonment, that some of the most important of his epistles were written: and by means of faithful delegates he still directed the Churches which, in his less restricted labors, he had established.

Among the successes of this restricted but most active toil, none could have been more delightful or encouraging to the Apostle than these converts of his in "the household of Cæsar." For not only were these the Christians with whom, because of the character of his imprisonment, he would be brought most frequently into contact; but they were also the fruit of his bonds; they were the successes of a ministry abounding in temptations to despair; they had been saved in the midst of the most powerful enticements to abandoned lives.

So, from this second picture suggested by the text, do we learn a lesson of encouragement, in work undertaken by us, however unpropitious the circumstances in which it is going forward. What slaves of immediate success we all are! How impatient to behold the seed ripening and bearing fruit in the very hour of its planting! How despairing we become in the presence of difficulties! Minister and people alike; the teacher teaching in the school; the parent training his children; the friend laboring with friend. How quick we are to see the difficulties of the work before us! How slow we are to find the advantages, which are sure to lie somewhere even in our difficulties! Over against this despair, I put this second picture of the text. The picture ought to exorcise despair, and inspire every one engaged in work for the redemption of men from sin. The moral of this picture of Paul—the captive, the prisoner, the aged—directing the Churches, educating the saints at Rome, winning souls for Christ in the very "household of Cæsar," is obviously, that you and I, if earnestly engaged in Christian work, have no right to be despairing about its results, whatever the obstacles that encompass it. The very law of Christian work and triumph is this: that God's noblest victories are victories plucked from the very grasp of the enemy, by feeblest agents, and with feeblest instruments. Had not Paul the right, in virtue both of inspiration and of large experience, to announce this law? And where shall we find it formulated in words as eloquent as his? "But God hath chosen the foolish things of the world to confound the wise; and God hath chosen the weak things of the world to confound the things which are mighty; and base things of the world, and things that are despised, hath God chosen, yea, and things which are not, to bring to nought the things that are."

Of all whom I address to-day, there is not one whom God does not call, by His Word and Providence and Spirit, to some work for men; work encompassed with difficulty, and demanding self-denial and exhausting toil. All Christian work is self-denying work. "If any man will come after me, let him deny himself, and take up his cross and follow me." In all Christian toil, there is something which makes it difficult of accomplishment. If we look for the difficulty we shall soon discover it. But there is no such difficulty in the toil, or in our circumstances as related to it, as should make us recoil from it in despair. There are obstacles, and great obstacles, in the way of the fulfillment of your mission as a Christian parent. It is doubtless a work filled with crosses, so to train your children, that they shall meet unharmed the temptations of the world; and be prepared for God's presence, and the bliss and holiness of heaven. But in all this, is to be found no reason why you should not move forward in your labors full of faith and hope. God purposely appoints his people to work, which in itself seems hopeless; in order that they may learn to find their hope, and strength, and inspiration, directly in Him. He brings his people, as of old, to the shores of deep seas: and, calling them to trust to Him, says now, as then; "Speak unto the children of Israel, that they go forward." What difficulty and danger, might Israel not have discerned on that day of flight from Egypt, in the journey to which God called them: the sands of desert; the pursuing enemy; and the awful deep! But the word of the Lord came unto Moses, saying: "Speak, that they go forward." And as they *obeyed*, the waters divided, the desert was left behind, and the enemy was engulfed. Our work may seem hard and hopeless as the apostle's at Rome. But it is not irreverent to say, that God's delight is to set before His people tasks, so full of obstacles, that, at the last, their success shall be the more signal, and their reward more glorious. Let us find hope, therefore, in the very disadvantages and difficulties of our work; remembering that God will proportion our strength to the labor to which he calls us. Let us remember the promise to every faithful soul: "as thy day is so shall my grace be;" and thus find ground for hope in all labor; even though it seem as hard and hopeless as this work of Paul's, had he forgotten God, must have appeared to him. Let us never forget, that it is not impossible, even while prisoners, to win saints of God out of the very "household of Cæsar."

III. I have thus endeavored to impress the lessons, to be learned from the pictures of Christian *life* and Christian *labor*, suggested by the text. There is still another, to which, in closing, I can allude, in only the briefest way. It is a picture of Christian *love*, persisting against the obstacles of both absence and distance; and binding together, in a strong affection, those who were widely separated in space and circumstance. The saints at Rome, in the household of Cæsar, saluting saints, across the Mediterranean and Ægean seas, in Philippi of Macedonia.

Those, whom Christ appointed as the apostles of his religion, affirmed the brotherhood of man. But they dwelt also, with peculiar delight, on the family relation, which unites the disciples of the Redeemer. They are members of a household, into which they have been received as adopted children. They are brethren, united in that Elder Brother, of whom the whole family in heaven and on earth is named. By the members of the Apostolic Churches, this relation was both deeply felt and highly valued. Though absent from each other, though separated by seas, and of different nationalities, they felt, that they were bound together by the most tender and most sacred of all ties. The power of one Name broke down all barriers, destroyed all intervening distance, and united them in faith and hope and love. It was the profound conviction of each Christian man, and of each Christian Church, that, as the power of that Name increased on earth, the love of man to man would grow, until the nations of the world would live in concord, and men would learn war no more. The bond of a common Savior, uniting them anew to one Father, was the one cord which they believed strong enough to bind in one brotherhood the race of man. And in the spirit of love to their fellows, they sought to spread abroad, throughout the world, the knowledge of Jesus Christ and Him crucified.

With this hope, and in this same faith, are we called to labor for the spread of the Gospel of Christ. Poets have sung, and seers have prophesied the coming of the day, when

"Man to man shall brother be."

And how often, in these days, do men talk glibly of a religion, whose only dogmas are the fatherhood of God and the brotherhood of man! *But how shall we make real this dream of a human brotherhood?* Is it supposed, that men can be bound together, by the mere iteration of this fine sentiment of God's fatherhood and men's brotherhood? A dream more baseless was never dreamed. I know but one source of the knowledge, which man has, that God is our Father. The heaven saith, it is not in me; and the deep saith, it is not in me. Man knows it, only through that revelation, which tells him the glad news, that, "God so loved the world, that He gave his only begotten Son, that whosoever believeth on Him might not perish, but might have everlasting life." And this Gospel, which reveals God's fatherhood, is the one bond strong enough to bind men in a common brotherhood. Therefore, to-day, as ever, is devolved on the Church of Christ the duty, announced in its great commission: "Go ye into all the world, and preach the Gospel to every creature." In this Gospel of God's grace alone, resides the divine power, that can unite in fraternal love, not only "saints at Rome" with the saints in Philippi of Macedonia, but the isles and continents of the earth, through the Redeemer and Elder Brother of all.

In view, then, of these great and blessed truths; in view of this inherent power of Christianity to overcome the greatest obstacles, and to persist to its purposed achievements; why should you wonder, that we speak of the Gospel, as "the power of God unto salvation to every one that believeth;" and call on you to believe in the Redeemer, whom this Gospel reveals? In Christ alone, the ideal goodness, which charms you in your better moments, is possible. In union to Him alone, therefore, can there be "saints in Cæsar's household." In the history of the Gospel of Christ alone, do we read the record of continuous labor for men culminating in triumph; though carried forward in difficulties the most formidable, and in an atmosphere the most enervating. It is only, therefore, when, like Paul, you shall have become co-workers with Christ, and shall have been imbued with His Spirit, that you will deem no sacrifice for your fellows fruitless, and will "call no man abandoned."

It is in Christ alone, that we discern our relationship to the whole family of man. And, therefore, it is in Him alone, that the race can be united in peace and holiness.

Wonder not then, I say, that we call upon you to believe in Him, as your only hope, or as the only hope of a world lying in iniquity. A spiritual life, born of a source less divine, must die in the atmosphere of the world's temptations. Philanthropic labor must be temporary and ineffective, when uninspired by the lofty motives and eternal rewards, which made the aged Apostle triumph in his chains. And charity itself will fail to take in the brotherhood of man, save when its view is enlarged by communion with Him, who, though equal with God, is not ashamed to call men his brethren.

Let your life, therefore, be hid with Christ in God. Let your labor for men be labor for Christ. Let your love be constrained by his love, who gave Himself to death for men. Your spiritual life will become eternal life. Your labor for men will never be in vain. And your love, embracing the race, will repeat the ancient prophecy,—and hasten its fulfillment—of the brotherhood of man.

III.

THE COMPLETION OF MAN IN CHRIST.

And ye are complete in him, which is the head of all principality and power.—COLOSSIANS ii, 10.

There had appeared in the Church of Colosse vital religious errors. These had their origin, partly at least, in an endeavor to unite certain oriental speculations with the Gospel of Christ. The Colossians had adopted, as their belief, a theory of the rank of the Redeemer in the orders of being, inconsistent with his essential Deity. They were led thus to question whether the salvation of Christ is the *ultimate* and *complete* salvation. They were disposed to regard it as an intermediate process; and to regard Christianity as an intermediate dispensation, which would be superseded by another, just as it had superseded Judaism. All this sprang from their belief, derived from these oriental speculations, that Jesus is one, and that not the loftiest, of a series of descending beings, which fills the long interval between God and man.

We are indebted to these errors, for some of the most sublime assertions of the Redeemer's Deity, to to be found in the New Testament. It is in this connection, that the Redeemer is said to be the image of the invisible God; the first-born of every creature; the One, by whom all things were created; by whom and for whom,—whether things visible or invisible, in heaven or in earth, thrones or dominions, or principalities or powers,—all things consist; who in all things has the pre-eminence; and in whom dwells all the fullness of the Godhead bodily. Depending on this pre-eminence of the Redeemer, is the truth announced in the text, namely: *the completeness of his redemption of man.* "And ye are complete in Him, who is the head of all principality and power."

It is the completeness of the redemption in Christ, then, which the Apostle here declares. The statement is not, you will observe, the redemption of Christ is now complete in you. But ye are complete in Christ, the Redeemer. There is a wide difference between these statements. It is not true that our redemption is now complete. Were it complete, Christianity might be judged as manifested in us. But this we will not permit without a protest. As well—we say to those, who would so judge our religion,—as well may you pronounce upon the beauty of a temple, before the walls are reared; while the scaffolding remains, and the unpolished stones are strewn around its half-built sides. Wait, until the top stone has been brought forth; and the idea of the architect has been made actual in the completed building. Wait, until the Gospel has wrought its work on man, before you pronounce upon the Gospel, as it appears in man. If you must judge an uncompleted building, go, not to the building itself, but to the plans of the architect. There you may see its proportions and details foreshadowed. And, if you must pass judgment upon an incomplete redemption, go, not to half-sanctified Christians, but to the plan of the Redeemer, in the New Testament.

The Gospel, then, contemplates and provides for *the completion of man.* Redemption will leave nothing to be desired. When it shall be finished, man will be complete. What is now fragmentary, will then be integral. The powers, which now act in conflict, will then be harmonized. The love, which is now borne down by selfish passions and combating interests, will then be regnant. The hope, which is now dimmed by obstacles to its fulfillment, will then be perfect enjoyment. The development of the soul, which is now hindered or distorted, will then be free, and in the direction of the infinitely perfect life. All this,—the Apostle tells the Colossians,—is not to be provided for hereafter; when Christ, as the Redeemer, shall give place to a loftier principality. But all this is provided for now. "Ye are complete in Him, who is the head of all principality and power."

The subject, thus brought before us by the text, I shall attempt to unfold in a series of propositions.

I. Of these, the first and most obvious is, that, as we can not *image the completed man,* we must accept the statement of the text, *by implicit faith in the Bible.* In this respect, the statement of the Apostle is like an unfulfilled prophecy; as, for example, the prophecy of the second coming of our Lord; belief in which is grounded, solely on our confidence in the Bible. It is unlike the doctrine of the presence of the Holy Spirit; belief in which is based, not only on our confidence in the Bible, but, partly, on historical evidence, and partly, on our own experience.

For we have never seen, and there has never lived on earth, a completed man, who once was sinful. We can not, therefore, portray one. This is true even of the *substantial* elements of man's completeness. These substantial elements are the traits, which, together, constitute perfect holiness. It might be supposed, that, in the attempt to conceive of these, we should derive sufficient aid from the recorded life of the perfect Man, Christ Jesus. But,—setting aside the personal union of his humanity with his divine nature, which led Paul to call his personality a "mystery,"— let us remember only, that his perfection is that of one *who never sinned*. Now, redeemed men have sinned; and this tremendous fact must forever give to their perfection a character of its own. Throughout eternity, though complete in Christ, their lives will be distinguished by activities, in which, for this reason, the man Christ Jesus can never engage; and by spiritual joys, which He can never share. In attempting to conceive of these, the life of the ever perfect Jesus lends us not one whit of aid.

The difficulty of portraying the *formal* elements of man's completeness is greater still. These formal elements are derived from his environment. To portray the completed man, therefore, it would be necessary, first of all, to see heaven, and the surrounding spirits of the just made perfect. We should have to know what is meant by the company of the angels; and what will be its influence on man; and what will be the changes wrought in him, by the perfected worship of God, and by celestial communion with Jesus, the Mediator of the new covenant. All this were necessary to the portrayal of the completed man. Imagination can not aid us here. For imagination constructs new images, only out of elements already familiar. And therefore, though perfect happiness and perfect holiness have been made known as the final heritage of the redeemed, yet for image of this redemption, we must wait, until we shall see God face to face, and know Him as we are known.

You will learn how impossible is the task proposed, if only you will attempt it. Tell me the elements of the perfect character and the final home. Gather them together in one harmonious whole, and by eloquence, or poetry, or painting, or sculpture, make that whole so vivid that I shall see a real image. Can you do it? If you can, you can do more than Christian art has yet achieved by poem, or sermon, or marble, or color, in its representations of the saints in light. All that we can do is to assert, just as the Bible does, of both man and heaven, mere negatives. We can say of heaven, that it will contain no sorrow, or sickness, or death. We can abstract positive moral evils and imperfections from man. But it is a feat beyond the power of genius, to image the completed man, with positive celestial virtues, and active in celestial engagements.

If, therefore, you ask me to describe the completed man; I can only turn upon you with the inquiry, but what is the completion of man? You can reply only: "Such a soul will neither sin nor suffer." You can not endow man with a single trait, of which you have had no observation. So the Bible proclaims the simple fact that we shall be complete; and its statement appeals to our faith, just as every prophecy appeals to it. The ground of its appeal is the truthfulness of God and the inspiration of his written Word.*

---

* There is no picture of Heaven in the New Testament. The twenty-first chapter of the book of Revelation is sometimes referred to as a description of Heaven. But it is not a description. Indeed, the chapter—we say it with reverence—becomes grotesque, when we "wrest it," by interpreting, what

Let us not, however, for this reason, spurn the promise. That were to condemn all faith. God assures us that all things are working together for our good. But he does not intimate the general method, which he adopts in making all things our servants. Nor in a particular case does he show us how our affliction is working for us the exceeding weight of glory. Shall we condition our faith, on his revelation, either of the mode of his procedure, or of the particular blessings which shall issue from our personal afflictions? That were to forget the function of faith. For the province of faith is just this un-

---

were intended to be symbols of the invisible, as though they were pictures of the visible. The cube is a *symbol* of perfection. But the figure of a city, whose length and breadth and height are equal, is not the *image* of a perfect city. And even interpreted as symbols—as they should be—the figures of this chapter do not convey detailed information. When we have named moral purity, perfect happiness, worship, and perpetuity, we have exhausted nearly, if not quite all, the elements of its revelation of the life of the redeemed. As to the material surroundings of the redeemed, the chapter can not be said to teach more than their unparalleled glory. And this unparalleled glory, it affirms by means of symbols, which become meaningless, the moment we press them to yield more than the most general truth. It were well, if modern writers would imitate this reticence of the Word of God. What was not revealed—possibly only, because it could not be to a world not "pure in heart," and unable, therefore, to "see God"—through inspired Apostles, can not be made vivid by the pens of modern *litterateurs*. The attempt to portray the details of the heavenly life, must result in pictures that are earthly and gross, just in proportion as they are distinct.

Nor has consummate genius failed to recognize the limits of the human imagination at this point. Dante, certainly, among the great poets, might have been expected to attempt a detailed description of the life of Heaven. His genius, as has been so often remarked, impels him to be definite, whenever definiteness is a possible attainment. Moreover, he lived at a known province between a promise and its fulfillment.

Let us, rather, in faith of God and of his Word, rejoice in the inspiring and uplifting promise of the text. The revealing spirit here brings to us the loftiest assurance ever uttered to man. This redemption, of which we are now enjoying the first-fruits, is the ultimate redemption. No power of ours shall fail of perfection. No circumstance shall be wanting to make our future life ineffably blessed. This salvation is no intermediate process. Ye are *complete* in Christ. He is no intermediate Saviour. He

---

time when Christianity revelled in sensuous forms; and when the Schoolmen employed their dialectic, in computing the number, in determining the relations to space and time, and in ascertaining the activities of the inhabitants of the celestial world. But the exact measurements of the Hell, and the vivid portrayals of the Purgatory, are not to be found in the Paradise of the Divine Comedy. The reason of this marked change, the poet himself states in the first Canto of the Paradise. He had seen the Paradise; because, gazing on Beatrice, he had been "trans-humanized." But he can not interpret the vision in human language; nay, he can not even recall it.

> "Within that heaven which most his light receives
> Was I, and things beheld which to repeat
> Nor knows, nor can, who from above descends;
> Because in drawing near to its desire
> Our intellect ingulphs itself so far
> That after it the memory can not go."

Because the intellect so "ingulphs itself" in the superhuman task of portraying the perfect life that even recollection fails, the Paradise is both the least distinct and the least intelligible member of the trilogy. The Hell, the poem of darkness, with just light enough to make forms stand out in the boldest relief, Frederick Schlegel calls, the *plastic* part of the poem. In the Purgatory, the light is increased, reflected, and refracted; so that colors beautify the scenery; and this, he calls, the *picturesque* part of the poem. "But in the Paradise," says Schlegel, "*there remains nothing but the pure music of light; reflection ceases,*

is the *head* of all principality and power. Redemption is not a single, forward, and upward step in an eternal series. It is ultimate destiny. The life of heaven is not a new discipline like the life of earth. It is God's gracious and final reward. Man is not again to be subjected to suffering, in order to purge away remaining evil. He is to be blessed as God is blessed. Beyond the Son of God there is no loftier Redeemer. "Ye are complete in Him, who is the head of all principality and power."

II. Our sense of the value of this special revelation will be deepened, if we consider, secondly, the truth that, without it, *man would not have dared to think of the next life as the ultimate life of the redeemed.*

---

and the poet rises gradually to behold the colorless pure essence of the Deity." Carlyle, also, finds no difficulty in understanding the first two parts of the poem; but, of the third, he says, "The Paradise is a kind of inarticulate music to me."

No one, who has read the Paradise, can doubt that its lack of form and color, as contrasted with the abounding form and color of the preceding poems, was *purposed* by the poet. That Dante could have portrayed a heaven filled with distinct though earthly images, the Hell and the Purgatory furnish sufficient proof. That such a heaven might easily have tempted him, and must have tempted a man less spiritual or with less genius, will be clear to all who will reflect on the sensuous forms which distinguish Mediæval Christianity. That he escaped, or, at least, overcame the temptation, is itself strong proof of his spiritual character. That, while refusing the aid of definite forms, he is still able to leave on the reader a distinct and profound impression of the infinite glory and sublimity of Paradise, is perhaps the highest achievement of his literary genius. Indications are not wanting that books, whose chief title to popularity will be their descriptions of the heavenly life, are to be multiplied. If, tempted to yield ourselves to their influence—which, so far as they shall be descriptive must be unspiritual—let us remember the reticence both of the book of Revelation itself, and of the spiritual Dante.

I do not doubt that man would have regarded the next life of the *impenitent* as ultimate. For nature and conscience alike intimate absolute penalty alone, for the breaker of law. But, let us suppose, that God, in revealing the purposes of his mercy, had forbidden the removal, even for an instant, of the veil, which hides the future world. Man would still have endeavored to conceive of the elements of the life to which death introduces us. But, even with the truth of God's mercy made known to him, would he have dared,— I will not say to believe,—but even faintly to hope, that any man, in the life immediately next this, will stand "complete" before God?

Remember, how thoroughly our minds are saturated with Biblical truth. We seldom realize, how nearly impossible it is to rise out of the region of religious thought, in which Biblical conceptions are dominant. In our religious speculations, we fall back, without purpose, and even without consciousness, on the written revelation; and so mistake its declarations for natural beliefs. It would not be strange, therefore, if we were to leap to the conclusion, that, even though heaven were unrevealed, all would believe, that if God is a God of grace, the next life must be the ultimate life; and the redeemed spirit be complete. But we would find it difficult to state the steps, by which we reached our conclusion. What is there in either man or nature to suggest it? The last glimpse, which we obtain of the dying Christian, is far from being an apocalypse of perfect manhood. If we may trust his descriptions of himself, he has never been more deeply conscious of his sinfulness, or of his need of the unmerited grace of God, than he is, at the moment, when his spirit flies to the spiritual world. In the absence of an authoritative statement, we should be compelled to believe, that the movement of the redeemed into the next world is but one of a countless series of movements upward toward perfection? We should look forward to the immediate future, as a state, in which the fires of new afflictions will still further purify us; and, in which, new disciplines will chasten us to a higher spiritual beauty. Nor should we dare to prophecy, after how many lives, and in what far off æon, the declaration will be made to our perfected spirits: "Ye are now complete, in the head of all principality and power." Who would dare to say,—unless he could appeal to the written revelation,—that by the purging fires of a single life, the sinful spirit can be fitted for communion with the immaculate God?

The truth stated in the text, then, is distinctly a revealed truth. Unlike the existence of God, or the guilt of sin, or the future judgment, the sole ground of our belief of it is the written Word of God. The best that we could have believed, without this declaration, is that belief in an ascending series of partial redemptions; which, it would seem, false teachers at Colosse attempted to unite with the Gospel of Christ. If this Bible is not, in the narrow and exact sense of that phrase, the one divinely inspired Word of God, we have not a scintilla of evidence—even though we dare to hope that the Lawgiver of the universe is a God of grace—we have not a scintilla of evidence, that the life of the good hereafter is a life either of perfect holiness or of perfect happiness.

But the declaration of the Word of God is clear. For the Christian, the next life is ultimate. And here arises the solemn question. If his life is ultimate, is not the next life of the wicked ultimate also? In the light of the text, what a tremendous import is seen to belong to this brief and brittle career of ours! Imperceptibly the movement of time is bearing men forward to the end of life. But where does it place them? In a new probation? Where does the Bible, even, suggest that belief? Certainly not in the truth that I am repeating. If not here, where else in the Scriptures? And, if not in these Scriptures, where? In the revelation of God in Nature? I know no such intimation anywhere. All things in Nature point to the life beyond as the life of destiny. From every place, whence comes any intimation of the future world, comes an intimation like the announcement made by the preacher in the metaphor, "If the tree fall toward the south, or toward the north, in the place where the tree falleth, there it shall be."

III. We shall gain a new impression of the value of the text, by holding before us a third truth, namely, that the completion of man which it predicts, *involves the perpetuity of the human personality.* "Ye are complete in Him." The completed man will forever remain human; and his surroundings will be adjusted to his humanity. The perfection, which the human spirit will attain in Christ, will be personal; after its own kind.

This seems only a truism; but personal immortality is a distinctively Biblical revelation. The greatest ethnic religions, in their promise of immortality, make immortality of no effect.* They teach that

---

* I refer of course to Brahmanism and Buddhism. It is not disputed, I believe, that the absorption of the individual into the universal soul is the highest promise made by Brahmanism to the devotee. The question whether, in Buddhism, Nirvāna is absorption or extinction divides scholars. But it is still true, that, if Buddhism offers immortality at all, it offers it only in the form of absorption into the infinite and impersonal being.

man is immortal, only as he is swallowed up and lost in infinite and impersonal being. But the Word of God, in its promise of completion, does not make "a promise to the ear" which it "breaks to the hope." It does not offer a stone to those whom it tells to hope for bread. It does not promise completeness to men, and then describe a completeness which destroys humanity, or even individuality. Whatever shall be the surprises of the future life; between the imperfect soul here and the perfected soul hereafter, there will be the bond of the same unity, that exists here between the child and the man. The two lives will be two lives of one person. And just as hope now looks forward to that future life, so memory will then look back over this present life. On whatever new objects they shall be employed, we shall possess the faculties and capacities which are ours now in the life beyond. It is *ourselves*, who are complete in Christ.

This truth should dissipate the doubt which sometimes pains us, touching recognitions in the future world. There are few who have not asked the question: "Shall I know those from whom death has separated me?" And thoughts of their completion in the presence of God, in the company of angels, and by means of celestial activities, awakened doubts, and sometimes caused new and more poignant griefs.

But let us remember, that whatever is involved in our completion, it is still ourselves who shall be completed. The Abraham, with whom we shall sit down in the kingdom of God, is the same Abraham, who, even when on earth, looked for a city which had foundations; with a vivid recollection still of that awful trial when the word was spoken: "Take thy son, thine only son: and offer him for a burnt-offering." The Moses, who came from heaven to a mountain in Canaan, is the same Moses, who went to heaven from a mountain of Moab. If we shall know these, doubt not, that we shall know those also, whom God has taken from our care or love. It doth not yet appear what we shall be. But we shall be ourselves, at least. And friends, gone before us, will still be friends; and we shall know and love them, there, as here.

IV. I remark, in the fourth place, that this completeness will consist largely in *perfect and eternal harmony* between the powers of man himself. I suppose that a chief result, as well as proof, of the incompleteness of man, is the war within himself. Who does not know what I mean, when I speak of the war of contending tastes and passions and powers in the same man? Each of us is the theater of an incessant battle. We are conscious of the shock of it every day; and our very dreams attest, that sleep itself brings no cessation of the warfare. Men of all beliefs have confessed it. The heathen poet, who has written: "I see and approve the right—I detest and follow the wrong;" and the Christian Apostle, who has recorded the confession: "I find a law in my members warring against the law of my mind." The animal and the spiritual natures, the tastes and the moral sense, the physical appetite and the nobler ambitions—I need only to repeat phrases like these, to summon before all of you a picture, which each one knows to be a faithful portrait of his own career: a career, of which the distinctest feature, is an incessant and destructive war with himself. This war, as I have said, is the result, as well as the evidence, of the incompleteness of man.

But when man shall be perfected, this war will

cease. The Apostle tells us, that we shall be complete in Christ, because Christ is the *head* of all principality and power. Before we can rest from this battle in ourselves, our powers, now warring with each other, must be united in loyal devotion to an inspiring object. All of us know, that when such an object is vividly before a man or a people, internal strife dies; and the man or the nation develops through its unity before uncomputed strength. Thus, internal contests died, when the thought of supreme peril awakened our people's latent love of country. And there resulted on the instant, an amazing development of natural resource. So does a man become a unit, and discover new power, and rise toward completion, when he gives himself to the all-inspiring Object. So, powers and tastes, which before warred with each other, are united and developed through their loyal devotion to their common Lord. Thus we become complete in Christ. And it is vain to think of completion without Him. In this, as in every other view of man's relations to Christ, there is none other name given under heaven among men whereby they can be saved. For Jesus Christ is the only object that can harmonize man's powers *perfectly and forever*. It is not needful that I dwell on this truth. It is enough to say that because He is God, He is inexhaustible by man. It is on the Deity of Christ that the Apostle dwells with emphasis in connection with the text. His kingdom embraces the universe, and is without end; for He is the head of all principality and power. The end of this kingdom—the historical unfolding, to the view of the universe, of the glory of its King—is the loftiest which can appeal to man. And in the King himself, dwells all the fullness of the Godhead bodily. Man may exhaust other objects, as motives and inspirations. But throughout eternity, new discoveries of God's nature, and new developments of his universal kingdom will educate the powers, and intensify the holy feelings of the redeemed.

I have thus, in simplest outline, endeavored to explain the meaning of man's completeness in Christ. As I have said, it is impossible to portray the completed man. But enough has been said to make evident the truth, that Jesus Christ is a necessity in order to our completion. We find within us colossal powers as yet undeveloped, and infinite capacities. We find the former engaged in each other's destruction; and the latter unsatisfied by the world in which we live. The result is a misery which grows apace; and which points, not uncertainly forward, to hopeless woe. We are tempted to cry out, "Why hast thou made man in vain?" I put to every thoughtful man and woman, the question; if the daily round of eating and drinking, of buying and selling, is to be the outcome of the powers with which you are endowed,—is it not true that you have been made in vain? Is life worth the living, if this is all? Does it not become a conscious curse, in proportion as we are conscious of our powers and godlike capacities? But, here is the revelation of another destiny. We may be complete in the head of all principality and power. The dignity which we now feel to be only possible, may become actual in Him. This living temple may be rebuilt. These powers may be harmonized and unified. They may find objects worthy of their most loyal devotion. This is the meaning of Redemption. Thus the Gospel which announces it is a Gospel of eternal life, indeed. When the Word of God says to us: "Believe on the Lord Jesus Christ, and you shall be saved," it means unspeakably more than that we shall escape an external hell, and be given an external heaven. It means the union of all these scattered and warring powers in Christ. In asking you, therefore, to submit yourselves to Him, I appeal to the sentiment of self-respect within you. For the perfect man is possible, only in Christ. Without Him, all that you possess of wealth, or reputation, or talent, are less than nothing and vanity. For you possess nothing apart from Him, that shall save them in the day of visitation. Give yourselves, therefore, to the Redeemer of men. All talent will find its aim, all powers their appropriate objects, all capacity its fulfillment, in Him who is the head of all principality and power. You will be satisfied with His likeness; and become in character, as in title, redeemed children of the Most High.

One word more, and I have done. The preacher of the Gospel must always feel that he is addressing suffering people; needing to hear some truth of consolation. Such a truth is this great promise, upon which I have spoken this morning.

We are bewildered by the events which befall us; so many of which are disappointing; so many others of which are sources of positive and terrible suffering; all of which, so far as their final issue is concerned, are, to the view of reason, mysterious. What is the reason, what is to be the end of them, we can not tell. But read again these words of the inspired Apostle: "Ye are complete in Him, who is the head of all principality and power." What a sublime and inspiring truth do the words announce! The truth that there is One above all the hosts of God, and above all the forces of Nature, guiding all, controlling all, Head over all, that we may be complete in Him. This is the revelation of God. And what, if we can not single out each event, and tell its special meaning and mission? Christ is head over all things for us. Therefore, all things are ours;—whether Paul or Apollos, or Cephas or the world, or life or death, or things present or things to come,—all are ours; and we are Christ's; and Christ is God's.

IV.

THE UNIVERSALITY OF THE CHRISTIAN BENEVOLENCE.

And let us not be weary in well-doing; for in due season, we shall reap, if we faint not. As we have therefore opportunity, let us do good unto all men.—GALATIANS vi, 9, 10.

Three things are involved in personal Christianity. It is a relation, a growth, and an outgiving. The relation is in order to the growth; and the relation and the growth are in order to the outgiving. The first thing that the Gospel does for man, is to renew his relation to God in Jesus Christ. He is forgiven, he is accepted, he is justified. Henceforth, he stands in an entirely new relation to God, to events, to death, and to the future life. All things are his; for he is Christ's, and Christ is God's.

But his justification does not terminate in itself. It is the condition of his sanctification. He is accepted in Christ, that he may grow into the likeness of Christ. This is the second element of personal Christianity.

But we have not yet exhausted it. No man liveth to himself. This is true especially of Christians. We remain in this world for others. Here we come upon the third element of personal Christianity. This new relation in which we stand to God, and this growth of our souls into the image of Christ are in order to the outgiving of our lives for our fellow men. This *Christian benevolence* is the element of the Christian life which the text brings to view: "And let us not be weary in well-doing; for in due season, we shall reap, if we faint not. As we have opportunity therefore, let us do good unto all men."

I shall not go beyond the text, in speaking of the Christian benevolence. We shall find subjects enough to employ our time, and interest enough to engage our attention, in the various aspects of the single quality of *universality*, which the text indicates as its distinctive trait. What I mean by the various aspects of the universality of the Christian benevolence, will be understood, when I say these five things of it. Its objects are all men; Let us do good unto *all men*. It seeks their whole welfare; Let us *do good* unto all men. It employs the whole Church; Let *us*, that is, all Christians, do good unto all men. It seizes every occasion; *As we have opportunity*, let us do good unto all men. It believes that all Christian outgiving will be blessed; Let us not be weary; for in due season, *we shall reap*, if we faint not.—I shall dwell briefly on each of these aspects.

I. First, then, the Christian beneficence contrasts all other beneficence, in that it contemplates *the race*. It looks out on men as men; as members of one family. It does not regard the adventitious differences which separate them. Differences of race or of station, even differences of morality, prove no barriers to the outgoing of Christian love, and the outgiving of the Christian life. It contemplates men as made of one blood, as involved in a common ruin, and as in need of the same salvation. It sets aside no man as too abandoned for redemption. It overlooks no other man as too good for spiritual destruction. In this sense, as in another, it is true, that in Christ Jesus, there is neither barbarian, Scythian, bond nor free. Christ is not only all in all, but all to all. "Let us do good to *all men*," says the Apostle to the Churches of Galatia.

How strikingly this trait appears in the invitations of the Gospel! There are special appeals in the Gospel to special classes. But the tenderest appeals of Prophet, of Saviour, and Apostle, are those which are meant to find a response in every heart. Isaiah is never more eloquent than when he cries; "Ho! every one that thirsteth, come ye to the waters." Our Lord never more strikingly reveals his love than when he says; "Come unto me, all ye that labor, and I will give you rest." In one of the most profound discourses of Jesus, preserved in the New Testament, the statement is made, that the outlook of the Father's love was toward the race. "God so loved the world, that he gave his Son, that whosoever believeth on him might have life." The Saviour's last commission imposed on the Church the duty of preaching the Gospel to every creature. And the last invitation in the New Testament, is the invitation; "And whosoever will, let him take the water of life freely."

Statements like these are so familiar, that we fail to grasp their significance. But a moment's reflection will show, how strikingly they place the Gospel as a system of benevolence in contrast with other systems, and with the beneficence of individual men. For other religions are limited by racial or geographical boundaries. Other acts of beneficence are intended to benefit single classes. Other promptings of love need to be reinforced by considerations which bound the gifts of charity. It is a class in the community for whom we labor. It is the fact that they belong to our family, or to our neighborhood, or our country, that excites our sympathies and impels our aid. You will not misunderstand me, of course. I am not decrying the philanthropic labors or sacrifices that are addressed to the alleviation of the wretchedness of specific classes. Not at all. I do not impugn the motives of those engaged in them. This kind of beneficence but illustrates the glory of the Gospel itself. For it is most abundant where first the Gospel has given character to the people. But this also is true: that the Gospel of Christ alone, teaches us to look out on men as men. It alone sees in every child of Adam a child of God. It alone teaches every member of the human family to say "My Father which art in heaven." It alone assures us that there is no one "so vile, or unlovely, or lost," but he may be fitted for fellowship with angels, and immediate communion with God himself. "I, if I be lifted up," said Christ, "will draw all men unto me;" and the history of the Church of Christ has made nothing more clear, than the adaptation of Christianity to the people of every age, and of every land. Hence the Christian faith has ever been a missionary faith, looking forward to the conquest of the world; predicting a universal peace, a universal brotherhood. No race is favored in the consummation of all things. The glory and honor of the kings of the *whole earth* are to adorn the new city of God.

This being the outlook of the Gospel, the Gospel must promote a like beneficence in Christians. And so it does. Paul, though a Hebrew of the Hebrews, becomes the Apostle to the Gentiles; but his devotion to the Gentiles does not weaken his love for his "kinsmen according to the flesh." Peter,—though sent to the Jews, and though at the first a narrow man,—under the influence of Christianity, rises above his prejudices, leaps all national barriers, and rejoices that on the Gentiles is poured the gift of the Holy Ghost. So, to-day, Christianity alone is missionary to all peoples and to every soul.

Without dwelling longer on this aspect of our subject, let me say only, that it behooves you and me to see to it, that we have caught this spirit. There is a way, common enough in our churches, of quoting the proverb, "Charity begins at home," which means, I fear, "Charity should stay at home." This, whatever it is, is not the Christian spirit. The cause of Foreign Missions deserves our support, if for no other reason, because it lifts us above the spirit of class, and sect, and neighborhood; yes, and the spirit of patriotism—for there is a higher spirit than patriotism—and associates us with Him who loved the world, and gave Himself for the world, and bade us believe that the world will one day be redeemed to God.

Moreover, this spirit of universal charity can inspire every Christian labor, however limited in space or the number of its objects. We can labor for men as men; and in our labors for their well-being, we can regard no man as hopeless. I do not doubt, that you are brought into contact with many souls, who seem utterly incapable of receiving any real good. Do not despair. The Gospel is for them. Christ came to all men; to call sinners to repentance; to seek and to save the lost. We shall be putting dishonor on Christianity, if our love and our labor are not given to them, in the full assurance of hope.

For their wants are what our wants were; and, if between us and them there seems to be a radical difference, it is because we are what we are, only by the grace revealed in the Gospel of the Son of God.

II. But the Christian charity not only seeks all men as its objects. It contemplates their *entire welfare.* "Let us *do good* unto all men." The word, here trans-translated good, is made specific by the definite article. Literally, it is "the good thing," the thing which in the circumstances is the best. And it suggests, if it does not formally state the truth, that the Christian beneficence aims at accomplishing the central and so the controlling good. This also is a trait, which distinguishes it from all others. I do not criticise the aim of other benevolence. I state only a fact, when I say that benevolence, when not inspired and directed by Christianity, stops with good which is not central and dominating. It regards its objects in but one or in but a few of their relations. Usually, it is prompted by the sensibilities, which have been powerfully wrought upon by specific forms of human misery; and to these it applies specific remedies.

Now, the beneficence, that is born of Christianity, while it excludes no form of charity, always attacks the central and radical misery of humanity. Its theory is, if you relieve that, you will finally relieve all. Thus its great Founder healed every form of disease, and pointed to his miracles of mercy as evidence that he was sent of God; but He did not announce to them the crowning proof of his divine mission, until he told the messengers from John, that to the poor the Gospel was preached.

The conduct of the Church of Christ, from that day until now, has been formed upon the conduct of her divine Head. Her path throughout the world and down the ages, has been illumined by institutions to alleviate all forms of human suffering. She has made, in the human society which she controls, the dogma that "only the fittest survive," an untruth; by her care for the poor, the crippled, the blind, the dumb, the insane. Nor is her beneficence accurately measured by annual statistics. Those, who have given study to the subject, assure us, that were the gifts in our Christian land directed to their proper objects; were they made economically to flow in proper channels, no man or woman would want bread.

But the Christian charity does not end with the bestowment of bread; the temporary relief of special sources of misery. In making the conversion of man from sin its aim, it strikes at the central evil, the root of all the rest, and so provides for every kind of good. I say, it so provides for every kind of good; and bestows it too, if the history of Christianity proves any thing. This, at least, is the aim of the Gospel. It leaves no human want unprovided for. It leaves no human relation unblessed. When Christ saves a nation, He transfigures the whole national life. When He shall save the world, men will not only be redeemed from the punishment and dominion of sin; but a higher beauty will adorn the products of art, a purer social life will bless the homes of men, the blood of immortal youth will course through their veins, and even unconscious nature will put on a new glory, at the manifestation of the sons of God. So, too, when a single man is saved. It is not alone that there is no more condemnation, and that a new character fits him for heaven. The whole life is redeemed. A new joy lights up the home; a new pride of life gives birth to honest labor and self-respect; a higher mental life is born of his communion with

God; and though he remains, for the time, subject to death, yet will he one day rejoice in the redemption of his body: for death shall be swallowed up in victory.

Thus the outlook of the Christian beneficence is not only as wide as the world. It is also as deep as the longings of the human heart. It not only goes out into all the world; but, on its journey, it leaves no relation of life untouched, or unblessed. It not only leaps the bounds of class and neighborhood; but it leaps also the bounds of sense. It provides not only for time. It fits man also for eternity.

I wish that we might have clearly before us this aspect of the universality of the Christian beneficence, when giving and laboring. In giving your lives to the redemption of men through Christ, you are redeeming the *whole man unto God*. For the Captain of our salvation does not mean that his conquest of this world shall be a partial triumph. His victory will be the restitution of all things: and there is not a faculty or a lofty possibility of man's nature, which will not join in the anthem of praise unto Him, who has loved us, and redeemed us by his blood unto God.

III. But the Christian beneficence is universal, not only because it contemplates the whole world and every want, but also because it employs the *whole Church*. Let *us*, that is, all *Christians*—not ministers alone, but people; not people of five talents only, but of one talent—"Let us do good unto all men."

It is true, that in founding his Church, our Lord appointed special officers for the fulfillment of special duties. He gave some apostles, and some prophets, and some evangelists, and some pastors and teachers; for the perfecting of the saints, for the work of the ministry. And we should observe his order, and honor the offices which He has appointed. Free as we are in this dispensation of the Spirit, there is a divine economy for the Christian administration. The Christian man, or association of men, that fails to observe this divine order, will find labor wasted so far forth. But it is also true, that there is not a man, or woman, or child, whose talents are not intended to be employed. To every man, Christ gives his work. "Let him that heareth say, come," is the divine call. Nor will he accept the excuse that our talents are too few, or our opportunities too narrow, or our means too limited, for the outgiving of our life in beneficence. In the parable of the talents, in the story of the widow who gave her all, in the assurance that out of the mouths of babes He has ordained praise, in the eloquent words of the Apostle, that God hath chosen the things which are not to bring to naught the things that are; we are taught, that in the Church of Christ there is intended to be no useless, no ineffective material. The entire Church, as one body, is to labor for the redemption of the world.

Let us learn the lesson of this sublime truth. My friend, poor though you may be, or weak, or sick, with but two talents, or but one, you are called to do no unimportant work in the conquest of the world. There is a work, which you are better fitted to accomplish, than any man on earth; than any angel in heaven. Are you looking for it? Filled with love of God and men are you seeking it, or doing it? Even if you are separated from all others, you can pray; you can aid the Master by at least saying, from your soul, "Thy will be done;" for—

They also serve who only stand and wait.

God grant us each grace— for each is called—to see his work for the world, and in the spirit of Christ to do it.

IV. But not only because it seeks all men, and provides for every want, and employs the whole Church; but also because *it seizes every occasion*, is the Christian beneficence universal. Let us do good unto all men, *as we have opportunity.*

The charity of the world is a thing of times and seasons. Designed to meet special wants, and to benefit special classes, it awaits special opportunities. But since the wants for which the Gospel provides, and the perils which it averts, are those of every man, and exist or threaten every day and every hour; every place and every circumstance provide fitting occasion for the outgoing of Christian love. Of course, I do not mean to say, that every place or hour will furnish the opportunity to preach a sermon, or to address a man or woman on specifically Christian subjects, or even to relieve physical want. But there is no place and no hour, in which we can not let the light of our love shine, so that men seeing our good works will glorify our Father in heaven. The Christian beneficence is protean in its forms. Like the air of heaven, and the light of heaven, and the water which God in mercy has poured around the world; like the great unseen forces of the universe, which bind the worlds in harmony, and bathe them in beauty; it adjusts itself to all times, all places, and all men. There are no surroundings, from the midst of which it may not continuously issue as a spiritual energy. Think not that you have done revealing it when you have given money, or taught your children, or spoken with your lips for Christ. Was our Lord beneficent, only when he healed the sick, or proclaimed the glad tidings of great joy? Was there a moment of his life in which his love did not warm and illumine the world he came to save? So must it be with us. For, in the last analysis, the Christian beneficence is the loving and self-sacrificing spirit of Christ; and this spirit, we can carry everywhere. No surroundings are too secular to hide it. If within us, it will shine out at home, in business, among the poor, in the church, on the street. But why try to catalogue the places and times befitting its outgoing? It is for all times and for all places. By its constant outshining more than in specific labor, is this world to be rescued from its sins.

V. Once more, not only because its outlook is the whole world,—because its end is the redemption of the whole man,—because it engages the whole Church, and seizes every opportunity,—is the Christian beneficence the universal beneficence; but also because it proceeds in the faith, that *all its outgoing will be successful.* Let us not be weary in well-doing. For in due season *we shall reap,* if we faint not.

There are two verses of Scripture which I am never tired of repeating; and which, as you know, I often repeat from this pulpit. When I despair of unraveling the tangled skein of occurrence; when I am about to fall into despair at the many afflictions that befall the righteous, and the calling away from earth of good men—I recall the sublime declaration of the inspired Apostle: "All things work together for good to them that love God." When I am despondent about my own work as a minister, disposed to believe, as all of us are, that I am of little use; that my weakness is insufficient as against the obstacles to successful work for Christ—I reanimate my drooping hope with the not less sublime assurance: "No labor is in vain in the Lord."

It is the union of these two assurances of God that I would press upon you this morning. Your labor, if in the Lord, shall not be in vain. And this, not only because you will be blessed, but also because the universe is on your side. All things are yours; all things are working together for your good. And just this is the truth which the Apostle brings to view in the context. Christian beneficence is the outgoing of the soul in love and sacrifice; and so is the outworking of a great law that never fails. He that soweth to the spirit shall reap of the spirit life everlasting; not for himself alone, but for mankind. Therefore, he adds, "Let us not be weary in well-doing, for in due season we shall reap if we faint not." "We shall reap." That is the promise. "He that soweth shall reap." That is the law. No labor is in vain in the Lord. If we believe the Gospel, if we believe in God the Father Almighty, and in Jesus Christ his Son our Lord, how can we doubt this assurance? Let us go forth to Christian labor for men and women, inspired by this great truth. We are sowing seed, whose abundant harvest God has predicted.

> "Let us set the plow with a joy akin
> To the joy of putting the sickle in."

Let us pray for more faith in this great consummation. To-morrow and to-morrow, and again to-morrow, let us labor and faint not. We may not see here the victory which we are winning. We may not see the fruit whose seed we are planting. But, if God be true, our labors can not fail. In due season,—whether in time or eternity,—in due season, we shall reap if we faint not.

From the subject, thus imperfectly brought before us, let us learn, first, the majesty of the Gospel. I know no aspect of the Gospel that more strikingly reveals its sublimity than this. It is no narrow religion with which as Christians we are allied. It is no small scheme to which we have pledged our souls' support. The world is its field. Every want of the soul is its object. All time is its opportunity. The whole Church is its missionary. The whole universe is its ally. Did such a Gospel spring from man? Was it conceived and brought forth on the earth? The greatness of the conception, alone, is enough to make reasonable the belief in its Divinity.

Let us learn, also, to be ashamed of our lack of faith in the Gospel's triumphs. If victory does not wait upon a Gospel to be described, as this has been; "Who will show us any good?" I know the sinfulness of the human heart. But, where sin has abounded, grace much more abounds. Could the Church, in the spirit I have described, move forward to the conquest of men, the redemption of the earth would soon draw nigh. And if we, each in his own lot, would labor in the same spirit, doubt not, that we also would soon see the strongholds of sin and wretchedness fall before our eyes.

Finally, in this spirit, would I call on all before me to accept the large provisions which God has made for them in the Gospel. This redemption is for you; because it is for all men. It is the redemption you need; for it provides for every want of your souls. It is the only redemption offered you; or, if there seems to be another, this is the only real redemption. The Christian beneficence that would bestow it is, as I have said, the Spirit of Christ; of Him who seeks and saves the lost. He is even now speaking to you in infinite love: "You are lost, I will save you. You are wretched, I will give you perfect bliss. Your spirit is hungry for righteousness, I will feed you. You are naked, I will clothe you. You are in prison, under the condemnation of the law, I will release you." Hear and heed the words of the infinitely benevolent Son of God, and Saviour of the world.

V.

THE CHRISTIAN CASUISTRY.

I, therefore, the prisoner of the Lord, beseech you that ye walk worthy of the vocation wherewith ye are called.—EPHESIANS iv, 1.

The field of moral indifference, which lies between the region of the inherently good and the region of the inherently evil, is a far wider field than most of us, perhaps, suppose. It is on this field, that most of those acts are committed, which constitute a man's career. It is not true that these acts possess no moral character. Their moral character is derived, however, from something outside of themselves. It is derived from the motives which prompt the man to commit them, or from his individual relations to others upon whom the acts in some way may terminate. It requires but little reflection to reach the conclusion, that these acts, morally indifferent in themselves, can not be tried as a class. Each of them must stand by itself. The same act, committed by two persons, may in the one case, be a bounden duty, and in the other case, be a flagrant wrong. Each makes a distinct case, to be adjudicated in the court of conscience.

Out of this fact, have arisen a phrase and a word.

The phrase is "Cases of Conscience;" and the word is "Casuistry." Every one, who has a case before his conscience, is, at that moment, a casuist. And a case of conscience is one, in which a man or a woman endeavors to determine, whether an action, neither right nor wrong in itself, is right or wrong, because of the circumstances in which it has been committed, or in which it is proposed to commit it. The large majority of these cases of conscience may easily be decided. Comparatively few require for their decision more than a moment's thought. It is not to be denied, however, that there are cases not so easily determined; cases in which one may for a long time honestly halt between two opinions, all the while praying for guidance.

This is true, especially, of some of those cases which are called cases of Christian conscience; cases whose peculiarity is due to the fact that the actor is a disciple of Christ. What should a Christian give up? What amusements, and occupations, and companies, should he forego? What rules of life should he lay down for his guidance in the new sphere in which he moves? Is there any thing, which one not a Christian may do without sin, which a Christian can not do sinlessly? If this or that amusement is wrong for one man, is it not equally wrong for another? There is scarcely a Christian before me, I suppose, who has not proposed questions like these to his conscience, and who has not been perplexed about their answer. Spiritual teachers, parents and companions are called upon to determine for others what their duty is in numberless cases, in each of which, while the act is indifferent in itself, the questioner fears that it has gained moral quality from the circumstances of its proposed commission. It does no good to respond: "Let your conversation be as becometh the Gospel of Christ;" for the very question is what, in this case, is the conversation becoming to Christianity? And there are not a few, whom it seems impossible to satisfy, unless another can be found to take the place of their own consciences; and to assume the responsibility of deciding on the moral quality of a particular act or habit. What is more lamentable, there are not a few who are prepared to take this position and to assume this responsibility. I regret, while speaking on this subject, to feel compelled to say, that a crying sin of some religious instructors is, that they are ready, when advice is asked upon a delicate and difficult case of this kind, to go further than the declaration of the principles of the Gospel, and to decide for others their duty before God. From such presumptuous care and watch of souls, all who are Christian teachers need most devoutly to pray for deliverance. It is given to no Christian teacher, as such, to take the place of another's conscience; to decide, for any other than himself, as to the moral quality of acts themselves not immoral; and he should be careful lest he incur the displeasure of Him who said: "Judge not that ye be not judged."

There are, however, in the New Testament certain clearly defined principles, which should be honestly applied in each case; and these general principles, it is the function of the Christian teacher to announce and explain.

It is my purpose, at this time, to show that on this subject the New Testament uniformly employs the language of *general principle*, as contrasted with the language of specific rule; to state the *reasons* for this peculiarity; and to repeat and explain the *principles themselves*, which the New Testament thus affirms for the guidance of the Christian.

It is my hope that any of you, who are perplexed by questions such as I have described, will, by this brief discussion, be aided rightly to answer them. But let no one forget, that the application of these principles belongs to each one for himself; never to one Christian for another who has reached the years of maturity. This right and this responsibility—for it is both a privilege and a duty—can not be delegated. It can not be placed by the people in the hands of the priests. If it can, it can be surrendered by the priests to the bishops; and if this can be done, it may just as righteously be given up to a supreme pontiff; and all below him, who refuse to yield to his declarations, on questions of morals, an implicit faith, may be declared under the ban of the Church. This, certainly, is not Christianity as we understand it. The application of these principles to cases of conscience is an individual right which can not be wrested. It is an individual duty which can not be delegated. If it is a privilege, it is indefeasible. If it is a burden, it belongs to a class of burdens of which every man shall bear his own.

I. First, then, I ask your attention to the fact, that, on this subject, the New Testament uniformly speaks in the language of *general principle*, as distinguished from the language of *specific rule*.

Among the many contrasts between the form of the Old Testament and that of the New,—the substance of the two being the same,—no one is more obvious and striking than just this; that the former seeks to promote morality by means of specific command and prohibition, and the latter by means of principle. The Israelite was hedged about by a system of the most minute rules. The Christian, on the contrary, looks in vain in the New Testament for such a system. It is abrogated. Of the ceremonies of the Hebrew ritual there remains only the memory; while the Decalogue itself is condensed into the two all-including precepts of love to God and man. Here, Christ as the great Teacher, placed himself in antagonism to the scribes, whose labors resulted in the multiplication of rules of conduct; and so careful was He, that He would decide no special case brought before him. Instead of pronouncing judgment, He declared fundamental principles; the application of which He invariably left to those immediately interested. When, for example, a criminal case was brought before Him, and his judgment solicited; instead of deciding in favor of the accusers or the accused; instead of bidding the former either to stone or to release the latter; He merely stated a principle, which He left them to apply: "He that is without sin among you, let him first cast a stone:" and, that the accusers did make the application, is evident from the words which follow: "And they which heard it, being convicted by their own conscience, went out one by one, beginning at the eldest even unto the last; and Jesus was left alone and the woman standing in the midst."*

---

* While using the incident of the woman taken in adultery as illustrating our Lord's method of dealing with specific cases brought before Him, I do not forget the mass of external evidence against its right to the position which it fills in the fourth Gospel. But though a probable interpolation, there is no good reason to doubt the actual occurrence of the incident. It would be difficult to assign a motive for the fabrication of the story. Moreover, the conduct attributed to the scribes and Pharisees harmonizes with their conduct on similar occasions, as the conduct attributed to Jesus harmonizes with his. Dr. Vaughan, the

So, also, when a case, involving the right to a particular inheritance, was brought before Him by one who supposed that he had been wronged, with the request: "Master, speak to my brother that he divide the inheritance with me;" the Saviour distinctly denied that, as a teacher of moral and religious truth, He was called to decide a dispute of that nature. "Man," said He, "who made me a judge or a divider over you?" And He then announced a general principle, by which, as He taught, men should control their conduct. "Take heed and beware of covetousness; for a man's life consisteth not in the abundance of the things which he possesseth." It is as if He had said: "I am not here to decide cases according to the law of conscience or the law of the empire. I am not called to judge and to execute judgment. I have been sent by the Father to proclaim the fundamental truths concerning your relations to Him and to your fellow men; and to impress upon the conscience of the world these great principles by which the life of man must be directed, if man is to be lifted up to fellowship with God; and, therefore, I refuse to decide this case. I refuse to speak to your brother about the inheritance. But I will announce, as becomes me, a principle, which men should remember whenever, and wherever, and however they have to do with property and its inheritance: 'Take heed and beware of covetousness; for a man's life consisteth not in the abundance of the things which he possesseth.'"

Master of the Temple, makes this admirable remark on the passage: "We hear sometimes of a *verifying faculty* to which, as to a sort of spiritual taste, revelation itself makes its appeal for a hearing in man's conscience. I question whether any ten or twelve verses of Scripture could appeal with more confidence to a tribunal thus constituted."

In exactly the way in which He dealt with cases of crime, and with cases involving the rights of individuals, He dealt also with the political questions which then agitated the Jewish people. As a religious teacher, He would take no side. In the exercise of his office, He would counsel neither submission to the Roman government nor rebellion against it. When a test question was directly put to Him;—a question which He could not answer categorically without taking a side—He refused to answer it; contenting Himself, as before, with the declaration of a principle; and leaving its application to the particular case, to those who approached Him with the question. He would not say, whether or not, it was lawful to give tribute to Cæsar. His only reply was: "Render unto Cæsar the things which are Cæsar's, and unto God the things which are God's."

The great Apostle to the Gentiles, who has treated this whole subject with some detail, followed closely in the footsteps of his Master. Declaring the Gospel, as he did declare it, to be the legitimate outgrowth of the Jewish religion, it was only natural, that, among those converted to Christianity through his agency, there should arise questions as to the presence or absence of obligation resting upon them individually, to observe certain rites commanded in the Jewish law: questions concerning fasts, and feasts, and meats, and days of ceremony and worship. I can not discover, in any of the Epistles of Paul, or in any record of his conduct, that he ever undertook to decide a particular case; that he once placed himself in the position of another man's conscience. He counseled charity; he taught liberty; he exhorted to self-denial; he proclaimed himself ready to eat no meat while the world stood, should the eating of it offend the conscience of a brother; and this, though he was persuaded of the Lord Jesus, that there was nothing of itself unclean. But that he ever decided another's case of conscience, I can not find the least evidence. He was always careful to speak in the language of general and abiding principle, instead of such specific and temporary command, as might be suited to a particular case.

II. For the adoption of this course, the Great Teacher and the Great Apostle had the most cogent *reasons*. This Gospel, which they preached, was not designed, as was the Hebrew religion, for one people and a definite period. It was a finality. It was meant to be permanent, uniform, and universal. It was intended to move down the centuries, the same yesterday, to-day, and forever; and across the countries and throughout the peoples, the same Gospel; until it had subjected all men and all nations to its sway. Had the inspired Word been encumbered with rules in regard to customs and amusements prevalent in one age; it would not have been suited to an age, after the customs had been abrogated, and the amusements had given place to others. Had it adapted itself, in this manner, to the people and the country of Palestine; it would, so far forth, have been useless to other peoples and other zones. Intended, like the atmosphere, to enfold the *world* in its embrace, and to infuse in all time a life throughout the human system; it was necessary that, like the atmosphere, it should be the same in every place, alike adapted to the tropics and the poles. Meant in its present form to be permanent as humanity; it was requisite, that its appeal be made in the language of permanent principles, to the abiding conscience of humanity; and not the language of special and temporary rules for special and temporary customs.

Nor was this all. Even more impressive, because more profound, is another reason that lay in the mind of Christ, for refraining both from the prescription of rules, and from the decision of special cases of conscience. Had He intended to shape men's conduct to a model; had his object been to place man upon some bed of Procrustes, and by violent measures to adjust him outwardly to a preordained standard; doubtless the New Testament would have abounded in rules and commands, the most comprehensive and minute. But because He sought rather to develop a character than to shape conduct; because he sought first to change the heart rather than the acts that proceed from it; his words embody principle instead of precept, and unfold great and permanent truths instead of specific and temporary rules. Beginning at the center of life, his words move thence to the activities of life. So He created man anew, instead of forcing new conduct upon an unchanged nature. So He regenerated the soul, instead of merely reforming the life. Rules might effect the latter. Vital and eternal principles alone could secure the former.

If any one, at this point, should be disposed to object to this description of the Gospel, as making it appear powerless to restrain vice, and to promote virtue; let him remember, that every principle, posessing vitality, when rooted in the soul of an intelligent being, will of necessity create its own rules of action. Let the principle of deep and abiding affection for his wife—for affection is a principle as well as a passion—govern an intelligent man. That love, outworking itself in all his conduct toward her, will create its own rules; and, by its own strength, will better control his life in his relations to her, than the best system of precepts for husbands that could be framed. On the other hand, let this affection be wanting; and no series of rules for the outward conduct, however detailed, however exacting, and however obeyed, will be able to take the place of the absent principle. So, let these principles of the Gospel of Christ be grounded in the heart of the disciple; and let him thoroughly submit his life to their guidance; and no case of conscience, too perplexing for decision, can possibly come before him.

III. And now, having prepared the way, by bringing before you both the fact that the New Testament employs the language of principle, and the reasons for it, I ask your attention to a statement of *the principles* themselves. I am sure, that it would be impossible to speak to Christians on a more important subject, than the subject, which brings before them the principles, by which they are to determine their duty, in the case of all actions, of which conscience affirms neither inherent right nor inherent wrong.

The first of these principles,—that which underlies all the others,—is *liberty*. I need not take time to prove that the New Testament, in the plainest terms, affirms the liberty of the individual disciple; his right to judge all his own proposed acts, not in themselves right or wrong. Let it be observed, that I do not affirm that each individual Christian is at liberty to *do* any thing not inherently wrong; but that he alone is at liberty, in each case as it arises, to judge whether he may. This right of private judgment in cases of conscience, can not be wrested from him. No man, by virtue of his Christianity, may assume to stand between a soul and its indifferent acts, and pronounce judgment. Christ plainly teaches this in the words which I have already quoted: "Judge not that ye be not judged." And in the method adopted by the Apostle to unfold this important truth, there seems to me to be some indignation expressed at those who might dare to doubt it. "One believeth that he may eat all things: another, who is weak, eateth herbs. Let not him that eateth, despise him that eateth not; and let not him which eateth not, judge him that eateth. Who art thou, that judgest another man's servant? To his own master he standeth or falleth. Let every man be fully persuaded in his own mind."

When a question, such as I have described, comes before a Christian man; when he is compelled by circumstances to decide, whether it will be wrong for him to indulge in an amusement or to begin or continue a habit, it is that Christian's inalienable right to decide for himself. This is a large and important part of the liberty, with which Christ has made us free. I may not specifically inform you of your duty in respect to these habits or amusements. You may not specifically inform me of mine. Each of us must stand or fall; never to his brother; but always to the individual conscience, and to our common Lord. This is a principle which the Church of Christ must respect. The recognition of this liberty is one of the highest exercises of that charity, which the Gospel so often inculcates and commends. Let us not forget, at the same time, that the liberty, which the New Testament emphasizes, is entirely different from individual liberty of action. It is only a freedom of judgment. You may not infer, that, because no one save yourself may sit in judgment on your cases of conscience, you have a Christian right to do every thing not in itself wrong. By no means. This, I fear, is a mistake often made. You have only a freedom to try and determine your own cases. For the right exercise of this judgment, free and indefeasible as it is, you are responsible to Christ.

Let us understand, then, that this liberty of judgment can not be invaded by the Church or by another Christian. But while it may not be invaded, the judgment itself must be under the guidance of the remaining principles of the Christian casuistry. Of these, I name, as the second principle clearly announced in the New Testament, the principle of *certainty*. A Christian has no right to perform any act, or to indulge in any practice, of whose moral character he is in doubt. This is clearly taught by the Apostle Paul in the words: "Let every man be fully persuaded in his own mind;" and more clearly, if that be possible, in the words which conclude his discussion, in the same chapter, in respect to the right to eat certain articles of food: "He that *doubteth* is condemned if he eat, because he eateth not of faith; for whatsoever is not of faith is of sin."

It would be strange, if most of us were not often placed in positions, which call for the brave and honest application of this principle. There are many acts and habits of whose moral character, or of the character of whose influence, as committed or indulged by us, we are unable thoroughly to convince ourselves. We know that they are not specifically prohibited, by either the written or the unwritten law of God. And yet we are unable to rid ourselves of the fear, that, in becoming responsible for them, we shall exert an influence against the interests of that spiritual kingdom, which our vocation pledges us to aid. The truth may be, that our fears are baseless. It may even be, that, while we entertain the fears, we are convinced, that but for unworthy but wide-spread and deep-seated prejudices, there would be no ground for the apprehensions we feel compelled to entertain. But the doubts or the fears are there; and, try how we will, we can not dissipate them. Is there a principle, then, clearly stated in the New Testament, by which a Christian thus perplexed is called to regulate his conduct? It is clear to my mind that there is; and that I have already stated it in this declaration of Paul: "He that *doubteth* is condemned if he eat." It is as if he had said: "While you are the sole judges of the influence and expediency of this proposed act so far as yourselves are concerned, you may not begin any course of conduct which requires reflection and judgment, until you have faithfully exercised the right of judgment, which, as Christians, you possess; until you are fully persuaded in your own minds. You may not eat the meats, therefore, while you suffer yourselves to remain in doubt. He that doubteth is condemned if he eat, because he eateth not of faith."

You see, at once, the Christian basis of the principle. A Christian is represented in the New Testament as one on whom God has bestowed a new life; and, because a new life, a new power of spiritual discernment. The possession of this power of discernment is the ground of his right to judge; for "he that is spiritual, judgeth all things; and is judged of no man." But the talent which God has given him, he has no right to hide in a napkin. He has no right to act as though he did not possess it. And so long as he is in doubt; so long as fears exist; so long as he does not, by means of this new power of discernment, and in the exercise of this spiritual privilege of judgment, reach a conclusion which permits him to eat the meat or indulge in the amusement; he must deny himself. This is no rule to restrain. It is not a covert attack on Christian liberty. On the contrary, it implies the liberty to judge, and simply compels its exercise.

The two principles, of which I have spoken, emerge out of man's individual relations to the Gospel. Liberty of judgment and certainty of conviction would be applicable to cases of conscience, though the man applying them were the only Christian on the earth. To these, however, we must add a third; growing out of his relations to his fellow-men. This is the principle of *self-denial;* or, more specifically, charity for the consciences of others.

Compromise of individual privileges is necessary to the existence of society. Social relations involve abridgments and restrictions. Separate a man from his fellows. Place him in a district apart from all other members of the human family. You enlarge his liberty of action; and he may do many things, from which, on his re-entrance into the busy walks of men, he must refrain. On the uninhabited prairie, or in the wilderness, I may build fires everywhere and discharge fire-arms in every direction with impunity. The moment, however, that I re-enter the thoroughfares of the city, I stand in relations to others, which properly abridge my liberty of action. My new position demands of me some regard for the welfare of those with whom I come in contact. If Christianity had to do, solely, with the relations of man to God and his own conscience; doubtless, the moment one satisfied God's written law and the demands of his own conscience, he might, as a Christian, do or leave undone every thing else. In that case he would not, as a Christian, at least, be called to debate many things in themselves indifferent. But this is not the New Testament account of the religion or of the mission of the disciple of Christ. "Ye are the salt of the earth." "Ye are the light of the world." "Ye are a city set on a hill which can not be hid." "Ye are epistles read and known of all men." In terms like these, does the word of God describe the mission of Christians to the world. Moreover, Christians are united to each other so closely, that the Apostle says of them, that they are members one of another.

Other lives than our own, both without the Church and within it, are molded by our conduct. Other destinies are suspended on our careers. We can not therefore, as Christians, release ourselves from the duty of regarding the influence of our conduct on society. Especially, must we be careful of those, to whom we are so closely bound, as our brethren of the household of faith. This truth, the Apostle states with clearness and emphasis both in the Epistle to the Romans and in that to the Corinthians. He takes the highest ground as to the duty, especially, which Christians owe to the consciences of their brethren. Listen to his words: "I know, and am persuaded by the Lord Jesus, that there is nothing unclean of itself. But if thy brother be grieved with thy meat, now walkest thou not charitably. Destroy not him with thy meat, for whom Christ died. Let us, therefore, follow after the things which make for peace, and things wherewith one may edify another. For meat, destroy not the work of

God. All things indeed are pure; but it is evil for that man who eateth with offense. It is good neither to eat flesh, nor to drink wine, nor any thing whereby thy brother stumbleth, or is offended, or made weak." And to the Corinthians he says of himself: "Wherefore, if meat make my brother to offend, I will eat no flesh while the world standeth, lest I make my brother to offend."

This, then, is the principle of Christian conduct growing out of our relations to others, as unfolded by Paul. It is the principle of charity or self-denial. I purposely refrain from illustrating it, by naming any of the customs and amusements which to-day divide the members of Christian communities, lest I should seem to attempt to take the place of the consciences of others. The principle is a clear one. We are bound, as banded together in Christ, to have regard for each other's scruples. Or, to put it in a form which will enable us easily to employ it, we must be careful not to offend the Christian sentiment of the community. We are under obligation not to do that which will prove a stumbling-block to other Christians. Because limited in time, I content myself with its bare statement. I can not, however, pass on to the statement of the next principle, without first remarking, that it is not always easy to say, just how far we must refrain on account of other Christians. There is a difficulty here, which often arises in practice. I can conceive of one pushing the principle too far. I can conceive of one, so oversensitive to the feelings of every fellow Christian, that he will become the veriest slave; who, by exchanging the bondage of rule for the bondage of a morbid and hurtful charity, may injure the very men, whose consciences he fears to wound. It is not true, that we are called upon always to conform our conduct, in indifferent matters, to the judgment of the Christians who are about us. Self-denial, in charity to our brethren, is not without limits. It may often become our duty, as more than once it became Paul's, to oppose, not only with steadfastness, but with vigor, the religious prejudices of weaker disciples. For the Kingdom of God is a more commanding object, than even the sentiment of a Christian community on courses of conduct in themselves indifferent. And when the two are in conflict, whatever else must give way, the interests of the Kingdom of righteousness have the highest right to determine our action.

And, thus, we are brought to the fourth of these great principles of the Christian casuistry—the principle of *loyalty;*—of loyalty to the Kingdom of God. Why are Christians suffered to remain here, subjected to the temptations and the sufferings of a sinful society? Why, if they have been forgiven and made heirs of God, are they not given the inheritance at once? The answer to this question can not be included in a single remark. Doubtless, they are here, partly for their own sakes. A higher type of perfection will be theirs, because of the struggles against sin which they are compelled to undergo while living in the world. Doubtless they are here, partly for the greater glory of the Redeemer. For his victory over the powers of evil, in the rescue of a soul from the dominion of sin, is greater, when that rescue is accomplished in this world; which is ruled, as we are taught, by these very powers. But, more than all, I take it, we are here to carry forward the work of Christ, in behalf of his own Kingdom. This would seem to be implied in the words of the Lord himself; uttered in connection with the prayer that his people should not be taken out of the world, but should be preserved from its evil. "As thou, Father, hast sent me into the world, even so have I sent them into the world." We are here to advance the interests of the eternal Kingdom of God. No duty can be more imperative than loyalty to that Kingdom. Loyalty to the Kingdom, therefore, is a principle,— than which none can be more commanding,—which we should not fail to apply to indifferent acts. We are bound to judge the tendency of every course of conduct. We are bound, as Christians, to subject it honestly to scrutiny, for the purpose of ascertaining whether it will advance or retard the Kingdom's progress to its predicted triumph. Nor must this principle ever be suffered to lie below consciousness. So Paul exhorts Christians: "Whether ye eat or drink, or whatsoever ye do, do all to the glory of God." It is, indeed, true, that we may not do evil that good may come. But every thing, except the commands of the law of God, must be made subservient to the Kingdom of Christ. A morally indifferent act at once loses its quality of indifference to the man, who, when tempted to commit it, sees that its probable influence will be inimical to the rule of God in the earth. This is so clear and indisputable that nothing need be added to its simple statement.

One more principle of the Christian casuistry remains to be mentioned: the principle of *imitation of Christ*. Here, we reach the crowning and governing principle of Christian living. Here, is to be found the ultimate test, in every case of conscience. When no other principle can, from the nature of the case, be applied to indifferent acts, this is applicable, because spiritual. "If any man have not the Spirit of Christ, he is none of his."

These, then, are the great and general principles of the Gospel, that we are to apply to every question, in that large field of actions, which, indifferent in themselves, may become right or wrong, duties or sins, from the circumstances of their commission. Here are no rules to restrain, but principles to constrain; no commands to be obeyed, but truths to inspire; no minute directions to repress the life, but broad generalizations to expand the soul. So, if conduct is not directly shaped; character is directly developed. So, if Christianity does not instantly repress outward vice; it touches the heart, and implants the seeds of a new spiritual life, itself divine and eternal, by whose power the soul grows to the stature of the perfect man in Christ Jesus. Liberty of judgment. Certainty before action. Charity for others' consciences. Loyalty to the Kingdom of God. Imitation of Christ. These are, at once, the great principles, which lie at the basis of the Christian casuistry; and the great traits, which make up the Christian character. I would, that they were graven, as with a pen of iron, on every Christian heart. I would, too, that God might give us all grace, fairly and bravely and always, to apply them to our lives.

There is a tremendous responsibility, Christian brethren, in being lifted, out of a life of bondage to rule, into the liberty a life guided by principle. It is the great remove from childhood to manhood. There comes a time to every boy, when the rules and formulas, the tasks and hours of home, are no longer imposed; when the youth breathes and walks, unrestrained by behests and prohibitions. Who, that has passed that period, does not know the exultant joy of the hour of the newly found freedom? What young man does not rejoice in the strength of his youth, and the ecstasy of liberty, when first he sees the world, with all its paths before him, free to choose between them all? But, the danger of the hour! The responsibility of the freedom! What, if no lofty principle guide his footsteps to the paths of right? What, if he drown the voice within, which bids him wisely choose? There are no rules, no hedges, no barriers. There is no strong arm of parent, to hold him back from destruction. He is no longer a child. God help him—for he sorely needs help—and hold his soul attentive to the voice within!

So do we stand to-day. When, at the death of the old Dispensation, its rules and ceremonies were abrogated, and the new Dispensation of principle was ushered in, the Church passed from childhood to manhood. The disciple of Christ is held to no code of laws, daily and hourly brought before him, in the ritual of his religion. That age of the Church has gone forever. The Christian of to-day stands in the midst of a world of ever increasing activity, with perfect liberty of judgment, and with no rule of life to guide him, save these principles of the Gospel of Christ. How solemn the position! And temptations are so many; and relations are so intricate; and pleasure so allures; and the world is so engrossing; and evil is so active; and destiny is so near. How solemn are the issues of his conduct! No wonder that the hosts of heaven are intensely interested in the life of man.

Brethren, let us, too, seek to realize what a vocation ours is; what a problem Christian living is. To be perfectly free; and yet to walk worthily. O, let us hold fast by great principles of action! What need we have of them! What need of the strong agony of prayer; of every means of grace—the Word of God, the Church, the Sacraments! How cautiously do we need to walk; how valiantly to wrestle; how prayerfully to live! For sin is within us, as well as holiness. And temptations are around us, as well as the angels of God. And one is seeking to destroy us, as well as One to lift us to fellowship with Himself. And other destinies than our own are determined by our lives. O, let us watch, and study, and fight, and pray continuously; that we may walk worthy of the vocation wherewith we are called.

I may not close without one word to you, who, because you do not call yourselves Christians, may be congratulating yourselves, that you are not obliged to apply the principles of the Christian casuistry to the conduct of your lives. Do not suppose, that, for this reason, you enjoy a larger freedom. If you are not under Christ, you are under law. And law will hold you guilty of the violation of all, though you violate but the least of its commands. Law will heed no excuse, though you plead the strongest of temptations. Law will inflict its whole penalty, though the infliction result in eternal death.

VI.
THE GAIN OF THE CHRISTIAN IN CHRIST'S DEPARTURE.

Nevertheless, I tell you the truth; it is expedient for you that I go away.—JOHN xvi, 7.

It will be conceded by all, that suffering reveals, by calling into activity, man's latent selfishness; that the influence of sharp or long continued pain is to fix the sufferer's attention on himself; to induce him to emphasize his own claims and needs, and to disparage the claims and needs of others. When one finds himself in imminent peril of disaster, his first, and, usually, his prevailing impulse is, at whatever cost to others, to make certain his own escape. Before this impulse, all moral barriers easily give way. In the thronging crowd, hurrying from some dreaded and impending catastrophe, the cry of the hearts, if not of the lips, is: "Save himself who can:" and the strong relentlessly crush the weak, in the awful struggle for life. Had Jesus been a sinner, therefore, his sinfulness could scarcely have been concealed in the hours of his severest suffering. The crucial test of moral perfection is to be found at the point, where the temptation to selfishness is strongest. And it is at this point, precisely, that the character of the Redeemer stands forth as unique: as the Revelation, indeed, of the absolute unselfishness.

"Having loved his own, which were in the world, He loved them unto the end." As He approached his predicted passion, his anxiety was aroused, not by the agony which He was about to endure, but by the disappointments of those around Him. He did nothing to mitigate his own sorrow; He did every thing to relieve theirs. He refused the impetuous defense of an Apostle; but He healed the wound of an enemy. He declined the draught which would have dulled his own consciousness of suffering; but He did not forget to commend his mother to the loving care of a friend. He would not exert his miraculous power to ward off the blows that his foes were inflicting; but He prayed: "Father, forgive them, for they know not what they do." We shall search history in vain, for another example of absolute unselfishness, under the temptation of prolonged and unspeakable suffering. It were possible to Him, alone, who, though He knew no sin, was made sin for us, that we might be made the righteousness of God in Him.

Similar evidence of sinlessness—and evidence quite as strong—appears in the prayer, which He addressed to God, and in the words, which He addressed to his disciples, at the beginning of his passion. In both the prayer and the address, He dwells, not on the weight of his own burdens, but on the sorrow of those whom He is about to leave, and on the dangers to which they will be exposed after his departure. The prayer is not for Himself, but for them. The address indicates, that, while He appreciated what was about to be inflicted on Himself, his heart throbbed with a sympathy, deeper than mere man ever has felt, for those who so soon would forsake Him and flee away. It is to this absolute unselfishness, that we owe the great river of comfort, which, springing from the heart of the Lord, flows through this farewell discourse to his disciples. And it is to this, especially, that we owe the words, which I have selected as my text: "It is expedient for you that I go away."

As we are to recall, to-day, in the ordinance which He has appointed, the death of our Lord, we may appropriately attempt to answer the question: "What was the expediency of Christ's departure?" The inquiry is important. For there is no devout Christian, who reads his life without a feeling, akin to envy of the disciples, who walked with Him on earth; who heard his words of celestial wisdom; and beheld the works of almighty power, which attested his divinity. We efface with difficulty the impression, that personal contact with a character so lofty must have done far more, than the mere record of his life, however devoutly pondered, can ever do, to strengthen faith, and quicken love, and stimulate to self-sacrifice. The inquiry gains additional interest, the moment we recall, how greatly the personal benevolent work of our Lord was limited by his death. As one has well said on this subject: "It is, indeed, wonderful, that Christ should never have employed force to establish his kingdom. But above this height of wonder we may see another far higher; and that is, that He restrained his power in works of benevolence. It is difficult for good men to restrain their benevolent activities, even when these can not be well employed, or have ceased to be useful. How, then, could Christ, with his opportunities, forbid his undiminished love and power to do more for men?" Why did He voluntarily leave his work of mercy, when, it would seem, He had just begun it? Why was his ministry so brief? Why were his miracles so few; when He left a world still sunk in iniquity, and groaning with pain?

I can not, within the limits of a single sermon, answer this question exhaustively. All that I can hope to do, is to touch upon one branch of it; the gain of the Christian in the departure of the Lord. "It is expedient *for you* that I go away."

I. That we may have this gain brought clearly before us, I ask your attention, first, to a truth with which all of us are, no doubt, familiar: *that the sensations, excited by material objects, become weak, in the proportion in which the objects become familiar.*

Perhaps no line of English poetry is more often repeated, than that which begins "Endymion:" "A thing of beauty is a joy forever." The line is a household word, because it is the noble expression of a great truth. But a thing of beauty becomes a permanent joy only, when, vanishing from sight for a time, it gives opportunity to the mind to idealize it. If the bodily eyes see it day after day, it loses largely its power to excite the feelings. It must "go away" for a time, at least, or it can not be a joy forever. To bring this truth clearly before our minds, let us suppose a man standing, for the first time, before the falls of Niagara. A sense of awe in the presence of a power so incessant and so resistless takes possession of his soul; and if he leaves the scene, this sense of awe will become permanent. He will never think of the cataract, without a revival of the feeling which the first sight of it awakened. But, let us suppose that he builds a house in full view of the falls, and sees the rush of waters and hears their majestic thunder from day to day. You need not be told, that, though Niagara will not be less a thing of beauty, it will lose its power to enchant him, because of the very familiarity of his senses with the scene.

The sublimest object, which nature offers to the view of man, is the firmament at night, resplendent with countless suns. Profound must have been both the awe and the joy of the first man, when he beheld, for the first time, the vault of heaven above him, "glowing with living sapphires." When, first, for him,

> Hesperus that led
> The starry host, rode brightest, till the moon,
> Rising in clouded majesty, at length,
> Apparent queen, unveil'd her peerless light,
> And o'er the dark her silver mantle threw.

Why are not feelings as vivid nightly excited in every one of us? It is not because the heavens have lost any of their sublimity. But, rather, because the very familiarity of our senses with the spectacle has made it impossible for us to reproduce the feelings, which the first view of them awakened.

It will not be disputed, that the senses become wearied, or, at least, satiated, by the too continuous impact upon them of forms of material beauty or sublimity. The fact I do not stop to explain. Accepting it, for the purposes of this sermon, as ultimate, I go on to say, that in the light of it, we begin to see one element of the expediency of Christ's departure. Had He remained in the world, had his life continued longer than it did, or had his miracles been more often repeated, men would have ceased to be impressed by them. In order that the influence of the life of Christ on men might be a permanent influence; abiding with the world; it was necessary that he should "go away."

All who have read the history of the disciples, who, at this time, were mourning the predicted departure of the Saviour, know how much deeper was the impression, which they received from his life after his death, than was that, which they received while He lived. Within a few weeks after the crucifixion, they made far greater advances in growth into his likeness, than they had made during the years they were his companions. The longer He remained with them, holy and loving as He was, the less profound was the impression which his life made upon their souls. And this He saw; and therefore said of Himself: "Except a grain of wheat fall into the ground and die it abideth alone, but if it die it bringeth forth fruit:" and again: "I, if I be lifted up, will draw all men unto me." And now, just before the passion, which, as He knows, will culminate in his death, He reiterates the same great truth, in the words: "It is expedient for you that I go away."

There is nothing exceptional in this. We see the outworking of the same law in daily life. There is many a man upon whom, while she lived, the parental love and the Christian example of a devoted mother exerted little influence; but who, when she had "gone away," as Christ went away from these disciples, began to feel the worth of her love and the beauty of her example; and continued to feel them more and more deeply, until at last they transfigured his life. And, therefore, let me say to those, who are tempted to discouragement, as they seem to themselves, to see their Christian influence wasted on those whom God has given them; it will be but in accordance with a great law, that is operative in all society, if the power of your life shall not be manifest in the lives of your children, until God shall have called you away. You may do by your death, what you can not do by your life. Let no delay discourage you. It was so with the Master. Why may it not be so with the disciple? The impression of his life on them was beginning to be weakened, by the very fact of their daily contact. It was expedient for them, therefore, and for the world itself, that He should return to the Father.

II. Another element of this expediency will appear, if we recall the fact, *that the object of the Gospel is to form in man a character, independent of human help, and superior to circumstance.*

I state a truth, obvious to every one who has studied the Gospel, when I say, that its ultimate object, so far as this world and his fellow-men are concerned, is the character of the disciple. It may have a higher object so far as God is concerned, and so far as the future world is concerned. I believe, of course, that, as the highest act, which can engage the faculties of a created being, is the worship of the uncreated God; the end of the Gospel is to prepare man for immediate and adoring communion with the Father of spirits. But for this world, full of relations with his fellow-men, the end of the Gospel is the creation and development of a character like that of Christ himself; a character dependent on the fewest possible human and material aids. The ruin which sin had caused was so thorough, that, at the first, man was aided, in his endeavors to attain righteousness, by special interpositions; by miracles; by theophanies; by an elaborate ritual; by a detailed law; by a long succession of inspired prophets. He needed every human and material help that God could give him.

But the fullness of times came. A period arrived, when these detailed and abundant helps became, not only needless, but profitless; burdens instead of supports. Then appeared the incarnate Son of God; the end of the law for righteousness. His life and character became to men what the law had been. And, so it was, that his disciples leaned upon Him, just as before men had leaned upon the law, and the prophets, and the miracles, of the elder dispensation. And it was the design of God, that the disciples should thus imbibe Christ's spirit, and become strong with Christ's strength.

But a new danger arose. There is a leaning on another for support, the effect of which is, not to strengthen, but to weaken character. And in the case of the earliest disciples there was great danger, that, from their daily contact with Jesus, they would learn to rely on Him as a material presence, rather than on the spiritual strength, which his presence was intended to impart. Christ would thus have become an external reliance, instead of a source of personal inspiration. They would have turned to Him for directions, instead of imbibing from his life a spirit. They would have obtained from Him commands in particular cases, instead of forming upon his, a vigorous and self-reliant character. And it was because this danger could be averted by his departure alone, that our Lord said to his disciples: "It is expedient for you that I go away."

I do not know that I am understood. But I think that all will understand me, when I say, that there comes a time in the life of every boy, when it is the duty of the father to throw his child upon his own resources; when it behooves the father to refuse longer to make opinions, or to decide questions of conscience for him; when tutelage and restraint should cease; and responsibility, and liberty, and self-reliance should begin. There is a time, when the father must "go away" from the boy. Otherwise, force of character, and power to do great things, to resist great temptations, and to bear great burdens will become impossibilities. So is it with Christ and his people. It was the design of Christ that his people should walk fearlessly amid evil; strong not only, but self-reliant also, in the spiritual strength which they derive from Him. The lofty piety, the large self-sacrifice, the faith, and hope, and love, which have beautified the lives of so many of his disciples, would have been far more difficult than at present, if not absolutely impossible of attainment, had Jesus of Nazareth remained in the world. His people would have leaned upon the Man; they would have invoked his miraculous power; they would have sought refuge from personal danger in the omnipotence of their Master; they would have found strength only in his material nearness; and they would have been weak in proportion to their physical distance from Him. You and I are stronger to-day; we are better men and women every way, more like Christ himself; than we could have been, had his earthly life continued until now. It was expedient for us that He should go away.

III. We shall see another element of this expediency, if we call to mind the truth, that *the imitation of an example is corrected by the example's personal absence.*

We all know, that there is a lower and a higher imitation. The lower is mere servile copying. It seizes hold of nothing more permanent or noble, than the mere exterior; the peculiarities and manners. Infinitely above this, is the imitation, which we describe by the phrase, imbibing the spirit of another. This latter, of course, is the imitation which the Gospel expects of us, as the followers of Christ. Each one of us is expected to be able to say with Paul: "For to me to live is Christ." "I am crucified with Christ, nevertheless I live, and yet, not I, but Christ liveth in me." We can easily picture a man treading in the footsteps of Christ; beginning a ministry in Galilee; repeating the words that he uttered on its hill-slopes, and on the shores of the sea of Tiberias; refusing to dwell in one place; journeying through Palestine from Lebanon to the south of Judea; carefully seeking the spots made sacred by the presence of Jesus, in order that his life may in all respects be like that of his Master; and at last consenting to be crucified on the very hill, on which the Lord himself offered up his life in our behalf. But after all had been done, no one of us would think of affirming, that he had followed Christ as Christ commands his people to follow Him. And we can picture another, filled with a desire to be about his father's business like that which impelled the Lord himself in all things to seek his Father's will; living in a like communion with God; loving and sympathizing with his fellow-men; devoting all that he is and all that he has to their highest well-being: and, though such a man knows nothing of the geography of the holy land, and has scarcely imagination enough, to call vividly before him one single scene in the life of the Lord; we would still say, that the "mind is in him which was also in Christ."

It is this latter imitation, this spiritual following, this imbibing his spirit, that Christ would see in all of us. Without it all mere outward imitation is worthless. Yea, though we could repeat the very miracles of Christ himself, it would avail us not one whit, if below it all we had not this spiritual life that was his. How well the great Apostle to the Gentiles understood this, let his own words testify: "Though I have the gift of prophecy, and the tongues of angels, and understand all mystery and knowledge; though I have all faith so that I could remove mountains; and though I bestow all my goods to feed the poor, and give my body to be burned, and have not love, it profiteth me nothing."

There was danger,—and by no means slight danger,—that the disciples of Christ, living near his person, would give themselves to this lower and mere outward imitation; that they would copy his acts instead of imbibing his spirit. On more than one occasion did this tendency reveal itself. They heard their Lord's judgments pronounced on sin; and, imitating Him, would have called down fire from heaven. They beheld Him casting out devils; and themselves sought to cast them out. Like the Pharisees, who tithed mint, anise, and cummin, and forgot the weightier matters of the law, they seized upon that which was outward, and temporary, and exceptional in Christ's life; and failed to learn the secret of his life that lay below them all. And, therefore, He said to them: "It is expedient *for you* that I go away." How soon this expediency was revealed! For when He had gone, that which was outward and peculiar in his life went with Him. And, as they recalled their absent Lord, these outward peculiarities retired from the first place in their recollection. Memories of his deeper life became more vivid;—memories of earnest prayer, of a love for men that passed all knowledge, of a self-sacrifice that gave

Himself to death. And, as these stood forth before them when they sought to follow Him; you know, how their characters grew stronger, and their love deepened, until the spirit of Christ so shone in them, that, men took knowledge of them that they had been with Jesus. The Peter, who had denied his Master, preached Christ crucified before the council; and the Son of Thunder was able to write the fourth Gospel, and that epistle, in which he reaches a tone so Christ-like, in the words: "If Christ laid down his life for us, we ought to lay down our lives for the brethren."

And, as it was expedient for the first disciples, so it was expedient for us who have come after them, that Christ should return to the Father. Had He remained on the earth, repeating, from that day to this, the works He wrought in Palestine, we also should have lost sight of his spirit in the overshadowing history of his outward career. Our Lord remained on earth only long enough, to accomplish his sacrificial mission, and to show to men the spirit of the perfect human life. It is this spirit, that we must imbibe in our endeavors to become like Him. Not an outward mechanical copying, but an inward spiritual following of the Master, is the high privilege, as it is the duty of the disciple.

IV. We shall see still further proof of the expediency of Christ's departure, by holding before us *its relation to the universal triumph of Christianity.*

The proclamation of Christianity as the exclusive, the ultimate, and the universal religion, was not an after-thought of the Apostles. That it was in the mind of Jesus himself, we are not left to prove from a single declaration, like the declaration: "I, if I be lifted up, will draw all men unto me." The prediction of its universality is to be read, quite as clearly, in that sublime statement to the woman of Samaria, in which He places the heart of man, as the shrine in which God delights, over against both Gerizim and Jerusalem; and in the great commission: "Go, teach all nations, baptizing them in the name of the Father, and of the Son, and of the Holy Ghost."

But what progress, toward this universal supremacy, was made by his faith, so long as He lived in the world? His disciples were men of his own nation; they were, largely, men of his own province of Galilee. Only once, during his ministry, so far as we know, did He travel beyond the boundary of Palestine. What, during his life, was Jesus of Nazareth to the great outlying peoples of the empire? How lame and impotent a conclusion to a ministry, attested by stupendous miracles, was the little company of disciples, which the ascension of Christ left orphaned in a hostile or contemptuous world! Had the history of Christianity ended with the earthly life of Jesus, we should still have been compelled to assert the expediency of his departure; and this, for the reason, that the revelation of the grace of God, in the life of Jesus, though authenticated by "signs and wonders," failed to secure the belief of his own people, and made no impression upon the world at large. And, what seems remarkable to the casual reader of his life, the longer He remained in the world after his first provincial and external successes, the more conspicuous his failure became. There seems to have been a point in his ministry, when the crowds, which first had followed Him, began to fall away. From that point onward, not a day seems to have passed by, on which some did not turn back from following after Him. Miracles were no longer needed, to provide food for the crowds of listening and excited people. And, at the last, betrayed by one, denied by another, and forsaken by all of his chosen companions; He is left in the hands of his malignant foes, to suffer and to die alone. Where, now, is the promise of his conquest of the world?

Contrast—if you would know the expediency of his departure—contrast this apparent failure, with the movement of Christianity after He had definitely "gone away:" after the crucifixion, the resurrection, and ascension. At once, the spiritual power and the universality of Christianity were revealed. The first Christian sermon was addressed by Peter to men who represented three continents; and the conquest of the world, by the faith of Christ, was begun. From that day to this, the movement of Christianity—retarded, though it has often been, by the unbelief or the corruption of the Church—has been an advance toward its predestined triumph. And whatever else has checked it, it has never been checked by the barriers of climate, of nation, or of race. For, having "gone away" from earth, the presence of Christ, at any moment, is limited to no country. No people may monopolize Him. No city is the exclusive capital of his spiritual Kingdom. Nowhere is the center; everywhere is the circumference of his gracious and redeeming presence.

V. But all this and more, on which I can not dwell, is included in the words of the Lord, which immediately follow the text: *"If I go not away, the Comforter can not come."* We lose the material presence of Christ, that, through the indwelling Spirit, the power of Christ may be within us. We lose the external help of his nearness, that we may possess the internal might, which the Comforter bestows, in taking the things of Christ and showing them to our spirits. The change is from the exterior and temporal to the interior and eternal; from the relation of friendship to the possession of character. We can not hear his words, but we can imbibe his spirit. We may not touch the hem of his garment, but we may be clothed upon with Him. There may not be an outward walking with Him; but, what was largely an impossibility for the first disciples, there may be a communion of our souls with Him. It is not possible, indeed, to invoke his miraculous power to aid us in our lives; but we may, as they could not, be strengthened with might by his spirit in the inner man. Every way, therefore, is there gain to the disciple and the world. The Church is not limited by the possibility of nearness to his body; but his spirit is everywhere. The Church's shrine is no longer in Jerusalem alone; but wherever men lift their hearts in believing prayer and praise. Religion is spiritual, and therefore eternal. Let no heart mourn to-day, then, because we can not look upon the body of Christ, or talk with Him at his table, as men talked with Him when on earth. Let no one imagine this to be no real communion, because we can not see Him face to face. His spirit is with us; and our hearts, as they throb in sympathy with the great love which impelled Him to the sacrifice which we remember, can hold communion with Him, who now is present, wherever two or three are met together in his name. Let us rejoice that He has gone away; knowing the truth of the blessed paradox, that He returned to the Father, that He might be nearer to the world.

These words will have been spoken in vain, if they do not leave, on all of us, a profound impression of the spiritual character of the religion of Christ. The Gospel is satisfied with nothing except a character and life like Christ's. It is not content that we shall rest in any thing outward: though it be as sacred as the house of God; the sacrament of Christ's death; yea, as the very body of our Lord. With reverence be it said, our Lord would remove from his Church this blessed eucharist, as He removed Himself from his disciples, if He saw that it was standing in the way, or in the place of growth into likeness to Himself. Nothing but that likeness will satisfy Him; and nothing but that likeness will satisfy our own hearts. The outward is ever for the inward. The material is in order to the spiritual. The Church is in order to life. The sacrament is in order that we may be sanctified. If Christ would not prolong his earthly life, knowing that his disciples would make it a hindrance and stumbling-block, a minister of spiritual weakness instead of spiritual might; if it was expedient for them that He should go away; think you that He will look with satisfaction upon us, as we rest ultimately in these outward services of his Church; these songs of praise, this eating and drinking in his name? No, my brethren; there is something loftier than these services. There is someting more sacred than the sacrament. There is the spirit of Christ. There is a love like his, which loves all men, and overcomes all obstacles, and endures through all time. There is the image of God to be recovered, and confiding communion with Him to be achieved. O, let us learn to look, through all these material and worldly aids, to the ultimate, the spiritual, the eternal bestowments of the Gospel! These aids, like his visible life, are earthly and temporal. The Supper itself will abide only till He come again. But the spirit that was his, and that may be ours, is the very end of all his sacrifice, and should be the end of all our prayer and our endeavor. For that spirit is, itself, the great inheritance of his people; and it alone, of all the objects that we can now attain, is incorruptible and undefiled, and fadeth not away.

Finally, the truth, which we have had before us to-day, may well be employed—as it certainly is calculated—to dissipate the impression, that the Redeemer, whom we proclaim to you who thus far have not accepted him, is valuable only as a shield to interpose between you and the future punishment, which your conscience proclaims to be your desert, and distinctly prophesies to be your destiny. He is valuable, indeed, as such a shield. But the supreme blessing, which follows his acceptance, is the bestowment of this perfect character, of which He is both the source and the example. Holiness floats as a dim and distant vision, indistinct and unattainable, until Christ is seen. To use language now quite popular,—without Him, man must adjust his life to his material environment, and be directed by his lower and sensual impulses; and the holiness, which sometimes attracts him in the distance, must remain distant forever. In Him alone—now that, by his going away, his life and death can exert their legitimate influence on men—in Him alone, is holiness made known, and made possible to our souls.

I come, then, to you, O, men and women, who, though sorely sick with sin, and tempted to despair of its removal, still see in yourselves the ruins of a godlike character, which you sometimes dare to hope may be rebuilded. I hold forth Jesus Christ; in union to whom this hope will grow to full assurance. He came with this high object: to restore in man the image of God. For this, He lived a human life. For this, He died a sacrificial death. To bestow this greatest, all-including blessing, He even limited, in time and in number, his miracles of blessing; and went away. God has approved his work, and raised Him from the dead. Nothing remains, but that you accept Him as your Redeemer; and, living in communion with Him, catch his spirit, and grow into his image evermore.

VII.
THE SANCTIFICATION OF THE SECULAR LIFE.

Whether therefore ye eat, or drink, or whatsoever ye do, do all to the glory of God.—I. CORINTHIANS x, 31.

We speak familiarly of John as the Apostle of love, of James as the Apostle of works, of Peter as the Apostle of character, and of Paul as the Apostle of doctrine. But we do not mean any thing more, than that each of these subjects, respectively, is the one, upon which the Apostle, to whom it gives a title, chiefly dwells. Above all, we do not mean to assert, that any one Apostle intended to depreciate any subject, which gives special tone to the writings of either of the others. I have spoken of Paul, as the Apostle, especially, of doctrine. At the same time, it would be difficult to find, in John's epistles, a more impassioned assertion of God's love, than the statement: "I am persuaded that neither death nor life, nor angels nor principalities nor powers, nor things present nor things to come, nor height nor depth, nor any other creature, shall be able to separate us from the love of God which is in Christ Jesus our Lord." It would be difficult to find a more emphatic affirmation of the necessity of Christian character, even in the epistles of Peter, than this extract from Paul's letter to the Galatians: "But the fruit of the Spirit is love, joy, peace, long suffering, gentleness, goodness, faith, meekness, temperance: against such there is no law. And they that are Christ's have crucified the flesh with the affections and lusts." And if James is the Apostle peculiarly of good works, I am sure that he does not assert their absolute necessity, with more clearness and decision, than the great Apostle to the Gentiles, in every epistle that bears his name.

It is a peculiarity of Paul's letters, that, if in the beginning of them, he dwells almost exclusively on great truths; in their concluding portions, he presses on the attention of those, to whom he is writing, counsels, exhortations, and precepts, all designed to make them feel deeply the necessity of glorifying God, by the good works, which will commend them to their fellow-men. Such an exhortation is the text. It is the more forceful, because, as we read it, separated from its connections, it seizes hold of two acts—those of eating and drinking—which we seldom connect with religion; and teaches us that, even in these animal acts, as well as in every higher act, we may worship the Most High. "Whether ye eat or drink, or whatsoever ye do, do all to the glory of God." Such an exhortation needs no extended explanation. We see, at once, that it is intended to enforce upon Christians, the duty of serving God in their week-day life; the duty of making sacred their most common and secular affairs. This is the subject, on which I purpose to speak at this time.

I suppose, that in respect to no other subject, is

our ordinary mental habit so vicious. It requires a mental struggle, not to connect religion exclusively with technically religious acts and states; with prayer and the Bible, and the services of the Church, and the sacraments. We call these religious or Christian; and the remainder, and by far the largest part of our activities, we describe as secular. We set the one class over against the other; and, thus, are tempted to indulge in that pharisecism, which can be devoted to God on the Lord's day, and quite as thoroughly devoted to worldly interests, throughout the remaining six days. Moreover, when we place a statement, like the text, side by side with the actual necessities of life; we are tempted to despair. To be told, on the one hand, that God demands all our time, and all our talents; and to find, on the other, that the severest labor during all the week scarcely suffices, in the terrible strife for bread, to gain a competency for the vast majority of men,—is, often, to excite the suspicion, that the God of Providence and the God of the Bible are not one; and to start the question; if God would have us give our lives to Him, why has He made the conditions of life what they are?

I do not intend to answer this question directly. Rather, do I hope, that we shall find no necessity for asking it, when this sermon shall be concluded. Instead of replying to it, I take up the text again. I ask you to reflect on the great truth, which the Apostle deemed so important; the truth, that this secular life, with all its struggles for food, with all its anxieties at home and in business, with its afflictions and amusements, with its eating and drinking,—that this common and daily round of toil may become one ceaseless act of worship; an act of worship, as real and grateful as any of those, which we associate with church or closet; the offering of incense, as acceptable to our Father, as prayer or song or sacrament. This is what Paul means, when he says: "Whether ye eat or drink, or whatsoever ye do, do all to the glory of God."

In addressing you on this subject—the sanctification of the daily life—as brought to view in these words; I shall speak, only of the possibility and the method of this sanctification. I shall answer the questions: Can we obey the Apostle's injunction? If we can, how shall be obey it?

I. In considering the possibility of sanctifying the daily life, let us turn to the word of God for aid. And let us begin, by calling to mind the truth, that the Old Testament not only teaches this possibility, but ascribes even to inanimate nature the function of glorifying God.

I speak of the Old Testament, especially, because it is supposed by many, that the older volume of the Scriptures gives special support to the distinction, between sacred acts and secular acts; because the life of the Jew was so divided by the law of Moses, that he knew what time to devote to God, and what to give to his own affairs. The ceremonies of his religious worship were so specifically ordered, and the precepts of his religion were so exact and various, that we are disposed to think, that it was natural for the Jew, to call compliance with, or obedience to them, the worship of God; and to call the rest of his life his secular life. Phariseeism, the divorce between religion and daily life, is, therefore, really thought by many, to have sprung out of Judaism, as naturally as the fruit springs out of the flower. But this opinion is the result, either of absolute

THE SANCTIFICATION OF THE SECULAR LIFE. 105

ignorance of Judaism, or of a false interpretation of the Old Testament. A careful student of the laws of the Hebrews will find in them not the slightest germ of phariseeism. On the contrary, he will see, on every page, an evident and most painstaking endeavor, to connect the glory and the worship of God with every, even the least important, act of daily life. If these laws have any design apparent in them, it is to impel their subjects to think of Jehovah, not only in the stated worship of the tabernacle or temple, but in buying and selling, in eating and drinking, in paying taxes to the government, in household employments, and in public holidays. The entire national life, public and private, is studiously associated with the worship of Jehovah. It would be impossible to imagine a code of laws more thoroughly unified by a single purpose, than is the Mosaic Code unified by the purpose of educating the Hebrew people, in all things, even eating and drinking, consciously and purposely to glorify God. Nothing is secular in the Hebrew life, as its ideal is portrayed in the Old Testament.

So it is, that Hebrew poetry, animated by the spirit of the Hebrew religion, ascribes even to inanimate nature a religious life. Poetry addresses itself to a habit of mind, congruous to the life of those, for whom it is written. If it did not, it would find no response. The poet would speak in an unknown tongue. His lyrics would be unsung. His epics would be unread, and would soon be forgotten. He speaks in loftiest language, or sings in harmonious strains, the thoughts of his people; but which they know not how to utter. Thus the true poet becomes the true voice of the nation. Thus the universal poet becomes the voice of humanity.

We will not let the name of Shakespeare die; just because, in fittest words, he tells us what we ourselves have thought or felt, but which, try how we might, we did not know how to say. So did the great Hebrew poets. They gave voice to the people's unuttered thoughts. Therefore, they found response in the people's hearts. So, for centuries, have the children of Abraham sung the songs of Zion; and pored entranced over the great drama of Job; and repeated the lofty harmonies of Isaiah. And, I ask you, is the ideal life, of which these are the poems, a life in which secular affairs and religious duties are set in sharp contrast? Is not the highest practical lesson, taught in this body of poetry, the lesson, that God may be glorified in all life, and is glorified even by the inorganic world in its ordinary movements? It is a Hebrew poet, who tells of day uttering speech to day, and of night showing to night the glory of God. It is a Hebrew poet, whose spiritual vision so clearly discerns the power of lifeless matter to worship the Most High, that he sings: "Praise the Lord, ye sun and moon; praise Him, all ye stars of light. Praise Him, ye heaven of heavens, and ye waters that be above the heavens. Let them praise the name of the Lord. For His name alone is excellent. His glory is above the earth and heaven."

This is the religion, of which we are the heirs. Nay, this is the religious thought, on which we have advanced. And if it was easy for them to associate religious thoughts even with the stars; if their religious life not only permeated their daily careers, and gave tone and purpose to their secular life; but also sanctified, as they beheld them, the movements even of unconscious nature,—ought it to be an unheard of or an unusual attainment among us, to achieve a mental habit so spiritual, that our daily life will be sanctified; and that, whether we eat or drink, or whatever we do, we shall do all to the glory of God.

But, turning from the Old to the New Testament, let us observe the light, thrown on this subject by the life of Jesus Christ. Not less clearly than our Redeemer, is Jesus presented in the New Testament as our example. That we might possess an ideal, as well as a Saviour, He took upon Him our form, and lived a human life. We all confess his spiritual perfection. No taint of sin defiles Him. What piety and virtue! What intimacy of communion with God! What submission to his providential will! How untiring his benevolence! How tender his compassion! How self-sacrificing his love for men! "This is a character beyond human conception." Man could not have invented it. It must have been real. It is the revelation of God, to men, of the perfect human life. You and I, at least, have accepted Him as our example. We profess to follow Him. We have called ourselves by his name. And, looking over the New Testament, we find that this imitation of Jesus is the great demand everywhere made upon us. His own words are: "Deny yourselves, and take up your cross and follow me." And throughout the Epistles, we meet with statements like the statement: "If any man have not the Spirit of Christ, he is none of his;" and with exhortations such as: "Let the mind be in you which was also in Him."

Now it is obvious, that if Jesus glorified God at all, He must have glorified God in secular affairs; in eating and drinking; in a career of ordinary and constant intercourse with the world. For Jesus of

Nazareth lived a secular life, just as you and I live secular lives. You will recall the fact, that He asserts this of Himself, when contrasting his career with that of his great forerunner. "John," he says, "came neither eating nor drinking. The Son of man came eating and drinking." Were John the Baptist held forth as our example in the New Testament, we may be sure, that we would have pressed upon us no exhortation like the text. John was ascetic. He lived apart from men, in the desert. He appeared among them, clothed in strange garb, and uttering the voice of solemn preparation for the advent of the Son of man. His message delivered, he sought the unpeopled wastes, until the Spirit again impelled him, suddenly to cry in the populous valley of the Jordan: "Repent, for the kingdom of heaven is at hand." How sharp a contrast this, to the life of our great Example! He, like John, comes from the wilderness to his work; but the wilderness has not been his abode. And when He comes, almost his first act, it would seem, is to attend as a guest a marriage feast; and his first miracle is performed, in order to enhance the joy of his fellow-guests, by turning the water into wine. Like John, He begins his ministry among a busy population. But, unlike John, He makes the city in which He preaches his home. The life of Jesus, even during his public ministry, was crowded with secular duties and associations. Nor let us forget, how small a portion of his life was taken up, in prosecuting this public ministry as a teacher of religion. Only three out of thirty-three years. During the remaining thirty, He lived, in the city of his reputed father, an ordinary human life. He was a Galilean villager. He grew in stature. He increased in wisdom. Year by year his character matured; and, discovering itself to those about Him, He increased in favor with man as with God. He was the carpenter's son, and was subject to his father. He labored at his father's trade. Such was the life of our great Example; of the only man who, in all things, did his Father's will. Here is no separation, in interest or in actual life, from worldly affairs; no exclusive pietism; no rapture too unworldly for the work; no gloomy asceticism. In its external incidents, the life of Jesus, for thirty years, was as commonplace as that of any man or woman before me. But his purity, his benignity, his obedience, his gentleness, his integrity, his self-sacrificing love, transfigured it. Each daily duty, as done by Him, became, through his love of God and men, an act of worship. And whether He ate and drank at a marriage feast, or labored in his father's work-shop, or played with his companions, or addressed his disciples on the loftiest themes, or wrought miracles, or consented to the death of the cross,— He did all to the glory of the Most High God. His career was a continuous psalm of adoration and of praise. Do you wonder, therefore, that one of his Apostles, with the record of this life before him, with the revelation of its acceptance by God, as the one perfect life ever lived—do you wonder, I say, that this Apostle should count it not impossible, that a disciple should sanctify even the most common and secular elements of life; and that, in writing to a company of believers, he should say: "Whether, therefore, ye eat or drink, or whatsoever ye do, do all to the glory of God"?

You see, therefore, that the Old Testament and the New unite, in proclaiming it to be both our duty and our privilege, so to consecrate to God our whole week-day life—including even the mere physical acts of eating and drinking—that all shall contribute to the glory of God; so to make all sacred, that, in money-getting, and pleasure-seeking, and in the various rounds of household duties, we shall honor and worship Him, who has called us to the dignity of sons and daughters of the Most High.

II. Having thus seen the possibility of obeying the Apostle's injunction; having seen, indeed, that just such a life, as that which the injunction calls before us, is contemplated by the sacred books of both dispensations; we are prepared to answer the question, how shall we go about sanctifying this secular life? What methods shall we adopt, what helps shall we make use of?

In replying to this question, I ask you, first, to observe, how much may be done by us to sanctify our secular life by that habit of mind which we call *association*. You all know, that when an event occurs, which takes strong hold of our feelings, every other event seems to us altered by it; and every physical object wears a changed aspect. Instinctively, we associate every thing else with the one all-controlling occurrence. Do you not recall, how different nature appeared to you, during the first few days after you felt the shock of a sore bereavement? The sun, the sky, the trees all associated themselves in your mind with your terrible loss, and in some way seemed to sympathize with, or to add to your woe. The Poet Laureate of England but speaks the feelings of humanity, when he calls the death of a loved and admired friend—

> "that reverse of doom
> Which sickened every living bloom
> And blurred the splendor of the sun."

And in describing his own, he describes our association of nature with our grief, when he writes:

> "With weary steps I loiter on,
> Though always under altered skies,
> The purple from the distance dies,
> The prospect and horizon gone."

Do I speak of an unheard of, or even an unusual occurrence, when I tell you of a mother, who at an hour, when she will not be disturbed, goes to her room, and takes from its secure hiding place, perhaps, a lock of hair, or a pair of half-worn shoes, or a little child's dress; some object in itself trivial or valueless; over which she pores, as though it were gold or a precious stone. It has power to break up the deep fountains of feeling, and to call forth tears and prayers. The trivial or valueless object belonged to a lost or long absent child; and its power over the mother is an example of the power of the mind, in the act of association, to sanctify the most commonplace objects or events.

Every Christian parent, I dare say, recognizes this instinct of association, as a fact not to be disregarded in the training of children. You warn your child against this or that habit, not because, in itself, it is morally wrong, but because its associations are vicious or vulgar. "It is my custom," said an intelligent Christian man, "not only to indulge my children in all household recreations, not sinful or expensive, but also to join in their games. And I do this, in order that, when absent from home, at college or elsewhere, these very recreations may be associated with home, with a father's care and a mother's love. I am sure, that this association will both put a restraint upon indulgence, and, at the same time, enlarge the number of objects which, when they shall have left it, will make their image of home a perpetual joy."

These examples,—and they might be multiplied indefinitely,—show us the possibility of making our secular life religious, by associating it with God. Indeed, this association of all things with God is the one central and unchanging element of religion. Stripped of its accidents, and of the elements which belong to its dispensations rather than to its essence, religion, on its intellectual side, is the recognition of the living God, the first cause of the universe, in all his works. On its active side, religion is the determination of all conduct, by the truth, that God is the final, as well as the first cause, of the universe. Let our conduct be determined by this fundamental truth; let all our secular life be thus associated with God; and the prayers offered in our closets will not be more religious than is the business transacted in our counting-rooms. This is the truth, which George Herbert has so finely expressed in his poem, called the "Elixir," a part of which, I am sure, whether familiar with it or not, you will thank me for repeating:

> Teach me, my God and King,
>   In all things thee to see;
> And what I do in anything,
>   To do it as for thee.
>
> All may of thee partake;
>   Nothing can be so mean,
> Which with this tincture, *for thy sake*,
>   Will not grow bright and clean.
>
> A servant, with this clause,
>   Makes drudgery divine:
> Who sweeps a room, as for thy laws,
>   Makes that, and the action, fine.

> This is the famous stone
> That turneth all to gold;
> For that, which God doth touch and own,
> Can not for less be told.

The truth is, that there is no more inherent difficulty in making our daily work the service of God, than there is in making it the service of the family. And just as the association of our labor with wife and children so dignifies its drudgery, that it is no longer drudgery; so the association of our labor with God lifts it into the realm of the religious life, and transforms it into worship.

But we can not, by the mere exercise of the will, habitually associate daily duties with God. The mere volition will be overborne by temptations. We must, therefore, seize the aid which God has furnished us, in the privilege of *prayer*. If you ask how you can make your secular life an act of worship; I answer, take your secular life to God in prayer. You can not glorify God in eating and drinking, if you do not ask his direction in eating and drinking. On the other hand, such prayer, in itself considered, and altogether apart from the strength and direction which it seeks from God, will give to the entire life the character of worship. If you are a parent, engaged in training a child, you will see, at once, how true this statement is. I will suppose that the intercourse between you and your child is unrestrained; that the child confides in you, and confers with you, as to all his plays and plans; that day after day he comes to you to obtain your direction. Such a life, on the part of your child, honors you in all its phases. It glorifies you as much in its pleasures, as in its obedience. In this way, precisely, can we make all our work and all our pleasures, our very eating and drinking glorify our Father. We can take them all to Him. We can ask his will. Ah! brethren, I suppose that we glorify God, only in what we call our "religious life," simply because we pray to Him about that alone. I will show you "a more excellent way." Go to God with your business cares. Take counsel with Him about your conduct of business. When, to-morrow morning, the work and anxieties of the week begin to harass and perplex you, consult Him in earnest prayer, determining to be guided by the leadings of his Spirit and his Word. How long a time will be required, to form the habit of associating all things with God? But this, I fear, is not our conduct. In business and pleasure, we are not on terms of confidential intercourse with our Father in heaven. If we were, we should see nothing strange in the Apostle's injunction: "Whether ye eat or drink, or whatsoever ye do, do all to the glory of God."

But this is not all. If you would glorify God in secular affairs, you must test your conduct of them, habitually, by the requirements of *God's law*. It is not enough that you pray. For if you pray about duty, God will, more forcibly than ever, remind you of the great law of duty, written on your hearts. Now, there is no stronger temptation than the temptation, to set up the customs or the average life of the business community, instead of God's law, as the standard of business life. How common is the remark: "I propose to adjust my conduct in business, not to any unattainable standard, like the law of God, but to the average conduct of those about me. When one is in Rome, one must do as Romans do." Well, brethren, I put the question: whom does such a state of mind glorify? God, or Rome? Certainly not God. But let me suppose a man, after careful consideration and prayer, to say: "I may often yield to temptation; but I am resolved, come what will, in all things, to make the dictates of conscience, and the revealed will of God my rule of life." Such a man may often be overborne by his lower nature; but his religion will, at least, be no mere "Sunday habit;" it will be a spiritual force, permeating and ennobling his whole being. His eating and drinking will be the worship of God.

Let me add only, that if you would glorify God in your secular life, you must keep in view, constantly, the truth that Christ died to *redeem it;* to sanctify and glorify it. At last, not merely the spiritual element of our personality will be saved. Our bodily life,—with all which that imports,—will be rescued from the great destroyer, and death will be swallowed up in victory. Nay, this world itself, it would seem, will be renewed by the refining fires, which God has appointed; and the curse, now on it, be removed. Doubt not, that a secular life will then be lived. Though we can not describe or conceive of it, yet this is implied in the statement, that the body and this world will be redeemed. It becomes us, dear Christian brethren, so far as may be, to anticipate that final life even now, by consecrating all work and all pleasure to the redeeming God.

And now, in view of the possibility of glorifying God in daily life, let us examine our lives. Let us bring to the examination another truth of the most solemn character. If we fail to sanctify our secular life, we shall certainly secularize our religious life. This is the alternative before us. Two powers are in strife for the mastery of our whole being. One is the spirit of Christ; the other is the spirit of the world. One or the other must conquer us, and, by the conquest, must determine the character of every act of our lives. If, at last, we shall be possessed by the spirit of Christ, "whether we eat or drink, or whatsoever we do, we shall do all to the glory of God." But if we shall be possessed by the spirit of the world, religious activity, in any true sense of that phrase, will be impossible. There may be the excitement of constitutional sensibilities; but religious character will be wanting. There may be the appearance of religious activity; but this appearance, though not perhaps a pretense, will be an appearance only. Of the activity of a religious spirit, there will be none. For the essence of religion is the love of God. But the spirit of the world will be our spirit. And, "if any man love the world, the love of the Father is not in him."

In conclusion, let me say, that the injunction was addressed to Christians, and implies a union to Christ by faith. And this suggests the statement, that so long as a man is separated from Christ, so long is it impossible for him to glorify God. If through Him, we do not rise above this material life, and compel it, as the servant of our free and redeemed spirits, to glorify God, we must become its slaves. The slaves of business, of money, of eating and drinking! There is no other alternative. And, as its slaves, our hopes and ambitions will grow more earthly, until, at last, all our interests will be bounded by the term of our present life; and we shall see in death only a tyrant, who robs us of all our enjoyments. From this narrow earthliness the Gospel comes to free us all. And this it does, through Christ alone.

VIII.
THE GOSPEL A HOPE.

"Blessed be the God and Father of our Lord Jesus Christ, which according to his abundant mercy hath begotten us again unto a lively hope by the resurrection of Jesus Christ from the dead, to an inheritance incorruptible, and undefiled, and that fadeth not away, reserved in heaven for you, who are kept by the power of God through faith unto salvation ready to be revealed in the last time."—I. PETER i, 3, 4, 5.

The text is the Apostle Peter's ascription of thanksgiving to God for the Gospel of his Son; an ascription in which he describes the Gospel with singular felicity and power. It is to Peter's description of the Gospel; to his description of our religion, that I ask your attention this morning.

A description of Christianity, by such a man, can not fail to prove an instructive study. There are unnumbered definitions of Christianity, to be found in religious and general literature; written, some by friends, and others by enemies; definitions by professedly neutral historians, by friendly theologians, by hostile critics, by *littérateurs*. Their very multitude has produced confusion in many minds. Possibly, they have produced in your minds such confusion, that, if you were asked the question: "What is

Christianity?" you might be startled by your own inability, satisfactorily to answer it. May we not, therefore, at least hope to clarify our own minds in respect to this question, by adverting to this description of the Gospel; written by a man, who was one of the earliest and one of the most trusted disciples of Jesus; who was probably at his baptism; who heard his Sermon on the Mount; who listened to his last discourse; who saw the Transfiguration; who was present during a portion of his last trial; who, first of all, entered his emptied tomb; who saw Him ascend to heaven; who gave his life to the propagation of the faith of Christ; who sealed his devotion to his Redeemer by a painful death; and who is honored by the largest, if not the purest, of the Churches of Christendom, as the Primate of the Apostles, on whom Christ founded the Church, of which he prophesied, that the gates of hell should not prevail against it. Surely, brethren, we may give very appropriately this morning's hour to answering the question, in the light of this thanksgiving: what was the Gospel of Christ, as apprehended by this great Apostle Peter?

I. And first, you will notice, that it existed in his mind as, and exerted upon his life the power of a *living hope.* "Blessed be the God and Father of our Lord Jesus Christ, who hath begotten us again unto a *lively hope.*"

Whatever we shall find, in our study of the text, to be the object of this hope, it is important, I think, that we seize, at once, the great truth, that Christianity, as understood by Peter, was not a system of burdensome duties. If hope is the word that best characterizes the Gospel, a good many popular mistakes have been made in respect to it. We can imagine, with what astonishment, with what indignation, indeed, this man—who of all men had a right to an opinion on the subject—would have read, that "Christianity is a system of repression; that the voice of the pulpit is a whine; that its psalm is a *miserere*." The truth is, that, in the days of Peter, the one thing, that was not enchained by the giant Despair, was the Church of Jesus Christ. I have often directed your attention to the state of society, when the Apostles, dispersed by the persecutions of the Jews, carried the Gospel throughout the Roman Empire. Let me recall it to your attention. A great living classical and Biblical scholar has said, that, "to see the world in its worst estate, we must turn to the age of Juvenal and Tacitus—the age, also, of Peter and Paul—when all the different streams of evil, coming from east, west, north, and south, the vices of barbarism and the vices of civilization, remnants of ancient cults, and the latest refinements of luxury and impurity, met and mingled on the banks of the Tiber." It was the age, in which Nero reigned, and perished

> by the justest doom
> Which ever the destroyer yet destroyed.

It was the age in which slavery was most widely spread, in the worst form in which slavery can exist. It was the age whose vices, as satirized by Juvenal and described by Tacitus, I dare not even name before a Christian congregation. It was a worse age than the age which immediately preceded it; the age constituted by the decline of the Republic. And, describing this better age, Sallust tells us, that "lust of licentiousness, of low debauchery, and of every sort of luxury spread abroad. Men and women publicly offered their chastity for sale. For the sake of filling themselves with food, they sought all things by land and sea; they slept before any desire for food had come; they waited neither for hunger, thirst, desire of coolness, nor for weariness; but anticipated all in their luxurious indulgence. The spirit steeped in evil arts did not easily restrain itself from any lusts; it was only more prodigally devoted, in all ways, to venal advantage and to extravagance."*

What could such a state of society produce, except despair? What, after vice had wrought satiety, and debauchery had been succeeded by reflection, could men forbode but utter destruction? And they did. Murders were equaled in number only by suicides. And suicide was the loftiest act that lofty man could perform. The best men were the Stoic nobles. And the Stoic nobles could only "wrap their cloaks around them," or seek, in self-inflicted death, separation from the awful impurity they were utterly powerless to remove.

In this gross darkness, the only ray of light shone from the hill of Calvary. Amid riot and orgy, of which the expected end was an awful doom, the only voice of hope was the voice of the Gospel of Christ. But just this it was to men surrounded by or sunken in this terrible sinfulness. It was as a hope, that the Gospel was preached throughout the Empire. It called the victim of hard and dry remorse, to pour

---

* "The Conspiracy of Catiline," Sec. XIII. I quote above the translation of Dr. R. S. Storrs: Appendix to Lect. VIII, "Divine Origin of Christianity." But worse than the vices and crimes to which Sallust thus refers, was the perversion of the moral judgments which attended them. Roman society had earned the woe, denounced on those who "call evil good and good evil." "Righteousness," says Sallust (Sec. XII), "was held to be malice." *Innocentia pro malevolentia duci cœpit.*

forth tears of hopeful penitence. It bade the man, bent on suicide as his only escape, fling away his sword and gaze into the opened heavens. It called on the Jew, mourning over the destruction of Zion and the desolation of the Holy of Holies, to behold his Messiah. Its message to all the children of men, dead in trespasses and sins, was: "Ye may be born again." Thus the Gospel was apprehended by Peter. Thus he preached it, and explained it in his letters to the Churches. Because it was a hope, he suffered for it, and died its witness on the cross. And, therefore, in this Epistle, thanking God for the Gospel of his Son, he so describes it. "Blessed be the God and Father of our Lord Jesus Christ, which according to his abundant mercy hath begotten us again unto a living hope."

And, brethren, this description of the Gospel has lost none of its force and none of its pertinence by the lapse of eighteen centuries. It is a hope to-day. It is not a system of duties. It is not a series of burdens. It is not a collection of ceremonies. It is not, in its ultimate form, even a system of doctrine. Above all, it is the dawning of a new light on the horizon of the world. It is a voice of hope, to such as sit in darkness and the shadow of death. For is it not true, that, though we are not sunk into the depths of vice, in which society then lay, despair as to the ultimate condition of man is the dominant feeling, alike of literature, of science, and of conscience? You have read the current literature to little purpose, if you have not observed, that its voice, uttered through those best inspired, yet not inspired by the Gospel, is one of lamentation over man's soul. Philosophy, that is not determined by the Gospel, is just as dark and dreary. And science, with its latest generalization;—the remorseless destruction of masses, that the few fittest may survive—what is this but the very gospel of despair? And then when you listen, if you dare to do so, to the voice of your own conscience, what do you, what can you hear, but the foreboding of utter misery?

I say, then, that this description of the Gospel has lost none of its force and none of its pertinence. If it ought to be preached to-day at all, it ought to be preached, above all else, because it is a voice of hope sounded in the ears of despairing men; and the Doxology that should be heard, above all others, in the Church of Christ, is the thanksgiving of Peter: "Blessed be the God and Father of our Lord Jesus Christ, which of his abundant mercy hath begotten us again unto a living hope."

II. But Peter not only describes the Gospel as a hope; he brings into view, also, the *ground* on which it is based; and that ground is the abounding *mercy* of God. "Blessed be the God and Father of our Lord Jesus Christ, which, according to his abundant mercy, hath begotten us." What does the Apostle mean, by the mercy of God being the ground of man's hope?

I answer, that, as we look around us on nature, we see that we are subjects of a government which lives and moves and has its being by law; law that is everywhere operative; law that is uniform in its movements. Now, it is characteristic of law, that it is no respecter of persons. It never asks, what palliating circumstances may be connected with a single violation of it. It moves with resistless and unheeding progress, from the violation of command to the enforcement of penalty. It refuses to take into consideration, station, or age, or ignorance. Fire will not burn the less, because it is an unthinking child, that has been caught within the circumference of the flame. An earthquake will not pause to permit the better classes to escape. Law has no respect for individuals. It asks alone, has precept been transgressed? And, if this is true of the law whose domain is the physical universe; not less is it true of that moral law, whose subjects are the responsible spirits of men. It, also, is relentless. It is uncompromising. It holds the least transgressor guilty. It holds him guilty of the violation of the whole law. It visits upon him the entire penalty. Protest and quarrel as we may, this is the system under which man lives; this is the government which nature reveals; this is the law, whose precepts conscience announces, and whose sanction it threatens in tones of thunder. Men are transgressors, and therefore they are in despair. Therefore, they raise their voices to heavens, which are "resonant only with the echoes of their unavailing cries." Therefore, they cry in despair: "How shall man be just with God?" Therefore, they complain that God is a God, hidden back of a system of remorseless law, which He has substituted for Himself, and which will not regard the individuals that are enfolded in its iron and remorseless embrace.

Now, the mercy of God consists in his breaking through the environment of this system of law, and appearing to individual man; in his willingness to listen to his cry; in his desire and design to interfere, and prevent the crushing movement of this awful system on those who have insulted its majesty. Hence, the proper antithesis of the mercy of God is the law of God. Law does not regard individuals. Mercy does. It hears prayer. It takes into account special circumstances. It intervenes. It comes between precept and penalty. It mediates. It restores. It saves. Law is the expression of the hidden God. Mercy is the expression of God, no longer hidden in the clouds which He makes his pavilion, but breaking through them, and coming over the mountains of man's transgression to his succor and salvation. And the Gospel, in Peter's view, was a Gospel of hope, because it was grounded on the truth, that back of relentless law, and ready to come forth at the cry of the least of his human creatures, is the loving and redeeming God. And this, friends, is the Gospel to-day. It is hope grounded on the mercy of God. It is the love of God, above the law of the universe. It is a living hope, springing forth out of the truth, that on the throne of the universe is a heart throbbing with infinite love, and ready to move to each single soul, however sinful, in offices of sympathy and redemption.

III. But men might have said to Peter: "A great, an unspeakable benediction is such a hope as this, and a better ground on which to rest it, than this mercy there can not be, if indeed there be such a mercy. But what is the *pledge* of it? What pledge is there, that God will thus come forth through the meshes of his law to succor the children of men?" And, Peter, therefore, in his description of the Gospel, states not the hope only, and the ground of it, but the pledge, also, that this ground is a real and a safe ground. And this pledge is none other than a historic event; an event in which God did come forth, and in which He triumphed over the mightiest of visible laws, the law of death itself. "Blessed be God who, out of his abundant mercy, hath begotten us unto a living hope, by the resurrection of Jesus

Christ from the dead." The "resurrection of Christ from the dead!" This is the pledge which Peter offers, that the ground of man's hope is real and safe.

We are sometimes at a loss to find the precise place, which belongs to the resurrection of our Lord in a systematic statement of God's way of redemption. It does not justify us, as his obedience does. It does not sanctify us, as the promised Spirit does. It lies between the two great parts of redemption, apparently belonging to neither, and having part in neither. It was when Christ died, that He said: "It is finished." And it was when the Spirit came, that the work of sanctifying the world began. And yet, throughout the Acts of the Apostles, we read continually that the Apostles went throughout the Empire, preaching "Jesus and the resurrection." And when a Roman ruler speaks to another ruler, of an accusation brought against one of these Apostles, we find the burden of the charge against him to be his declaration concerning "one Jesus, which was dead, but whom Paul declared to be alive."

What is the meaning of this continuous emphasis? What, but that the resurrection of Jesus is the pledge of the reality of all that has occurred before it. Peter journeys throughout the world, telling men that God is a God of mercy; that He is ready to forgive; that He will listen to prayer; that He will give to individual men and women power to overcome sin; that He will bless them with everlasting glory. "Yes," they might answer: "Beautiful beyond our imagining is the Gospel that you preach. Better than the golden age, would this age be, if that were true. What is the pledge you offer us, that there is such a God, above the just but awful law, that now holds us to despair and foreboding?" And Peter's answer is, that, already, has the Omnipotent One come forth from his hiding place, and told men of his love and readiness to help their infirmities; and, that they might know that the voice is indeed the voice of the Almighty One, He rent the rocks; and broke the seal of the Empire; and called forth from the grave his own Messenger, whom men had crucified and slain.

And this—not that there are not other pledges, like the witness of the Spirit—is one great pledge that we offer to-day. God is a God of mercy. He is not bound by his physical laws which deal with classes only. He can and will overcome them for you, if you but look to Him and cry to Him for help. And, for pledge and evidence, we point you to the emptied tomb of Joseph, and the pierced hands and feet and side of the risen and glorified Jesus; and bid you hear his words: "Peace be unto you;" and watch Him as He ascends from Olivet to heaven. Thus it is, that the Church, testifying in all ages to the reality of this event, keeps sacred this first day of the week; and raises in her temples the ascription of thanksgiving: "Blessed be the God and Father of our Lord Jesus Christ, who, of his abundant mercy, hath begotten us again unto a living hope, by the resurrection of Jesus Christ from the dead."

IV. But the Apostle, in his ascription of praise, not only describes the Gospel as a living hope, and points out its ground, and announces its pledge. He also states specifically, what is the *object* of this hope.

For a hope may be good in its ground and pledge, that is to say, there may be a certainty of its fulfillment; and yet, in its fulfillment, it may be valueless. Men had a right to ask the Apostle: "Suppose this great hope, you speak of, fulfilled, is it adequate to make us happy, to redeem us from our misery, to still the foreboding of coming woe?" And, anticipating or answering this question, Peter announces the object of this hope, in language that we can not too earnestly study or too often repeat. The object of the Gospel hope is "an inheritance incorruptible and undefiled, and that fadeth not away."

Recall, I ask you, the state of society in which this announcement was first made, and which I have already attempted to describe. Degraded; wretched; evil almost beyond comparison; entirely hopeless; its only amusements excitements, which, in their reaction, deepened despair, and gave new poignancy to remorse; recall this society, and ask yourselves, whether a more adequate object of hope could have been announced? Could a Gospel of better news, of tidings more glad have been proclaimed? I can not dwell on the Apostle's words. I ask you only to observe, that, at once, they remove the thoughts and aspirations of men from the sin and turmoil of this world, to the calm upper world where the spirit rests forever in the immediate presence of the loving God. They reveal to men, not a condition of peace only, but a place of peace, for Heaven is "an inheritance;" an inheritance not only of joy, but of joy which neither time nor disaster can impair or destroy; of joy followed by no satiety, but "incorruptible;" of joy followed by no remorse, but "undefiled;" an inheritance for which no destruction is reserved; for it "fadeth not away." Nor has the Gospel changed the object of the hope which it inspires, since Peter thus described it. Still, does it point us to the satisfying and abiding joys of our eternal inheritance. In this world, indeed, it offers help, and consolation, and peace. But the help is ours, and the consolation and the peace are ours, most of all, because there shines, on the horizon of this world, the eternal light of the city, in which there is neither pain, nor sorrow, nor sickness, nor death; and into which we, if we will, may one day enter. And I ask, has the unchanged Gospel lost any of its pertinence? Society is better than it was in the days of the Cæsars. Life is purer, and larger, and longer, no doubt. But pain is here; and so are poverty, and sickness, and disappointment, and bereavement, and death. Still, is it true that "vanity of vanities" may be written on most earthly things. And still, is it true, therefore, that our highest songs of praise are due to the God and Father of our Lord Jesus Christ, because, in begetting us unto a lively hope, He has made it, the hope of "an inheritance, incorruptible, and undefiled, and that fadeth not away."

V. But, finally, the question might have been put to the Apostle Peter: "Great as this hope is, and sure as its ground is, and satisfying as its pledge is, and inspiring as its object is; what if we should fail to attain it, what if we can not reach the portals of the incorruptible inheritance?" And, not to dwell at length upon his words, let me say, that the Apostle makes reply by announcing the blessed truth, that the God of love, who has provided the inheritance, keeps those who trust Him from failing to attain it. It is an inheritance, "reserved for you, who are kept by the *power of God*, through faith unto salvation." Of which the meaning is, that our entrance into heaven, our attainment of all the joy which the Gospel promises, is dependent at last, not on our poor and feeble efforts, but on the God who has promised and provided it. A blessed truth it is that salvation, both in its inception, and in its consummation, is not of works, lest any man should boast. Boast, indeed! with our yieldings and neglectings, and backslidings! Boastings, with our worldliness, and enslavement to the flesh! Thanks be to God, our attainment of heaven is not dependent upon us. At last, as now, when the gates of the city shall receive us, and we shall enter into that joy which eye hath not seen nor ear heard, nor heart conceived; our redeemed spirits will first of all sing the song: "Not unto us, but unto Thy name give glory." For not by our might, but by the power of God, we shall have been kept, through faith unto salvation.

This, then, is the Gospel as understood and proclaimed by Peter. A hope against the world's despair. Its ground, the mercy of God. Its pledge, the resurrection of Christ from the dead. Its object, an inheritance, incorruptible and undefiled, and that fadeth not away. The certainty of our enjoyment of it, dependent not on our poor sinful powers; but on the might of the omnipotent God, by whom we are kept, through faith, unto salvation. If this is the Gospel, let us not wonder, that Peter's epistle opens with a psalm of praise. Nay, let us not wonder that his whole life was a life of gratitude, manifested in continuous labor and self-sacrifice. And should our praise be less fervent; should our lives be less devoted than his? Have we been rescued from a condemnation less severe, or from a condition less wretched? We profess to believe this Gospel. What are we doing to publish it? What are we doing to magnify in life, and labor, the God of mercy, who hath begotten us again unto a lively hope, by the resurrection of Jesus Christ from the dead? God grant us grace, to be more loyal to this Gospel, which it is the office of the Church to proclaim to men. God grant that our labors in its behalf may be more abundant, our gifts larger, our sacrifices more thorough and more cheerful.

And, if there are any here, who have been perplexed by the question: "What is Christianity?" let them carry away this description by the Great Apostle. Christianity is a hope offered to you; a hope grounded in the mercy of God; pledged to fulfillment by the resurrection of his Son; a hope of everlasting bliss, assured to you by the might of the indwelling God. It is a hope offered; but for that reason, it is a hope that must be accepted or rejected by you. To accept it is to believe; to reject it is to return to the world; to live for a time in its fleeting, unsatisfying pleasures; to be satiated with them; but to return to them, at last, in desperation; as they do, who say: "Let us eat and drink, for tomorrow we die."

IX.
THE BURDEN OF THE BODY.

"For we that are in this tabernacle do groan, being burdened."—II. CORINTHIANS v, 4.

In the last two verses of the preceding chapter, the Apostle states one of the most important truths to be found in the New Testament. He tells us, that if we look at the things which are unseen and eternal,—that is, if we are spiritually minded,—our affliction can not harm us; we shall be prepared for it; we shall make it our servant; and it will work for us a far more exceeding and eternal weight of glory. In illustrating this truth, he takes the extreme case of affliction, the case of death itself; the "dissolution of this earthly tabernacle," in which we live. Let even that occur, he tells us, to one, whose habit of soul is such, that he may be said to "look at the things which are unseen and eternal;" and the dissolution of his earthly tabernacle will work for him a far more exceeding and eternal weight of glory; for it will be the means of introducing him, the sooner, to the house not made with hands, eternal in the heavens. He is thus led to describe the condition of the spiritually minded man in this earthly tabernacle;

which he does in the words I have selected as my text: "We that are in this tabernacle do groan, being burdened."

Presupposing, as they do, on the part of those to whom they are addressed, this habit of spiritual-mindedness, or, to employ the Apostle's phrase, "a looking at things which are unseen and eternal," these words are addressed to Christians; and they state the truth, that the present conditions of their existence are so unfavorable to the development of the Christian life, that they "groan, being burdened."

I am sure, that it is well for us, Christian brethren, to dwell, at times, upon this unfavorable side of the life that we live in the flesh. We shall find it a subject of the most practical character. On the one hand, it will aid us in "toning our desires for time's rewards down to a degree befitting time's brevity." On the other, it will help us to a better appreciation of the opportunities for spiritual culture, which our life in the body affords.

It may serve to prevent any misunderstanding of what I shall say on this subject, if I preface my remarks with the statement, that a life in bodies formed as ours are, and in the relations made possible by these physical frames and senses and appetites, is not without advantage to us, as sinful beings whom God is educating with a view to their perfect holiness. The preacher of the Gospel, in the exercise of his teaching function, needs to be careful, lest he substitute mere individual speculations for the revealed truth of God. But it is not improper to say, that—though modes of administration, inconceivable to us, are possible to the omniscient God—we are unable to see, how a fallen man could be regained to allegiance to God; how holiness could be re-developed within him; except for the residence of his spirit in a body. Certainly, it is obvious, that the pains, the trials, the perplexities, through which, in the actual administration of his grace, we are brought back to the love and the service of our heavenly Father, are possible only in an existence like ours, who "in this tabernacle groan, being burdened." Let any one endeavor to call before him those "providential visitations,"—as we aptly denominate them—by means of which, he has been led to think of God, and to believe Him, and at last to love and live for Him; and he will not fail to recognize the force of this remark. All of these visitations,—the sicknesses, the losses of property, the deaths of friends, the trials, and the dangers of life,—of which our Father has made use, in turning our hearts to Himself, are possible, only because we are creatures of sense, as well as immortal spirits. Let any one think of himself, as possessing only a spiritual nature, as without a physical frame; and then think of himself as a sinner. Let him, with this image in his mind, attempt to picture, or to conceive of a process, by which he could be brought back into harmony with a holy God; and I have no hesitation in saying, that he will find that he has set before him an impossible task. It does not become one to speak confidently on one of the most mysterious subjects, referred to in the sacred writings; but it does not seem to me at all improbable, that we have here a partial explanation, at least, of sinful man's redemption; as contrasted with the fact, so clearly revealed in his Word, that God never interposed to save those purely spiritual beings, who fell from their high estate. It was man's body, that made it easy for man to fall. And it would seem to be man's bodily life, with its complex relations, that makes man's salvation possible. It was a physical appetite through which man was tempted into sin. And the glory of man's recovery, the greatness of God's triumph in securing it, is in his large employment of this same physical nature, through which man fell, to bring him back to holiness.

This is the view, that we should ever keep before us, of our life in the flesh. It is true, that "we groan and are burdened;" but we are held to our life in this tabernacle, in order that we may be prepared for the house not made with hands, eternal in the heavens. Sickness comes, and bereavement, and poverty, and pain—and all of them, you will observe, are events possible only in our present state—in order that we may attain that holiness, without which no man can see the Lord. The material is always for the spiritual. The highest thing, that can be said of this material universe, which, from day to day uttereth speech of the glory God, is, that it is not its own final cause; but is the theater of spiritual activities; is in order to the unfolding of spiritual truth, and the development of spiritual character. And the real dignity of this life in the body is not to be found in itself; in the mere eating, and drinking, and sleeping, and seeing, and hearing; but in the fact, that it is the instrument employed by God to re-form in man the divine image.

It is only as we grasp this truth, that we appreciate the dignity and the sacredness of this physical life. The first man, Adam, was given dominion over the earth; because he was made in the image of God. God put all things under him, and made all things in order to his well-being. So his kingship was obtained. And it was lost, only when he placed the creature before the Creator; and chose, before spiritual obedience to God's commands, the earthly fruit that seemed good for food, because it was pleasant to the eyes. "Where sin abounded, grace much more abounds." The physical life, by which man fell from communion with God, is that, by means of which, he is to be brought back into God's fellowship and likeness. This is the dignity and utility of the life that we live in the flesh. This is the meaning of this earthly tabernacle in which we groan, being burdened. This is the virtue, that lies concealed in its troubles and pains, and toils, and death. So it becomes us to accept the earthly life; and so it behooves us to live it; else we shall lose its worth. And yet, while all this is to be said of it, it remains true, that "we that are in this tabernacle, groan, being burdened." It is an abnormal life, as we live it; and the spirit of man sighs beneath the weight of it. Let us take up this statement of the Apostle, and endeavor to learn the grounds of it; and, having done this, attend to the practical lessons, which the subject contains for us.

Notice, then, in the first place, some of the limitations of a life in the body—without reference to sin—which help to explain the Apostle's words. The most obvious of these relate to the material universe. We are limited in space. To what "a grain of sand on the high field of immensity," do these bodies of ours confine us! From day to day, we enjoy the sublime spectacle of the heavens above us. Who can tell the number of the stars, or grasp the distances which, as we know, separate them from us? What thoughtful man, gazing into the deep vault above, has not kindled into rapture as he has remembered, that he has a mind capable of appreciating all the glories of all the suns and systems that he beholds; that the members of his species alone, of all the living creatures upon earth, know the meaning of their movements, and the final cause of their existence? Who of us has not felt the glow of a pardonable pride, as he has recalled the wondrous secrets, which the glass of the astronomer has extorted from the unwilling skies? How wonderful that knowledge—how like to inspiration itself—which foretells the coming and the going of bodies so distant, that imagination falters in attempting to fly through the intervening space! No conquests of the human mind are more impressive, than those which it has made in the regions, which it has explored with the telescope. And it requires no undue exercise of the fancy, to think of the careful observer of the stars, as a visitor among the worlds, which he has so often gazed on, from afar. But being in this tabernacle, "he groans, being burdened." Contrast the distances which the astronomer's mind traverses, with the limits to which his body confines him. Were he able to lift himself even a few short miles above the planets' surface—which he can not do—he would be driven back to earth for air to breathe and food to strengthen him. The planets invite him to themselves, both by what they reveal and by what they conceal. But his body holds him down. He is confined in this tabernacle. And their rays come to him, as the daylight comes to the criminal through the bars of his prison house.

Or think of man's limitations in another direction. The wonders of astronomy are paralleled only by the wonders of geology. What rapid strides have been made by man, during the present century, toward a knowledge of the origin and physical history of the world on which we live! If the stars have been questioned, and made to tell their secrets, so have the rocks beneath us. With what precision, does the story, lately told, of the earth's career, move from chaos, now through revolutions, and now through long periods of slow development, on to the present era! How admirable the investigations, which have ended, in finding the secret of the mighty movements, which upheaved our mountain ridges, or opened the long and wide fissures, through which the great rivers flow to the all-embracing ocean! What a triumph of mind was the discovery of the process, by which the little pebbles, of which the conglomerate is formed, were held together and hardened into a solid mass; and then cut to a face, which suggests both the tools and the skill of a lapidary! That such knowledge is not too wonderful for man, tells of a mighty mind in man. But how short is the distance which man, because of his life in the body, can travel toward the center of the earth! I have already spoken of the near point above the world, at which he can live. But nearer still is the point within the world, where, could he go, he would die. Thus his body limits him in space, on every side. He is a prisoner in the tabernacle, in which he groans, being burdened.

But this limitation in space is not the only, or the most striking limitation of man's life in the body. We shall observe another, if we consider the close connection, in this life, between the exercise of his mental faculties and the condition of his material frame. The latest researches of scientific men have made the fact of this connection more certain; and, by their discoveries of its character, have made it the most impressive of physiological truths. I shall not, however, speak of any thing beyond the comprehension of any one of us. I shall refer only to the facts of the commonest observation and experience. Is it not, in the highest degree, singular, that, though the mind of man is his glory, in this life it is always at the bidding of the body? How weary the mind becomes, because of the "weariness" of the physical brain! When the mind is most active, and labors are most alluring and engrossing, how often is it compelled to cease from work, because the body must re-create itself, by eating or sleeping! How terribly does the body assert this power over the mind, when the latter rises in rebellion against the body's sluggishness, and works on and on, until it is hampered by the body's paralysis, or is lashed into renewed subjection by fever! How many years, from the beginning of life, must the mind wait for the body to develop, before it dares to put forth its strongest efforts! And how many years, before the close of life, is the mind compelled to rest from toil, only because the body is worn with labor! Has it ever occurred to you, how much more man might accomplish but for the incessant demands which his mere animal life makes upon him? Is not that a strange, unnatural condition, in which the greater portion of one's life is necessarily consumed, in caring for the material home in which he dwells? It is, as if one purchased a residence, and most of his days were given to its repair. So is man burdened in this tabernacle in which he dwells. It limits him on every side, in space and time alike.

But notice another peculiarity of this life in the body. Its keenest and most enticing sensations of pleasure are the shortest lived; and are followed by proportionate satiety. All of us know, that every appetite of the body, which cries to be satisfied, tempts us on, until, when it is satisfied, we are not satisfied, but cloyed. I need not stop to describe the methods, by which the body tempts men to drunkenness and gluttony and others sins, by holding out promises of ecstatic delights. Nor need I try to tell the price of weakness, of weariness, and of loathing, which they soon pay for their dearly bought joys. The cheated soul, in the tabernacle of the flesh, groans, being burdened.

Or think of the long catalogue—which time does not permit me to recite—of those accidental ills, to the perils of which each of us is every day subjected, because of the life that he lives in the flesh. The touch of infectious disease; the epidemic, that fills the air we breathe with the seeds of death; the frightful accidents of travel; the upheavals of nature; the bolt of lightning; the swift and deadly stroke of the meridian sun—these, the pestilence that walketh in darkness, and the destruction that wasteth at noonday, by which thousands fall at our side, and ten thousand at our right hand, are our masters, because of our life in the body. Let us not wonder at the Apostle's words: "We that are in this tabernacle do groan, being burdened."

We shall find other reasons for the Apostle's statement if we regard the body, as it was designed to be, as the instrument, by which the spirit expresses itself. I am speaking, of course, of the body as it is; not of the body, as it might have been had man maintained the holiness in which he was created. Doubtless his body, in that case, would have adequately expressed the life of his spiritual nature. It would have been finely sensitive to the spiritual feelings, and perfectly responsive to the spirit's volitions. What the body would have finally become under the culture of unfallen man, we can not of course tell. I do not doubt that man's power over nature would have been immeasurably greater than it is to-day. Certainly, the body would have been far less limited, than it now is, in expressing the mental and spiritual life which it enshrines. Of the limitations of the body in expressing the life of the spirit, who has not had painful experience? Let me refer to but one of these limitations. All will agree that man is, by no other physical power, so widely separated from the animal kingdom below him, as he is by the power of articulate speech. Language is man's noblest physical endowment. Its nobility lies in the fact, that it presupposes faculties—like the power by which we abstract and generalize, and the power by which we perceive universal and necessary truth—of which no brute animal possesses the rudiments. Of these high powers, language, whether vocalized or represented by symbols on the written page, is the bodily expression. It is the most far-reaching, the most subtle, the most elastic instrument of expression, that man possesses. How poor and clumsy, as instruments of expression, in comparison with speech, are those fine arts, which appeal to the senses by form, or color, or sound! Surely, if, in any particular, the body is an aid, and not a burden to man; it is in its power to articulate, in "words that burn," the "thoughts that breathe" from the indwelling spirit. But I ask whether it is not true, that here, also, "we that are in this tabernacle do groan, being burdened?" Setting aside, for the moment, the limitations inherent in language, there is a difficulty almost insurmountable, in thoroughly mastering the instrument itself. Who has not felt, in the act of speech—especially when the topic has been a lofty intellectual or spiritual theme—a painful lack of concurrence between the spirit and the body? What, indeed, is the genius of the great reflective poet or philosopher, but this: that the concurrence between thought and language, which is lacking in us, exists in him? It is not that we fail to perceive the truth, which he perceives and to which he has been able to give a more nearly adequate expression. Our highest tribute to his genius is the tribute, that he has said what we knew, but which, struggle as we might, we could not say.

Indeed, those, whose mastery of language has been the admiration and despair of their fellow-men, have, like the rest of us, groaned under the conviction of the poverty of their speech. However exceptional has been their "curious felicity" of spoken or of written language, they have felt, that they have only "prophesied in part." Perhaps, the most striking illustration of the truth, stated in the text, is furnished by man, when, struggling to speak out a great truth, he finds himself in only partial possession of the physical instrument of expression. A great living writer of prose has confessed, that he has, more than once, labored for hours on the construction of a single sentence. And I have often thought, that there must have been times, when a master of expression in the region of abstract truth like Thomas Aquinas, or a great poet like Dante, has wished that he could command the body, that separated between himself and his fellow-man, to fall away; in order that spirit might commune immediately with spirit, as face answereth unto face. Indeed, it may be stated as a law, that, just in the proportion in which thought is lofty and profound and spiritual, man, in the attempt to express it in articulate speech, groans, being burdened. Nor is this only because man himself has not mastered his instrument of expression. The instrument itself is limited. The spirit of man is greater than the power of speech. Man discerns truth, which speech can not adequately express. Thus language, while it partially reveals, also partially conceals man's knowledge. Socrates, therefore, in describing the perfect state, speaking of those whose lives are given to attempts explicitly to state the fundamental truths, which are implicitly the possession of each human soul, says: "Those who have duly purified themselves with philosophy, live henceforth altogether without the body, in mansions fairer far than these, and of which the time would fail me to tell."* So the Apostle Paul taught. It was not of this life; but of the life to come, that he said, not only: "We shall know as we are known," but also: "We shall see face to face."

I have thus far spoken of man only in his individual life. I had intended, if time permitted, to speak of him in his relations to his fellow-men; and to show, how the adventitious inequalities between men, due to relations made possible only by the body, are the cause of no inconsiderable proportion of the groaning of men in this tabernacle of the flesh. It was my purpose, also, to dwell on the limits, which his possession of a body puts upon his acquisition of knowledge; and, setting this over against his insatiable thirst for truth, to ask whether we have not in this fact another reason for Paul's statement that, man in this tabernacle groans, being burdened.†

---

* Phædo, 114. Jowett's translation.

† The limitations, placed by the body on man's power to acquire knowledge, are not due merely to the *small number* of senses,

But, brethren, beyond all these considerations, which give force to the words of the Apostle, there is another, that was directly before his mind, when he wrote this Epistle.

What that was, we shall understand, only as we remember, in what capacity and for what purpose, he was writing to these men and women in the city of

---

through which, as through windows, the spirit inspects the universe. These limitations are due chiefly to the fact, that man's knowledge in his present state, is dependent on sense-perception. For sense-perception being the avenue of knowledge limits it. I do not mean, of course, that it is the cause of knowledge, in the proper sense of the term cause. I do mean that sense-perception is the necessary *occasion* of knowledge. Intuitive truths emerge into consciousness only on the occasion of the perception of objects, in which the truths inhere as particular facts. Even, therefore, if the number of our senses were multiplied a hundred-fold, our knowledge, though it would be vastly increased, would still be limited in exactly the way in which it is at present. Nor would the spirit groan any the less in its tabernacle of a hundred senses than it does now in its tabernacle of six; though it might rejoice in the multiplication of the windows of its dwelling.

Sir William Hamilton [Metaphyics, p. 101] quotes a passage from the Micromegas, a philosophical romance of Voltaire, which finely illustrates this truth. The passage is a conversation between an inhabitant of Saturn, who has seventy-two senses, and is able to detect and classify three hundred essential properties of matter, and Micromegas, an inhabitant of one of the planets of Sirius, who "has very near one thousand senses." Micromegas confesses, that with all these senses, he feels continually "a sort of listless inquietude and vague desire, which are forever telling him that he is nothing; and that there are beings infinitely nearer perfection." That Sir William Hamilton uses this extract in the interests of a theory of knowledge, which, if accepted, must destroy our confidence in fundamental truth, does not make it less happy as an illustration of the truth, that mere sense-perceptions, however multiplied, can never aid us in attaining that knowledge in kind, for which man now cries in vain, because imprisoned in a "natural body." The

Corinth. We must remember, that he and they were conscious sinners. They were giving the labor of their lives to the throttling and the killing of sin within their own hearts, and to the destruction of sin in the hearts of those around them. Under the guidance of the Spirit of God, they had learned to know and to feel, as few of those, in whose society they lived, knew and felt the exceeding

---

"natural body" would not be changed into a "spiritual body" were the number of the senses increased a hundred-fold. What the spirit of man, in its search after truth, longs for, is not so much an improvement, through the multiplication of senses, of the present mode of attaining knowledge, as a new, that is, a *spiritual mode* of knowledge. This—apart from sin—is, perhaps, the profoundest reason for man's groaning in the tabernacle that burdens him. So Plato makes Socrates say in the Phædo [66, 67]: "Moreover, if there is time and an inclination toward philosophy, yet the body introduces a turmoil, and confusion, and fear into the course of speculation, and hinders us from seeing the truth; and all experience shows that if we would have pure knowledge of any thing we must quit the body, and the soul in herself must see things in themselves; then I suppose that we shall attain that which we desire, and of which we say that we are lovers, and that is wisdom, not while we live, but after death, as the argument shows; for if while in company with the body, the soul can not have pure knowledge, one of two things seems to follow; either knowledge can not be attained at all, or, if at all, after death. For then, and not till then, the soul will be in herself alone, and without the body. In the present life, I reckon that we make the nearest approach to knowledge when we have the least possible concern or interest of the body, and are not saturated with the bodily nature, but remain pure until the hour when God pleases to release us. And then the foolishness of the body will be cleared away, and we shall be pure, and hold converse with other pure souls, and know of ourselves the clear light everywhere; and this is surely the light of truth. For no impure thing is allowed to approach the pure. These are the sort of words, Simmias, which the true lovers of wisdom can not help saying to one another, and thinking."—Jowett's translation.

sinfulness of sin. They hated it. They determined, that, with the help of God, they would not permit it to reign in their mortal bodies. In this warfare, they were battling bravely, with the felt help of the Saviour, in whose name they were waging it. Paul wrote to the Corinthian Church, as to a company of such warriors against indwelling and surrounding sin. And it was chiefly because their life in the body made temptations to sin more powerful and more numerous, that he wrote: "We that are in this tabernacle do groan, being burdened." It is, as if he had said: "This body is the citadel of the sin, against which we, who are spiritually minded, battle. This body is the theater of our conflict. And so long as the life in the body continues, the conflict can not cease. So long as these appetites and passions exist; so long as this life in the body makes necessary engrossing business, and makes possible enticing physical and social pleasures; so long as it continually tempts us to long for and labor after, as the end of life, the things that are seen and temporal, the warfare must continue; and we must know, what the perils and the wounds of battle are. So long as 'we are in this tabernacle we shall groan, being burdened.'" Ah! friends, I do not need to explain in detail the meaning of the Apostle's words. If we are really striving against sin; if we are really endeavoring, with the help of God, to become holy, as Christ is holy; we feel better than words can describe it, the awful, the bitter truth of the text. The Apostle, in another letter,—so terribly did he feel the truth, which he here states,—connects his sin with his body so closely, as to say: "I see a law in my members, warring against the law of my mind, and bringing into captivity to the law of sin in my members. O wretched man that I am, who shall deliver me from the body of this death?"

Let us lay it down, therefore, as a maxim in Christian living, that it is to be a strife, and a terrible strife, until we are relieved of the body. There is no discharge in this war. It is ceaseless, until death crowns the faithful soul with triumph. For the body will not surrender its claims to be regarded as the highest portion of our being; and the life of the body will not cease its harassments of the spirit, until the earthly house of this tabernacle is dissolved, and we are clothed upon with our house, which is from heaven. Let me speak, therefore, to any who suppose that, because they believe in the Saviour, the days of agonizing and striving are over. The striving has but begun when a man has accepted Christ. Then, for the first time, the spirit and body war with each other in earnest. Paul's words : "O wretched man that I am, who shall deliver me from the body of this death?" were written twenty-five years after he beheld the vision of Christ near to Damascus. Each of us may well make his own the words of the familiar hymn—

> "Fight on, my soul, till death
>   Shall bring thee to thy God.
> He'll take thee, at thy parting breath,
>   Up to his blest abode."

There, and there alone, in the house of God, not made with hands, eternal in the heavens, having escaped the toils and temptations of the earthly house of this tabernacle, we shall no longer groan, being burdened. The statement of our Church's confession has, not only a positive basis in the Word of God, but a negative confirmation also in Christian experience. "The souls of believers are, at their death, made perfect in holiness, and do immediately pass into glory."

I close this imperfect exposition of the words of the Apostle with the bare statement of two or three inferences. And first, the text reveals to us the real significance of our present life. It is disciplinary. We are schooled by it for the enjoyment of a life of perfect holiness. Were this not true, it would be hard to reconcile it, with all its limitations and disappointments and accidents and conflict, with the love of God for his children. And if we would live it aright, we must ever keep this in view. We must look forward to the end of it. We shall find its burdens lighter, and our groanings fewer, just in the proportion in which we look forward to the house not made with hands, eternal in the heavens.

The text helps us, also, to understand the Apostle's statement: "For, to me, to die is gain." Even if we think of death, as nothing more than an escape from the ills of a life in the body, it is an unspeakable gain. Even though we knew far less of the future state, than we do know, through the revelation of God in Christ; to know that, in dying, we throw off the imprisonment which we now suffer; to know that we are freed by death, from the weariness and weakness, which here oppress us, and from the sin which burdens us, were enough to enable us to understand the longing, which the Apostle felt when he wrote: "I have a desire to depart, and to be with Christ."

Moreover, the text enables us to discern the completeness, which shall be given to the redemption of man by the resurrection of the body. The hope of the resurrection; "the lively hope begotten in us by the resurrection of Christ Jesus from the dead!" And what a hope it is! We have seen what this body is to us now; in every aspect of it, a tabernacle in which we groan, being burdened. God promises us redemption *from* the body. He tells us that it shall no longer burden us; that He will clothe us with another house, eternal in the heavens. But we love these bodies, burdens though they are. And when we lay those of our Christian friends in the earth, we grieve and murmur, though we know that, by their release from them, they have gained immeasurably. We ask whether it is true, that sin has conquered the body finally, though the soul has escaped. And, in no uncertain tones, God's Word says: No! Sin has not finally triumphed over the body. "Now is Christ risen from the dead, and become the first-fruits of them that slept." This body shall be saved as the soul is saved. It shall be like the risen body of Christ. Sown in weakness; it shall be raised in power. Sown in a natural body; it shall be raised a spiritual body. It shall no longer burden us; but, raised in glory, shall give new power to the transfigured soul, in its endless life of love, of labor, and of praise.

I said, at the beginning of this sermon, that these words of Paul were addressed to Christians, to those whose habit of mind is spiritual. It is true of all men, that they groan in this tabernacle. And in these days, they are not slow to confess it. A pessimistic philosophy asks the question, confident that only a negative answer can be given: "Is life worth living?" But if the spiritual habit of mind be wanting, what gain will there be in release from the body? Death is gain to him alone, who looks at the unseen and eternal. If we live, "looking only at the seen and the temporal;" if we have "the mind of the flesh;" if, in other words, we are not united by faith to the Redeemer, and baptized with the Spirit, the dissolution of the earthly tabernacle is the loss of all things. And, therefore, now, as always, we call you to come to Christ.

X.
THE RELATIONS OF RELIGION AND BUSINESS.

"Not slothful in business; fervent in spirit; serving the Lord."—ROMANS xii, 11.

No subject, more immediately practical, could engage the attention of a Christian congregation, than the relations between Christianity and business pursuits. I use the phrase, business pursuits, in its largest significance. All of us are business men and women; we buy and sell; we touch the world commercially. Out of this fact spring certain relations to our fellows; and it is to the demands that Christianity makes upon us, in these relations, that I ask your attention. Though my theme, therefore, ought to have special interest for those who are distinctively business men; all of us, as earning wages and spending them, or, as employing our powers in making money, may very well hear what the religion of Christ has to say on this subject.

When we turn to the New Testament for instruction, we find the Saviour intimating the presence of peculiar temptations, in the conduct of a life, whose end is the attainment of wealth; as in the words: "How hardly shall they that have riches enter into the kingdom of God." And, on the other hand, we find his Apostle, exhorting Christians to activity in business, as in the text: "Not slothful in business; fervent in spirit; serving the Lord." We find him teaching, therefore, that there is no necessary discord, between an active business and a sincere and devout Christian life.

If, from the New Testament, we turn to our condition and surroundings, we find ourselves part of a nation more actively engaged in developing its resources by mining, and manufactures, and commerce, than perhaps any other; and members of one of the largest manufacturing communities in the country. It is beyond dispute, I think, that the type of personal Christianity that is to prevail for years to come in the United States, and especially in communities like this, will be determined, largely, by the commercial character of the people. It behooves us, therefore, from time to time, to re-examine the teachings of the word of God on this subject; and to gather from them, a picture of the Christian in his business life. What principles should guide him as a Christian? What peculiar temptations beset him? What helps, if any, are there in his goods and accounts, by the employment of which he can more rapidly grow into the image of Christ. The subject is as large as it is important; and I can hope to touch, only briefly, on aspects of it, which it would be instructive to treat at length.

At the outset, we are met by a general fact of the most hopeful character. If any of us were asked, in what nations, to-day, lies the hope of the world; what countries are most active in their endeavors to hasten the universal triumph of Christianity, our answer would undoubtedly be, that among the foremost, at least, are the two great commercial peoples of Great Britain and America. So far as practical, aggressive Christianity is concerned, we may, I think, without doing injustice to others, assume that these two are doing—not indeed what they should do—but a large proportion of the Christian work of the world. If this fact is of any importance, it shows a harmonious relation between business and religion. It encourages the belief, that there is an affinity, rather than an antagonism, between Christianity and mercantile pursuits; it suggests the probability, that those, who give themselves to active business life, do not find such a life more full of temptations than another would be; it teaches that a large responsibility rests upon them; that we have a right to expect from them as signal illustrations of the graces, which constitute personal Christianity, as from any class in a community; and that they, of all men, have no right to plead as an excuse for distorted Christian lives, the pursuits in which they are engaged. But it is not my intention, to base any plea I may have to make, or any lesson I may wish to teach, on general facts like this; I shall dwell rather on those great principles of Christianity, which all Christians profess to accept as the rules of their daily conduct.

In order to ascertain the relations between Christianity and business, we must first of all place clearly before our minds the meaning of the word Christianity, which we so often, and, at times, so loosely use. What is Christianity? If I put the question to one, he will reply, that it is the system of truth, revealed by God, and contained in the Scriptures of the Old and New Testaments. If I put it to another, the reply will be, that it is union with one of the organizations which together constitute the Church of Christ. Still another will define it, as the one true method of the soul's worship of God. While a fourth will say, that it is the embodiment of the highest morality. And so in one, whenever the word is spoken, the dominant thought is truth or doctrine; in another, organization or Church; in another, worship; in still another, morality or character.

Now, though each of these views is partial, each one emphasizes an element, necessary to the adequate definition of Christianity. There is no Christianity without truth accepted; none without work, which instinctively seeks organization that flowers out into the Church; none without worship engaged in, whose one object is God; and none without a character, formed upon Jesus Christ, the Christian example of morality. I do not undertake to say what detailed articles one must accept in order to Christianity; or how close must be his relation to the Church, and with what organization he must be allied; or what must be the method of his approach to God; or how far advanced in character he must be. This were to go a length, which the Scriptures do not warrant. But the Scriptures do warrant us in affirming the necessity of acceptance of the truth; when they call the Christian "a believer." They justify us in bringing the Church into the description; when they speak of him as a subject of the "Kingdom of God," and a member of the "Body of Christ." They make it necessary for us to include the idea of worship; for they themselves continually dwell upon his relations to God. And as for character; the very end of truth, and church, and worship, so far as man and this world are concerned, is to create in him a perfect character; the image of the perfect man, Christ Jesus. Now if any one of us has been honestly perplexed, as to the relations between Christianity and business life; if any one has been seriously disturbed by the question: "How am I to be a Christian business man?" it is not at all improbable, that the perplexity has arisen, because of a too great emphasis, relatively, of one of these elements of the definition, and a corresponding depression of the others.

For example, we can easily conceive of one, before whose mind Christianity stands forth most prominently as a system of *truth*, to be believed, and proclaimed, and defended; and who puts out of sight, or at least throws into the background, all the other elements of a true definition of Christianity. Holding fast to this one thought of truth, of doctrine; and depressing other essential elements; as organized work for men, the outgoing of the soul in worship to God, and the growth of the whole man in a character like that of Christ; it is evident that his Christianity will resolve itself into mere orthodoxy; the acceptance and defense of certain statements, found in, or inferred from the word of God. It is perfectly plain, that such a view of our holy religion must tend to make faith less and less an act of the whole man, and more and more an exercise of the understanding alone; until finally the man will stand as the exponent of a mere intellectual statement. The relations between such a man's business and his religion, can not be very many or very intimate. Whatever time he gives to business life; he must take from the defense, or contemplation, or study of the truth. The bringing of his religion into business will be, solely, the use of the results of his business labors, for the propagation of the truths, that for him constitute Christianity. Nothing more than this. And no one needs to be told, that this is far from fulfilling the exhortation of the Apostle: "Not slothful in business; fervent in spirit; serving the Lord."

So, too, with one who, in his conception of Christianity emphasizes the idea of *Church*, and work for an organization, to the almost entire seclusion of the other elements, included in the term Christianity. The world has never been without such religionists. The idea of the Church is a sublime idea. The visible Kingdom of which the Lord Christ is monarch; the living temple built upon the foundation of the apostles and prophets, Jesus himself being the chief corner-stone! But it was the uplifting of this truth, and the depression of all the other elements of religion, that bred the Pharaseeism, which called forth such indignant denunciations from Christ. And the relations of business with religion in such a view of Christianity, is well suggested in Christ's own descriptions of those, who, compassing sea and land to make a proselyte, are yet able to devour widow's houses.

Or here is another, to whom the term Christianity stands exclusively for *worship;* the communion of man with God; and all the joys of such communion. One of the most inspiring truths, which the Word of God reveals, is that man can commune with God; that not only is God the hearer of prayer, but that He communes with his people; that there is a manifestation of Himself to them. But when this thought, great and blessed as it is, so takes possession of a man, as to exclude all other elements of religion, the result must be a degeneration of the religious life, until it becomes a life of mere emotions and excitements; in whose frequent recurrence truth is forgotten, and character is weakened, and work for God and man neglected. Surely, such a Christianity has no place in the midst of the labors and engrossments of business life.

Or take the man who, ignoring doctrine, church and worship, regards Christianity as *morality* alone, in his relations to his fellows. There is a tendency in us all to adopt the view, that, "to do justly, and hurt nobody, and to render to every man his due," is the sum of the Gospel, and that all else is but instrumental; that truth, work, and worship are means of which the end is this character. And, undoubtedly it is true, so far as man's life here is concerned, that the end, at once, of the truth which the Bible reveals, of the Church which it makes known, and of the worship which it enjoins, is the development of a character, like that of Christ himself. But such is the tendency in man to narrowness, that he, who fixes his regards on character alone, ignoring these essential aids to its attainment, will insensibly lower his ideal; and, robbing it of one, and another, of its traits, will, at the last, substitute, for the divine ideal, the ideal of mere honesty in business transactions; of which honesty, however much may be said in its praise, this can not be said; that it fulfills all the relations between religion and business, as these are suggested in the words of the Apostle: "Not slothful in business; fervent in spirit; serving the Lord."

Before we can state adequately the truth concerning the relation of these two lives—the Christian life on the one hand, and business life on the other—

we must grasp Christianity in its entirety. We must remember that the truth, the Church, worship, and character, all belong to it. No man goes to his business life as a Christian should, who does not carry with him these four great thoughts. No one will conduct his daily business as a Christian should— who, in his conduct of it, is not controlled by the truths God's word reveals, by the fact that he is a member of Christ's Church, by his worship of and communion with God, and by the character which, as a Christian, he is seeking to attain. And we shall best ascertain the relations of Christianity and business life by placing before our minds the influence, which these elements of our religion are severally designed to exert.

I. Taking them up in the order in which I have already named them, and premising that, within the limits of a single sermon, I can hope to do no more than state, not the whole, but the single characteristic influence of each of them,—what, let us ask, is the legitimate influence, in a business life, of the great body of distinctly *Christian truths* which the Christian accepts? I am speaking now of truth that is distinctively Christian; not the history or the morality of the Word of God, but that which is distinctive of the Bible—its revelations. What should be the influence of these, on the Christian, in his pursuit of wealth? And the answer must be a restraining influence. It should be to moderate his desires, to hold back his hands from a too eager grasp of the riches which it is the end of business to obtain. This influence of the distinctive truths, revealed in the Word of God, is brought out, in connection with the statement of one of them, in an exhortation of St. Paul to the Church at Philippi:

"Let your moderation be known unto all men. The Lord is at hand." For consider, what is the character of this body of distinctly Christian truth. It relates immediately, not to the seen, but to the invisible world: to the immortality of man; the eternal life of destiny; the infinite value of the soul; the life which is more than meat; a meat and drink which is to do the will of our Father in heaven and to finish his work; a glory with which the sufferings of this present time are not worthy to be compared; a God in whose image man is created, and who is our Governor, Father, Redeemer and Judge. These are the subjects about which the Word of God makes special revelations. And therefore we find upon its pages such solemn questions, as: "What shall it profit a man, though he gain the whole world, and lose his soul?" and such exhortations, as: "Seek ye first the kingdom of God and his righteousness, and all these things shall be added unto you;" "If ye then be risen with Christ, set your affection on things which are above, where Christ sitteth at the right hand of God;" and such descriptions of the Christian life, as: "We look not at the things which are seen and temporal, but at the things which are not seen and eternal." The Christian is a *believer* of this great body of truth, that relates to sin, to salvation, to God, to judgment and eternal life. If he does not believe it, he has no right to the distinctive name of Christian.

But such is the constitution of the world in which he lives, and such are his own condition and wants, that it is absolutely necessary for him to labor in some business, whose end is the possession of money. But what an influence must this spiritual truth that he believes exert in abating his desire for wealth!

How little, in view of it, must earthly possessions seem. If he has, indeed, tasted of the good Word of God, and the powers of the world to come, his moderation will be known unto all men. I do not forget that man has bodily wants and a social nature and tastes which not only may, but, within limits not easily defined, should be cultivated and gratified. God has given us the power of perceiving, and the feeling of joy in the beautiful; and He has so adorned the world in which we live, as to call out the power and excite the feeling. It can not be contrary to his will, therefore, to gratify our love of beauty, if we hold it subordinate to that love of holiness which is the new man's true crown. And yet, it is also true that he, whose faith in the distinctive truth of God's Word is living; who, therefore, has his regard fixed on God and life eternal, will tone down his passion for time's wealth, and beauty and pleasures. Just this is the legitimate influence of faith in Christian truth upon business life. The Christian man of business will not leave these revelations out of account, when laying plans for the business of the year or the business of life. The desire for wealth will abate, in proportion as his mind is fixed on the things that are unseen and eternal. Here is one point of contact between Christianity and business life. He may be not slothful in business; he may be active, and absorbed. But he will be more fervent in spirit, serving the Lord, than feverish in his anxieties for the riches that make to themselves wings and fly toward heaven.

If we could affirm no other influence of this great body of truth which God has revealed to us, on its believers, than the abatement of the fiery haste to be rich, so characteristic of our people to-day, what an unspeakable blessing this revelation would still be! This feverish haste, begotten of exceptional opportunities—can any one be blind to the fact that it is destroying the higher life of thousands? How earnestly do all of us—for there is not one of us who is not affected by the atmosphere we breathe—need to pray: "Lord, increase our faith in the great truths of thy Word;" knowing that a vital faith in these truths is the one medicine that can cure this terrible fever, which is consuming the spiritual life of so many of our fellow-men.

II. The first element of Christianity, then, is the truth revealed and believed; and its influence on business life is to moderate the desire for wealth. The second element of the definition of Christianity, we found to be the *Church*. The Christian is not only a believer of truth, he is also a subject of the Kingdom, a member of the Church of Christ. The truth revealed must be proclaimed; and this is the distinctive mission of the Church. "Go ye into all the world and preach the Gospel to every creature." The influence of the thought of the Church on the Christian in business life, is very different from the influence which faith in the truths just referred to exerts. The influence of such faith, as we have seen, is to moderate the desire for wealth as a personal possession. But the Church, by giving a new object, intensifies his labors for wealth. But for the thought of the Church and his relation to it, it is conceivable that a Christian, full of faith in God's word, might retire from the competitions and excitements of business life. But remembering the Church, and his relation to it; remembering the words of his Master: "As thou, Father, hast sent me into the world, even so have I sent them into the world," the believing disciple returns to his labors, and works more vigorously for wealth and influence in the interest of the Kingdom of Christ. So the influence of the truth, and the influence of the Church on his business life, modify and balance one another. The labors, which in the light of the truths alone were excessive and harmful, become religious duties in view of the mission of the Church of God. In this way, business life is sanctified; and money-getting, so it be honest, being labor for God and man, is more than right; it is holy, and well-pleasing to God.

We call ourselves Christians. We profess to believe the truths which our Lord has revealed, and to belong to the Church that He loved, and for which He gave Himself. Do we indeed believe the truths; are we indeed members of that Church which is to conquer the world for Him? If the Church had faith in Christian truth and Christ's Kingdom, such as Christ described: faith as a grain of mustard-seed—the seed which, below the light and sun, yet, responsive to the powers of heaven, pushes through the clods that vainly seek to hold it; and, by the power of its life, breaks not the sod alone, but nature's great law of gravitation, and rising higher, and pushing out on every hand, becomes the great spreading tree, on whose branches the fowls of the air find shelter;—had the Church, I say, faith like this in the great truths of God's Word and in the Kingdom of God, with what quickened industry would its members—their desires for personal wealth abated—still labor for riches, that they might be laid upon the altar for the redemption of their fellow-men. When Christianity shall so mold business life; when the missionary spirit shall animate business pursuits; who can doubt that the world will again feel the throes of a new awakening; that nations will be born in a day, and the kingdoms of the world become the Kingdom of our Lord? But, because there is apathy in the Church at large, we are not relieved of our responsibility to Christ. To every congregation of Christians, as well as to the whole body of believers—nay, to every disciple—come the words of God: "Bring ye all the tithes into the store-house, that there may be meat in mine house, and prove me now herewith, saith the Lord of hosts, if I will not open you the windows of heaven, and pour you out a blessing, that there shall not be room enough to receive it."

III. But Christianity is not only belief of the truth of God, and union with the Church of God. We found a third essential element, to be *worship* of and communion with God. Christ came as the new and living way to the Father. The Christian has thus the assurance that God is near to him, and is ready to reveal Himself to the believer. The Christian consciousness is a consciousness of God. This is a great mystery; but great must be the mystery of Godliness. Now what is the relation of Christianity, in this aspect of it, to business life? I answer, that as the belief of God's revealed truth must abate the feverish anxiety for personal possession, on the one hand, and the thought of the Church must, on the other hand, excite him to new labors for wealth to be used for the world and Christ; the communion of the soul with God allays the anxiety, which the Christian's new labor in his business for the Church, is calculated to awaken. In the thought of his responsibility, as belonging to the Church whose mission it is to conquer the world for Christ, is ground for anxiety, lest his labors may not suffice for the work to which he is called. But when to this is joined the thought of God, above the Church, yet always with the Church, supplementing its gifts from the stores of his infinite fullness; and this in the measure, not of the gifts themselves, but of the consecration they represent; the Christian labors in his daily calling with an unanxious heart; rejoicing in the presence and the power of the God, who has already so blessed the two mites of the widow, and the alabaster box of ointment, that they have not lost their power, and will not, until all men shall rejoice in his redemption.

IV. We found the last essential element of personal Christianity to be *character*. The complete definition includes, not only the belief of truths revealed, union with the Church of Christ, and communion of the soul with God, but, also, the possession of a character formed on that of Christ and daily growing more and more like his. Do you ask the relation of Christianity, in this last aspect of it, to business life? I answer, that while the influence of the preceding elements is exerted mainly in determining the mission, and in tempering the anxieties of business life, the influence of this last element is to be looked for, most of all, in the daily conduct of business. If one, remembering that Christianity means a growing likeness to Christ, would do business in this world as a Christian, he must conduct it on principles of the loftiest morality. I say, of the loftiest morality. Christ came as the example and embodiment of such morality. And if you ask what this means in detail; I answer, that it means a spotless integrity, a determination, with God's help, in spite of whatever surroundings of another character, to do nothing, to say nothing that would justify the slightest suspicion of dishonesty; a morality like his "whose eye, e'en turned on empty space, beams keen with honor;" a morality which, in every transaction, with buyer and seller, with employer and employed, from day to day, and from year to year, finds its rule in those golden words of the Master: "Therefore all things, whatsoever ye would that men should do unto you, do ye even so to them; for this is the law and the prophets."

Christian friends, I have thus endeavored, fairly and faithfully, to take up the essential elements of our holy religion, and, describing their legitimate influence in business life, to make plain the meaning of those words we hear so often: a "Christian man of business." Is there one before me who is disposed to respond to what I have said: "But you have presented an ideal too lofty, one that is unattainable"? I reply, it is the ideal of the word of God. And if it is lofty, it is not too lofty for a religion whose example is Christ, and whose end is the restored image of God. It is true that you may not attain it at once; the week of work on which you will enter to-morrow may be full of temptations, and once, and again, and again, you may fall far below your new ideal. But should you fall, remember that the Lord turned and looked on fallen Peter, and, like Peter, go out penitent to new labors for the Master and the world. You are bound by the profession you have made, to hold this ideal in full view each day you live, and, with Paul, to say: "I count not myself to have apprehended, but this one thing I do, forgetting the things which are behind, and reaching forth unto those that are before, I press toward the mark for the prize of the high calling of God in Christ Jesus my Lord."

There may be those before me who feel that these words are not for them, because they have not taken the Christian name. To whom, then, are you giving the labors of your business life? What is the end of your striving after wealth? Because you have not confessed Christ, think you that Christ has not the same claims on you that he has on those, who, in obedience to his commands and with much trembling, have taken his name and service as their own? The same Lord who has given talents to them, has given talents to you; and though you may not acknowledge Him, I repeat the truth He teaches when I say, that of you as of them, He will at his coming require his own with usury. May God teach all of us, that it is the Lord's talents we are using; and so guide us in the use of them, that each at last shall hear the blessed words: "Well done, good and faithful servant, thou hast been faithful over a few things, I will make thee ruler over many things; enter thou into the joy of thy Lord."

XI.

THE VALUE OF A RELIGIOUS ATMOSPHERE.

"And Saul went thither to Naioth in Ramah: and the Spirit of God was upon him also, and he went on, and prophesied, until he came to Naioth in Ramah."—I. SAMUEL xix, 23.

In order to bring clearly before our minds the single subject, on which I wish to speak from these words, it will be necessary briefly to recall the narrative from which they are taken. The envy of David's popularity, felt by Saul, and the fear, which the monarch could not conceal, that the conqueror of the Philistine might usurp the throne, had for some time been growing in strength, and had already shown themselves in acts of violence. At last, Saul's determination to put an end to David's life became so ungovernable, that he disclosed his purpose, not only to his servants, but to Jonathan his son, and commanded them to aid him in his capture. But the friendship of Jonathan for David led not only to the latter's escape, but also to a reconciliation with Saul; so that we are told, that Jonathan induced the king to swear: "As the Lord liveth he shall not be slain." And Jonathan brought David into Saul's presence; and he was there, as in times past. But war between Israel and the Philistines having been renewed, a new opportunity for the display of his skill and valor was given to David. He went out and fought with the Philistines, and slew them with a great slaughter, and they fled from him. Very naturally, the people of the kingdom were loud in their praises of the son of Jesse, as before they had been, when, single-handed, he met and conquered the chosen champion of their foes. And the song must have been repeated which rang upon the air at the death of Goliath: "Saul hath slain his thousands, and David his ten thousands." All this was so chafing to the envious monarch, that he either forgot, or purposely violated his oath to Jonathan, and again sought to compass David's death. But with the aid of Michal his wife, who was the daughter of the king, David again escaped Saul's vengeance, and fled to Naioth in Ramah.

Now Naioth was the home of the prophets of the Lord. It was the seat of a school of the prophets, over which the aged and devout Samuel presided. For the purposes of this sermon, it is necessary only to say of these schools, that they were the great centers of the moral and religious influence exerted on the kingdom of Israel. David fled to this school at Naioth, no doubt, because of his intimate relations with its great leader, Samuel. Of Samuel's character and influence, I need to say but little. How pure was the life, how great and beneficent was his influence, how commanding was his personal presence, how he held Israel during the change from the government by Judges to the Monarchy—all know who are, in the least degree, familiar with the history of the times. Before this man David always bowed in reverence, and Saul always crouched in fear. It is not surprising, that his own religious habit of life gave character both to the schools he instituted, and to the places in which the schools were established. A religious atmosphere surrounded Naioth; as an intellectual atmosphere surrounds a university town; as a commercial atmosphere envelops London or New York. Men found it difficult not to think of religion in Naioth, just as men find it hard not to think of learning in Oxford, or not to be full of thoughts of business amid the noises of Broadway or Wall Street. So impressive and influential, so all-compelling was this religious atmosphere in Naioth, that no one entered the gates of the city without feeling it deeply and at once.

To this town of Naioth, to the school of the prophets, and to Samuel's presence, did David flee from the power and hate of his royal foe. And, whether or not he had calculated upon it, it soon became apparent that he could not have selected a better refuge. Not, indeed, that its material defenses were better than those of other places; for he might have found a more impregnable position in the strongholds at Engedi, or a safer covert in the Cave of Adullam. But, for a reason which will presently appear, Naioth, though open to the king's messengers and to the vengeful king himself, stood the fugitive in better stead than any other place could have done at this time. For when it was told Saul that David had fled to Naioth; and Saul, in his wrath, sent messengers to take him, they came; but entering the city, the religious spirit seized upon them; and they, who had come upon a message of blood, began to pray and prophesy. Again he sent messengers; but they also failed to capture the fugitive; not because the fugitive had fled, but because they too began to prophesy in Naioth. A third time the monarch sent a company to take him; and on this third company the religious spirit of the place descended, and David was safe from their hands, because they fell under its influence. Then Saul himself arose; his wrath against David increased by the repeated failures to arrest him. No doubt, he determined that no influence should keep him from his victim. In anger he went to Ramah; and coming to a well at Sechu, halted and demanded, as king, to know where Samuel and David were. And when one said: "Behold, they be at Naioth," he went there. All aflame with wrath, he entered the city. But David was safe, because the Spirit came also on the king; and, like his messengers before him, he went on and prophesied. Indeed, so overcome was he, that he abased himself before the aged leader of the school, and lay down naked all that day and all that night. Wherefore, men said: "Is Saul also among the prophets?"

Without attempting to separate the natural from the miraculous in the narrative, you will be prepared, at once, for the subject it suggests, and of which it is so striking an illustration. I mean that, which, for want of a better name, we may call the *religious atmosphere*—the natural, spontaneous religious outgoing of the place. It was no purposely exercised influence upon Saul—so far as we can gather from the narrative—that led the king to withhold violence from David, or that induced him to prophesy. No one remonstrated with him. There was no special power exerted to restrain his body or to constrain his soul. The moment, however, he came within reach of the immanent influences of Naioth, he voluntarily desisted from the execution of his murderous intent;—and not only so, but he caught the religious spirit of the place, and prophesied before Samuel and before the Lord.

I. I say that it was the religious atmosphere of the place which exerted so great an influence upon the king of Israel. I call it atmosphere, because that best defines, or, rather, describes it. You all know what I mean by the term. We use it in common conversation to designate that unconscious influence which men exert—nay, which they can not help exerting, and exerting always—which they bear with them everywhere; which is both the outcome and the surrounding of their personality. We speak familiarly of the air of a man—that he has a "chilling air," or a "pleasant air," or that he moves along the streets with a "grand air." And before we have done describing the man, we mention this air of his. We add to his features, and form, and words, and doings, and position in society and the Church and business, this impalpable and often indescribable atmosphere which surrounds him always and everywhere—just as the air, night and day, and throughout all its journey in the path of its orbit, surrounds the planet upon which we live. And not only so, but we usually feel it more than we feel any thing else when we first come within the range of a man's personal influence. Let any one endeavor to analyze what we call his first impressions of an individual, in order to ascertain from what exactly in the individual these impressions were received. I think we shall all agree that, in most cases, they are received, not so much from what the person said or did, as from this something which usually eludes analysis, and which sometimes we call the "tone," but more often the "air of the man." It is Thackeray, I think, who, in one of his sketches, tells of two men going one after another to a hotel, seeking lodgings. Nothing was said by either of them about the character of the room desired. But, such was the air of one of them, that the clerk did not hesitate to send him to the attic, while the other, he did not dare to place in any but his best apartment. Do we not all know women, in whose gentle presence—though they themselves would shrink in fear from their own voices, were they to attempt the utterance of any thing like a rebuke—the roughest boor loses for the time his roughness, and holds his voice to gentlest tones? We have all heard that Daniel Webster, in the days of his power, would, by his presence and the air he had, influence and awe an audience as other men could not by their eloquence.

But I will not detain you with illustrations. There is such a thing as the atmosphere of a man, an institution, a church, a place; and there is an influence exerted by it, distinct from and in addition to the more direct influence exerted by such place or person. There is, too, such a thing as a religious, a spiritual atmosphere, the unconscious and permanent exertion of a religious influence on all with whom we come in contact. And if a man has this religious atmosphere surrounding him, he will not only impress others with the fact that he is religious; he will also influence them religiously. And just here at the outset, we must make this clear and important distinction. It is one thing, as you walk about the streets and mingle in the society of the world, to impress men with the fact that you are religious. It is quite another thing, if your life, as you live it at home and in business, influences men in behalf of the religion which you profess. It would have been of little value to David, if the only impression made upon Saul, as he came near to Naioth, had been that Naioth was a place where all who dwelt prayed and prophesied. The value of the religious atmosphere of Naioth to David was, that Saul himself imbibed the spirit of the place, the moment he came within the range of its influence; and, instead of pursuing David, gave himself to prophecy. We speak of the benefit which a young man, beginning business, derives from living in a business place, in a commercial atmosphere. But that atmosphere will do him little good, if it only impresses him with the fact that his surroundings are those of a mercantile character. If such surroundings have any value for him, it lies in the fact that, in breathing their atmosphere he imbibes their spirit, and becomes himself what we call a business man. This is an all important distinction. If our religion is such, that men recognize only that we are religious, we are condemned by Him who distinctly says: "Take heed that ye do not your righteousness before men to be seen of them." But if we not only impress them with the fact that we are religious, but so impress them that they are drawn toward our religion, then are we in the exact line of duty, for in the same discourse to his disciples Christ says: "Let your light so shine before men, that they may see your good works and glorify your Father which is in heaven." A Christian Church always, I suppose, impresses the world with the fact that it is Christian. But sometimes God's Spirit descends on such a Church; and there succeeds what we call a revival of religion. Then the Church not only impresses the men, who come within the range of its influence, with the fact that it is Christian, but it impresses its own Christianity in some measure upon them. We all know the difference between the same Church at ordinary times and in seasons of real revival. It is not that the same truths are not spoken, that the same instrumentalities are not used; it is in the constantly outgoing influence, in the religious atmosphere which envelops it.

II. Having seen the nature of this religious atmosphere, let us notice briefly its value as indicated by the influence which those whom it surrounds exert. And in the first place, it is to be remarked that the influence so exerted will always be *unobtrusive*. I suppose, that if I were to address myself to those that are professed Christians before me, and put the question: "Why do you not obey the command of God, 'and let him that heareth, say come?' Why are you not more diligent in pressing home upon the attention of your friends and companions the claims of Christ and his Gospel?" If, I say, I should address questions like these to the individual Christians before me—I would probably receive the reply: "We have no wish to obtrude the subject, or rather we have no desire to appear obtrusive. We fear that such appeals will be regarded as officious; and instead of advancing the interests of Christianity, we shall only make enemies for ourselves." And in such a reply there would be force. However we may attempt to account for it, men do regard such conversation as impertinent and obtrusive. It seems to suppose that they do not give due attention to the subject on which the appeal is made. It seems to them to imply also the profession of a high degree of sanctity by the person addressing them. And at any rate, the subject being a distasteful one to almost all irreligious people, they are very glad to excuse their inattention, by the counter accusation of obtrusiveness. Accordingly, it is very desirable, if it be possible, to exert on others a religious influence which shall not be liable to this most unpleasant charge. A father, for instance, wishes to exert a Christian influence upon the members of his family. He desires earnestly that all of them will become disciples of Christ. He fears—and that very rationally—that if he shall continuously talk about the subject, if he shall intrude it into all hours, all studies, and all plays, the result will be, that his children will revolt from the subject, and more harm than good will be done. I will not be misunderstood here. I am not inveighing in the least against religious conversation in families, and an earnest pressing of the claims of Christ by parents on the attention of their children. By no means. On the contrary, I greatly fear, that in these days there is a very widespread disposition to throw off the duty of religious conversation and religious training, and to lay it upon the Church and the Sunday-school. And yet, on the other hand, there is a well-grounded alarm on the part of many parents, that if they shall do what seems to them their duty in speaking on this subject, they will drive their children away from attending to it. Now the question may well be asked: "Is there any method by which the religious influence can be exerted, and the charge of obtrusiveness escaped? Is it possible to unite influence and unobtrusiveness?" And I answer, yes; and refer you to this religious atmosphere of which I am speaking. Let such an atmosphere surround a parent. Let the continual outgoing of himself, and the constant and natural expression of his life in his home, and in his intercourse with his children be Christian. Let the spirit of his religion shine through him; and whether he speak or be silent, he will not fail to impress the beauty and the importance of Christ's Gospel on all who are near him; and in neither case will he be regarded as at all obtrusive. Just this was the case with Naioth's influence on Saul. The change effected in his conduct was a revolution. He came to Naioth to murder; and when he came, he prophesied. And yet, so far as we can learn, no one spoke to him, no one rebuked him. The fact was, that in such a spiritual atmosphere as that in which the monarch found himself, murder would have been so unnatural, that he was unable to accomplish his purpose; and prayer and prophecy were so in accordance with the place, that even he could not refrain from them. And so, dear friends, do we not all know homes, in which the atmosphere is such, that neither parents nor children find it at all difficult to think of religion, of their duties to God and Christ and their fellow-men; where the Christian influence on children is powerful, yet unobtrusive; whose members all men expect will become Christians, and profess themselves such, and walk worthy of their high vocation? And do we not all know other homes, where, if the Gospel enters at all, it seems to come as an intruder and an unwelcome guest; an utter stranger; so worldly is the air that all its inmates breathe? In all kindness, let me put the question: to which of these descriptions, do the homes answer, in which you are training those whom God has given you?

A second element of the superiority of the influence, which I am endeavoring to describe, is to be found in the fact that it is exerted *all the time, and on all* with whom one comes in contact. One difficulty with religious work is, that it is so often fitful, spasmodic. At best, it is intermittent. The mind and body both need rest at times. Another difficulty is, that it can be performed in behalf of comparatively so few. One is tempted to despair, when he reflects on the number of those upon whom he should, apparently, exert a religious influence; and compares it with the small number whom he can directly influence. When a man in active business, or a woman engrossed with the cares of an active life, thinks of adding to them special religious work, what wonder that the question spontaneously arises: "Who is sufficient for these things?" And may we not believe that the reflection, that one has time to do so little and in behalf of so few, induces many to refrain from doing any thing whatever?

Now, I bring a specific for this despair and resultant indolence, so far as religious work is concerned, in this religious atmosphere, which I would have surround the life of every professing Christian before me. It goes wherever he goes, whom it surrounds; it is with him always; and in the measure of its own purity it influences all with whom he is associated. So it was at Naioth in Ramah. The religious spirit of the place was abiding; potential always, and on all who came there; on the first messengers whom Saul sent, as well as on the king. It is just this abiding, ever-powerful influence, that Christ most desires to have his people exert. He would have us engage in special labor for Him, indeed; but He would also have all labor, labor in behalf of his Gospel. He would have us give certain time especially to his interests; but He would also have all time consecrated. And in this world, in which we are placed, this can be done, only by carrying about with us into all our relations, home and business, and into the presence of all into whose presence we come, this religious habit, or spirit, or atmosphere; so that all places and times shall be consecrated, and all with whom we are allied shall feel, that whether we eat or drink, or whatever we do, we are doing all to the glory of God.

But a third element of the superiority of this peculiar influence becomes evident when we remember, that without it, all personal and purposed religious work will probably be *without fruit*. When I speak of personal and purposed work, I mean work intended to act directly upon another soul, like that performed by a teacher in the Sunday-school, or by a mother endeavoring to instruct religiously her children. Such work, I repeat, it is reasonable to believe, can not be performed successfully unless this immanent influence accompanies it. This is only saying, what all of us, doubtless, are prepared to admit, that "religious talk" alone is not enough to exert religious influence. Added to the words, must be the power of a corresponding life, before they can exert the influence intended. Respect for the character, and a conviction of the sincerity of the clergyman—these are elements of power, without which the mere sermon is weakness indeed. Christ's words—though He spake as never man spake—are not so mighty as Christ's character; and the power, which they possess, is largely due to the perfect correspondence between Himself and them. A friend not long since made this remark to me: "A clergyman does not preach well, and can not preach effectively, when he tries to soar above the reach of his own religious experience." What is this but to say, that words are not enough; that when one speaks to another on the subject of religion, he must be careful to speak out of his own experience; he must carry with him a religious spirit; he must be surrounded with a religious atmosphere; and this spirit or atmosphere—call it what you will—is that, which saves his words from falling dead upon the heart of him to whom he speaks.

Hence, the special need that all have, whose religious work is of this personal character, to be earnest and constant in prayer. It is not enough for parents who endeavor religiously to influence their children, or for Sunday-school teachers, or for clergymen, that they be well informed about the subjects, from which they gather religious lessons and appeals. There must be a spiritual preparation also. The teacher, the parent, and the preacher, must come to their work in the true religious spirit; surrounded with this religious atmosphere; else will their words be lifeless. So, friends, do we need to pray more; "to linger and meditate in the deep shades of Gethsemane, and near the cross on Calvary;" and imbibe Christ's spirit, without which our labors with others, if not our labors for others, will for the most part be in vain.

III. But, no doubt, the question has already suggested itself to those before me: "In what way is this religious atmosphere secured? What is its source? What is the secret of those who possess it?" There is no secret, friends. The elements of the atmosphere, which surrounds the globe, lie within the globe itself. The religious atmosphere, which enveloped the little town to which David fled, and which so mightily influenced Saul, was born of the religious life within the town itself. Those who possess, in any degree, this subtle religious power, owe it entirely to the spirit of Christ within them. The deeper our religious life, the wider will be the circle of this surrounding air; or, at least, the more effective will it be on those who come within its circumference. The candle of the Lord must burn within us, before we can so let our light shine before men, that they will be led to glorify our Father in heaven. So it is with the Church at large, and with each individual Church. There may be an artificial excitement, born of the use of extraordinary means and external appliances and stimulants. But there can be no true revival, without a corresponding life within the Church. Let us not forget this, brethren. The atmosphere of a man's life or a Church's life, the immanent, unconscious, influence exerted, is always and exactly determined by the life itself. So that I have to urge again, as always, the one great duty, which it is the mission of the pulpit to urge from week to week; the duty of living near to Him, and drinking into the spirit of Him, whose spirit is the life and light of men. How do we need to pray to, and commune with, and meditate upon our Lord? Without Him—let us learn it anew to-day—without Him, without his spirit within us, we can do nothing.

Just one word more; and that for the purpose of caution. Let us remember that, important as this ever present, and, in one sense, unconscious influence is, it is not every thing needed for the awakening of religious life in others. Without the atmosphere which envelops the earth, all forms of life would perish, and the surface of the world would be as barren, as that of the moon itself. But while the air is needed, it is not all that is needed. Life springs from the ground, obedient only to the shining sun and the falling rain. It is requisite, indeed, if we would have men saved from the sin that is in them, that they be brought within the range of influence like that, which I have very imperfectly described. But this is not all. Let us not make the mistake of believing it to be all. Before the divine life of Christ can be within them, the Sun of righteousness must shine upon them with healing in his beams; and the dew and the gentle rain of God's Spirit must descend upon them from heaven. To the earthly atmosphere must be joined these heavenly influences. And so the Christian and the Church, in all their endeavors for the good of men, must ever hold up Christ, and ever pray for the Spirit. And so, when the fruit of labor shall appear, and here and there shall spring up within the garden of the Lord new plants, adorned with beauty and bearing fruit—let not the Church take the glory to herself. But let her remember the shining of the Sun of righteousness, and the descent of the rain of the Spirit of God.

I suppose that there are those before me, who, though not Christians, are still inspired at times with noble ambitions to do good to their fellow-men; to lift them up to better lives. They are conscious, no doubt, that their own lives must be failures, unless they live for others than themselves. But, if they are honest, they will confess, I doubt not, that these ambitions and the labors that proceed from them are spasmodic, and issue in little that is satisfactory to themselves. Friends, we would give these noble impulses due praise. We would not deny to them nobility. But we would see them made something more than mere temporary and inefficient impulse. We would have them so transfigured, that your whole living will be a doing good. And this can be done only by coming to Christ, and drinking into his life. When this shall have been done, there will go out from you, unconsciously, a permanent influence to bless your fellow-men. You will not only do good purposely. But, like the sun in the heavens, at all times there will radiate from you spiritual light and warmth to bless and beautify the world. This is the blessed life to which we call you when we bid you come to Christ. This is the mission of Christianity; and this the method of its benediction. Men and women, whose hearts swell at times with noblest aims, it is in Christ alone, that they can be achieved. Only when you live in Him, the Light of the world, can you also become the light of the world.

XII.

THE COST OF DISCIPLESHIP.

"For which of you, intending to build a tower, sitteth not down first, and counteth the cost, whether he have sufficient to finish it? Lest haply, after he hath laid the foundation, and is not able to finish it, all that behold it begin to mock him, saying, This man began to build, and was not able to finish."— LUKE xiv, 28, 29, 30.

The text is an illustration of the absolute honesty of our Lord; of his desire to hide no difficulty that attaches to a life of discipleship. It is an illustration the more remarkable, because it follows, immediately, the parable in which the privileges of the life to which He invites men are spoken of as a feast, to which all are called; the parable in which occur the words: "Go out into the highways and hedges and compel them to come in, that my house may be filled." Side by side with this parable, which sets forth both the blessedness of the Christian life and the Lord's desire that all men shall enjoy it, is the parable of the unfinished tower; which, in the plainest language, informs men that their entrance on this life and its continuance will involve the sacrifice of much that they hold dear. More solemn and impressive than the parable itself, are the words which introduce it: "If any man come to me, and hate not his father and mother and wife, yea, and his own life also, he can not be my disciple."

We easily believe the statements of the Evangelists, that great numbers were attracted to the Lord by his miracles of healing, by his teaching, and by his manifest sympathy with all classes and conditions of men. Such words as these, which we find in this chapter—"and there went great multitudes with him"—are perfectly credible. And equally credible, when read in connection with a statement like the text, are passages like those, which we find toward the close of the Gospel narrative, such as: "Then all his disciples forsook him and fled." For it would seem that many began a life of discipleship, without an adequate appreciation of its hardships. Impulsively they accepted Christ, because He seemed what He professed to be—the Messiah predicted by the prophets—and they were quite ready to confess their loyalty, in order to share in the spoils that would be distributed after the destruction of the Roman power. Others—moved by personal affection—were ready to manifest their love by a confession of discipleship, without propounding to themselves the question, to what will this discipleship lead us? Others still were filled with admiration for a supernatural power, which, by a word, could compel disease to loose its hold on its victims, or could still a tempest, or call the dead to life again, and joined the crowd of his followers, moving with Him from city to city. And thus, from a variety of motives, men followed Him in increasing numbers, until the chief priests and rulers feared that He would capture the nation, and take their places in the temple and the synagogues.

It serves to show, how far they were from appreciating his method and mission; that, notwithstanding his own words, like those which constitute the text, these rulers still sought to put Him to death, as a seditious disturber of the people. A demagogue, an aspirant after worldly power, a man ambitious for the miter of the priest, or the seat of Pilate, or the scepter of the Emperor, would have been guilty of no such folly as that, which, on the supposition of these rulers, we must attribute to Jesus. And it does seem to me, that modern skeptical critics who take the same ground, namely, that Christ was looking to the establishment of a government on the ruins of those of Pilate and Herod, must sometimes be startled from their theories, by words like those which we find in connection with the text, which were designed to impress the hardship of his service, and were calculated to lead men to withdraw from his company. Indeed, we are expressly told, that, after an expression like this, many followed not after Him. On every occasion on which He could do so, He took care to inform the people of the severe side of discipleship; of his indisposition to bestow worldly rewards. He rebuked the people because they followed Him simply for loaves and fishes; and more than once said distinctly: "If any man will come after me, let him deny himself, take up his cross and follow me."

So, at this time, He turns to the very multitudes, to whom He had spoken a gracious parable of invitation, and addresses to them another parable; warning them against inconsiderateness and haste in beginning a life of discipleship; and bidding them consider well the hardship and self-denial which it must involve. "For which of you, intending to build a tower, sitteth not down first and counteth the cost, whether he have sufficient money to finish it? Lest haply after he hath laid the foundation and is not able to finish it, all men begin to mock him, saying, This man began to build, and was not able to finish." He calls before their minds a picture designed to make them pause; a picture which Jeremy Taylor has so finely drawn, that I can not forbear to quote his words at this point. "So have I seen," he writes in his sermon on "Lukewarmness and Zeal"—"So have I seen a fair structure begun with art and care, and raised to half its stature; and then it stood still, by the misfortune or neglect of its owner, and the rain descended and dwelt in its joints, and supplanted the contexture of its pillars; and having stood awhile, like the antiquated temple of a deceased oracle, it fell into a hasty age, and sunk upon its knees, and so descended into a ruin. So is the imperfect, unfinished spirit of a man. It lays the foundation of a holy resolution, and strengthens it with vows and arts of prosecution; its raises up the walls, sacraments and prayers, reading and holy ordinances; and holy actions begin with a slow motion, and the building stays, and the spirit is weary, and the soul is naked and exposed to temptation, and in the day of storm takes in every thing that can do it mischief; and it is faint and sick and listless and tired, and it stands till its own weight wearies the foundation, and then declines to death and disorder."

The text, then, brings before us the necessity, laid on every one of us—whether we have begun already, or are only expecting to begin a life of discipleship—the necessity of seriously setting before our souls *the cost of the Christian life.*

I. And we can do no better, in considering the subject, than to begin by asking what the Christian life is, as Christ presents it in the parable. "For what man of you, intending to build a tower," or, in the parable that immediately follows: "What king going to make war against another king?" Just here is a difficulty with most men. They do not consider the cost of Christian living, because they are so prone not to consider another question that lies back of it; the question, what is Christian living? I do not say, that they do not know what it is, but it is not a subject of earnest, serious consideration. It is too often true that men, moved toward Christ by a single governing motive, seize hold of but a single part of Christianity. They take a partial view of it; and this most often, the brightest view. So it was with this great multitude that followed Christ. "How mighty He is," cries one: "He raises the dead; He heals the sick. I will follow Him." "What words of heavenly wisdom are these we hear:" another cries. "He speaks with authority, and not as the scribes. I will be his disciple." "Surely," cries the third, "this can be none other than the Messiah, that shall conquer our enemies and reign in Jerusalem. Hosanna, to the Son of David! I, too, will be of his company." And thus, attracted, some by evidences of power, and others by signs of supernatural wisdom, and others by the hope of external blessings, they accepted Him but partially; not caring to consider what might be involved in the acceptance. They failed seriously to ask the meaning of discipleship. So it is with many now, who are quite sincere in their belief in the Lord. Their acceptance is not entire, they do not seize the significance of the Christian life. And, therefore, it becomes us to ponder well this parable, in which the Lord sets forth the life of a disciple, under the image of the building of a tower. He chose the illustration, for the very purpose of dissipating the false impression, that discipleship is a slight thing, whose duties can easily be fulfilled. It is as if He had said: "The life of a disciple is a life of construction. The man, who would follow me, must rear a character, a monument in himself, which, as it is like me, will show forth my glory. It is no slight work. It demands the forth-putting of all his energies; and this, not for a day, but for his life. It requires patience and earnestness. He will need all the love he can command to hold him to his work. He will require constantly and devoutly to study the model, lest he build wrongly. He must give himself to it with a whole-heartedness, else the unfinished building will mock him forever. It is because this work is so hard and so engrossing, that I say: 'except a man hate his father and mother; yea, and his own life also, he can not be my disciple.'"

Christian friends, do we carry about with us continually a realization of the meaning of this discipleship, which every one of us has professed? Do we keep constantly in view of ourselves the fact, that, on our part, it means the building of a character upon Christ, and like Christ. This is the tower of which the Lord speaks in the text; a character like his own; formed after his; built with his, as the pattern shown to us in the mount of communion and contemplation. Are there not many of us, who, when we think of our Redeemer, think of Him only as a shield from future misery, or as a master to impose duties, or as an Almighty friend, to whom we trust ourselves for forgiveness and the bestowment of external blessings? He is all these indeed, and such acceptance is a necessary element of Christian discipleship. But He is far more. To be a Christian is to have the spirit of Christ; to live a Christian life is to put forth continually, all the powers of our souls, in order to the upbuilding of a character like his, who was holy, harmless, undefiled and separate from sinners.

II. Such being the character of the Christian life, it need not surprise us that it will cost us something; that it will involve suffering; the taking up of crosses, which we shall often find very hard to bear. But it is important to notice, before considering the elements of this cost, that the only self-denial it involves, is that which necessarily grows out of the great distance between us and the character which Christ sets before us. In other words, the self-denial of the Gospel is no arbitrary imposition. It is not commanded by Christ for its own sake. There is no virtue in cost itself. This is a very important remark, and one that needs often to be made. For many Christians seem to be impressed with the belief, that the Lord makes self-denial a positive virtue, just as faith and hope and love are made positive virtues. This is not true. On the contrary, it is to be said that the highest life is a life in which there is not the least consciousness of self-denial, of giving up. And, therefore, the more nearly perfect the Christian becomes in this life, the less is he conscious that there is the least cost in the Christian life.

Cost or self-denial is a virtue, only when its end is virtuous. The world contains innumerable examples of self-sacrifice, to which we should not think of according the least praise. For there is no reward of money, or power, or honor, or ease, which man can attain without it. And, therefore, Christ does not command it of his disciples, as He commands faith. It is not a Christian grace, as faith is a Christian grace. Redemption is free; and self-sacrifice is a result rather than a command. It is the necessary consequence of a sinful man's endeavor to build a character like that of Christ. The work is so great, that it must involve tremendous sacrifice to such a man. But let no one of us suppose that he is called to exercise any other denial, than that necessarily attaching to the labor to which, by professing the name of Christ, he has consecrated his life. Just this, as it seems to us, is one of the errors of the Roman Church. Its fasts and penances are imposed arbitrarily, as though some magical virtue belonged to the fast or the penance. And just this, too, is the mistake that Christians often make in their thinking on this subject. Let us put it out of our minds, friends. God does not impose one single burden unnecessarily or capriciously. He does not teach that self-denial is a good in itself. On the contrary, he would have us enjoy to the full every source of happiness, which we can enjoy consistently with our growth into the stature of the perfect man. The beauties of nature, the triumphs of art, the joys of social life—these are not the less a man's right, because he has become a disciple of Christ. And the asceticism which would deny them to him, simply on the ground that self-denial is commanded by our Lord, does great injustice to, and is well calculated to bring dishonor upon our holy religion. No, friends; the only cost of building this character, which shall be forever a tower, alike of strength and of beauty, grows out of the facts that we are sinners, and the tower is a tower of righteousness; that we have to begin so low and build so high; and that we are continually impelled away from building it by appetite, and passion, and sin. The sacrifice thus involved, is the only cost, the only self-denial, that Christ commands.

Moreover, if we build in the right spirit, if we build in love for Christ, and in love of the character that we are constructing; the cost will be to us no cost, the sacrifice no self-denial. We all know how, in the realm of the religious life, love transmutes happiness into gratitude and desire into prayer, and stoical fortitude into sweet submission. But it does more than this. It not only transforms self-denial; it so changes its very nature that it becomes its own opposite; it becomes the most sacred joy. Here is a mother giving her life to her children, bending herself down to their pleasures, watching over them in sickness, ready to die herself if only they can live. Ask any true mother if she knows the meaning of self-denial. Tell her how much she is sacrificing; what countless pleasures she is denying herself; and you will learn that her self-denial is no self-denial, but her highest happiness. And when we, brethren, have the love of the Lord shed abroad in our hearts; when we know and appreciate the beauty and the blessedness of that holiness, for which, as Christians, we are professing to strive; we talk no longer of sacrifices and burdens, but, like Him, after likeness to whom we are striving, we say: "Our meat and drink is to do the will of Him that sent us, and to finish his work." No one rightly estimates the cost of Christian discipleship who leaves out this element of love. In proportion as this is present and mighty; the paradox becomes true; his yoke is easy, his burden is light, and he, who bears them, finds, *in the bearing,* rest unto his soul.

III. At the same time, it is true that, to us, as sinners, the Christian discipleship does involve real and great sacrifices, and it behooves us, carefully to count the cost. I can allude to the elements of this cost only in the briefest possible way.

Notice then, in the first place, that to live a Christian life at all, we must subordinate *every thing* else to Christianity. It must take the first place in our life, or it will take no place. The Roman Emperors, before Christianity became the state religion, were willing to give to the statue of Christ a place in the Pantheon, equal to that of any of the gods of any of the nations of the Empire. But this did not satisfy the disciples of Him, whom they adored as King of kings, God over all, blessed for evermore. And there are those, now, who are willing to accord to the religious sentiment as expressed by Christianity, a place in the soul, side by side with its other desires and sentiments. It will not do. Christianity will be satisfied with nothing less than complete domination. It must triumph over the love of beauty, over learning, and wealth, and power, and home, and friends, or it can not exist at all. In this sense, it is a tyrant. It abides, only where it can control. Indeed, it is a contradiction in terms, to speak of Christianity, as standing on the same plane with any thing else in man. The central idea of Christianity is the subordination of all claims and purposes to Christ, as the Lord of all. If the end of our religion is the upbuilding of character, it is self-evident that it must, in all things, have the pre-eminence. The contradiction is so palpable as to be ludicrous, in the conception of the construction of a character, which character must, at times, give place to other claims. It was this truth that the Saviour announced in the strongest possible language, when He said: "If a man hate not father and mother and wife; yea, and his own life also, he can not be my disciple."

I could show you, were it worth while to do so, that the endeavors of men to escape this great sacrifice which Christianity demands, are the fruitful source of unworthy religious *expedients*, like the Phariseeism and the Sacerdotalism, which occupy so large a place in the history of our religion. The history of not a few of the greater errors of the Church of Christ in the sphere of life, is but the history of the attempts of men to compromise at this point; to hold fast by the promises of Christianity, and, at the same time, to subordinate Christianity to worldly ambitions and interests. And the crowning, all-including, sin of the Church to-day—of ministers and people alike—in Christian pulpits, and Christian counting-rooms, and Christian homes, is the sin of endeavoring to comfort ourselves with the promises of the Gospel, while subordinating its claims to others, which our lower nature puts forward. Brethren, let us understand that no such compromise is a possibility. Character,—that is to say, the spirit of Christ,—is every thing or nothing in Christianity. The Lord must be first, or He is not our Lord. Let us hold clearly before our minds this great cost of the Gospel; and, in full view of what it means, choose—or confirm the choice already made—whom we will serve. Christ did not think so little of his Gospel as to be willing to place any thing, either before it, or in the same rank with it. The power to perceive beauty is a noble endowment, and the love of beauty is a noble love, and art, which interprets and re-presents the beauty of the world which God has created, is a noble pursuit.

But the Gospel sometimes calls the artist away from the contemplation of beauty, to hard, spiritual labor; and he must obey. The love of home and country and friends, is implanted within us by God. Not to feel this love, or not to cultivate it, is evidence of spiritual degradation. But the Spirit of God sometimes comes to one, in whom this love is peculiarly intense; and calls him, as God of old called Abraham, saying: "Get thee out of thy country, and from thy kindred, and from thy father's house." And, though the command involves hardships that we know little of, the claims of the Gospel are preeminent; and the command must be obeyed. And so I might go through every appetite and taste, and natural affection. We do not count the cost of discipleship, until we confess that, above all and commanding all, are the claims of this Christian life.

It would seem that this were cost enough. It would seem that nothing else could be said; that, when we make the claims of religion paramount, we exhaust the subject. But it is not all. There is not only the cost of the lower life, but the sacrifice of something, which, to some men, is dearer than all other passions—the *sense of pride in one's own power*. Involved in this discipleship is the confession, that, in our own strength, we are entirely inadequate to it. He, who would follow Christ, must first profess his intention to subordinate every lower claim to the building of a character like that of Christ himself; and, having done so, must confess his inability to make good his profession. This is the greatest sacrifice in the view of many men. I suppose that I am speaking to some to-day, who,— if I should speak to them, as one man addresses another, and should say: "Your lower worldly life holds you with such a powerful grasp, that you are unable to subordinate your desires to lofty spiritual character,"—would esteem themselves insulted. And yet the Gospel of Christ says this to every one of us. Of ourselves, we can do nothing. We subordinate character to lower things. We sacrifice it on the altar of business, or friendship, or power, or beauty. If confession of sin means any thing at all, it means that we are sacrificing character. More than this, if the soul's coming to Christ means any thing, it means that, without his help, we must, in our spiritual weakness, continue to sacrifice character until we are twice dead. What a cost is this confession, friends! What a denial of self! What a humiliating proclamation of weakness! Yet just this is involved in discipleship. We must make the confession, if we would be Christ's. Until the confession is made, and acting upon it, we seek Divine aid, it is impossible to build a character, which shall stand as a strong tower, when all things perishable are destroyed.

Nor is this all. In addition to this subordination, and this sacrifice of pride in one's own power, is another sacrifice, involved in discipleship. I mean the sacrifice of *the present to the future*. This is one of the most forbidding aspects of Christianity. In speaking of it, I do not refer chiefly to those only who find it hard to give up the grosser animal pleasures, or to those who give up all struggling after goodness, in their eager longing for the rewards of this world. I refer especially to another class. There is a skepticism latent in all of us, which disbelieves or doubts the possibility of lofty spiritual achievement; and which therefore decries earnest, agonizing struggle after a noble ideal life. "After all," it says, "the conflict is a doubtful one. Man is weak at best; he must often fall. Why prolong the useless combat? Let us not attempt the impossible. Such a character, if it shall ever be man's, will be his only in another world, in some far distant golden age. Let us live, therefore, in the *present;* content with such worldly goodness as we can at present easily attain."

Who does not know the spirit I am attempting to describe? Who of us has not felt the temptation to yield to it: a contentment with present attainment, based upon the impossibility of making actual the ideal we see in our Lord? No spirit could be further than is this from the spirit of the Gospel. The Word of God does tell us, that we can not finish this tower of character now. But it bids us look to the future, assured that, when Christ shall appear, we shall be like Him; and calls us to work and wait and pray, neither content with present attainment, nor expecting perfection on earth. And this is hard;—to toil and fight, knowing that to-morrow and to-morrow we must toil and fight, overcoming the same obstacles, conquering the same foes, until the end of the present life; to continue the conflict though the termination of struggle recedes as we advance. Yet just this sacrifice of rest in what we can accomplish now is an essential part of this discipleship.

And now, friends, let us who have made profession of this discipleship, ask ourselves, are we living this Christian life as those who have counted the cost of it? Do we think of it as a life in which every thing else is subordinated to the attainment of this Christ-like spirit, and do we subordinate every thing? Are we ready with the humbling confession, that we are not equal to it, and must have the might of God to aid us: and do we seek that aid in earnest prayer? Do we realize that we are engaged in a conflict in which we can expect a complete triumph only hereafter; and are we living for the future? What a solemn thing it is to be a disciple of Christ! This parable of the Lord supposes an awful possibility—the possibility of beginning this building without counting the cost, of giving up in despair, and of standing at last like the decaying tower, of which men say, mockingly: "That man began to build, but was unable to finish." I will not attempt to interpret this part of the parable. I will say of it only, that it contains a solemn warning, which should stimulate us to deeper devotion, to labors more abundant, to prayers more agonizing; fearing the dread decay and ruin, the possibility of which the gracious Lord himself announces.

I dare not conclude these remarks without one word to any, who may have been dangerously asking themselves the question: "But is the discipleship worth the cost?" Such questions may be considered, even though the soul dare not put them in words. And it would not be strange if some here were, half-consciously, letting this be a question. Permit me to reply, that self-denial, struggle, labor, are incident to every triumph in this world. You can not gain wealth without them. You can not attain any thing that men count worth attainment without them. And, after all, the soul must struggle for something. What it possesses of power must, by a law of its own nature, be put forth for some object. The question, then, is not, how hard shall we labor, and how thoroughly shall we deny ourselves, but, what shall we labor and sacrifice ourselves for? For character, or something lower? In the strength of Christ, or in our own weakness? For the rewards of time, or the glories of eternal life? To ask is to answer the question.

XIII.
THE CHRISTIAN CONTENTMENT.

"I have learned in whatsoever state I am, therewith to be content. I know both how to be abased, and I know how to abound; everywhere and in all things I am instructed both to be full and to be hungry, both to abound and to suffer need. I can do all things through Christ, which strengtheneth me."—PHILIPPIANS iv, 11, 12, 13.

If these words of Paul are not mere boasting, if they are the truthful expression of what the Apostle felt, they certainly deserve our most careful study. Here is a man, who, for thirty years, has been undergoing hardships of no ordinary character. His active labors have been intermitted, only when he has been enduring persecutions. There are few passages in literature, more touching than the one written a few years before this, in which he contrasts his ministry with those, who, in Corinth, had sought—and with some success—to undermine his influence with the Church which he had established in that city. "Are they ministers of Christ? I am more; in labors more abundant, in stripes above measure, in prisons more frequent, in deaths oft. Beside those things which are without, that which cometh upon me daily, the care of all the churches."

Here is a life marked by violent transitions, and filled with sufferings. If ever a man had a right to complain; if ever a man had excuse for bitterness, for cynicism, that man was the Apostle to the Gentiles. There is no one of us, who would not feel bound to hold back the story of his own distresses, before the recital of a career like his. We could easily pardon, indeed, we could applaud the murmurings of such a man. But of murmurings we do not hear a word. A prisoner chained to a Roman soldier, and awaiting a trial which he must have feared would result adversely to him; his only reference to his imprisonment is one of the most cheerful character. "I would ye should understand, brethren, that my bonds have fallen out to the furtherance of the Gospel;" deprecating, as best he could, any undue sorrow which his friends at Philippi might feel in view of his present condition. And when he writes of their kindness—fearing that it was due to their anxiety for his mental state—he makes haste to assure them, in the text, that he has learned, in whatever state he is, therewith to be content.

We could consider no more practical subject than the subject which the text thus suggests; the subject of *Christian contentment* as illustrated by the life of Paul. I shall confine myself to two points: the nature of this contentment, and the method of attaining it.

I. What is this contentment which the Apostle here affirms of himself? We shall best answer this question, by translating the sentence literally. So translated it is as follows: "I have learned, in whatever state I am, to be strong in myself." The condition is one of independence of outward and worldly surroundings. The state is not satisfaction. For satisfaction implies a harmony between one's self and one's circumstances. In satisfaction the outward and the inward blend. We shall never be satisfied in this world. Only when—made meet for the inheritance of the saints in light—the inheritance shall be ours; only when, to the perfect life of the soul, shall be added the joys of the city of God, shall we know the meaning of satisfaction. What heaven is, and where it is, have not been clearly revealed in the Word of God. For a reason, which is quite obvious, the details of its outward glory have been veiled from the view of man. We can easily understand, that had they been made known, man would have dwelt on them, instead of on the spirit requisite to enjoy them; on the streets of gold and gates of pearl, and the glory and honor of the kings of the earth, which shall contribute to the beauty of the celestial city, rather than on the holiness, without which no man can see God. Thus the discipline of life would have been lost. So the Israelites were held to the desert, and were not permitted a view of the land of promise, during the period of their education; else they had pressed forward to Canaan, and claimed the fulfillment of the promise, before they were ready to begin their new life. For the same reason, God has told us little of the life that is to come. But this much we know of it, that there will be a perfect adjustment between the soul and the outward things that surround it; a harmony complete between man and his circumstances. The delight which we now only anticipate, as we look forward to the future, will then be felt. Faith and hope will be sight and fruition. Then, and then alone, we shall be satisfied.

In this world this satisfaction is impossible. The adjustment, the harmony is wanting. There is a continual clashing between what man desires and what man possesses. It is impossible that a being with spiritual vision and appetite like man's should be satisfied with this world. And, therefore, the Word of God does not demand it. On the contrary, it bids man look forward to another life and another world. It makes satisfaction here less possible, if that could be, by revealing a future, with whose glory the sufferings of this present time are not worthy to be compared. And all its representations are determined by the endeavor to induce him to take his supreme affections from the earth, and to set them on things above, where Christ sitteth at the right hand of God. We must not, therefore, think of the contentment of St. Paul as satisfaction, or as at all allied to it. It is rather to be contrasted with it. It was content in the midst of that, with which he had every reason to be dissatisfied; from which he was taught to look away; and from which, in fact, he did gladly look for relief, in that death which he said would be gain to him.

Nor was Paul's contentment a mere indolent resignation of himself to present sufferings; as though he thought one set of circumstances in this life quite as desirable as another; as though he found it quite as enjoyable to be a prisoner at Rome, as he found it to be the loved and cherished Apostle of Christ at Philippi; as though hunger and shipwreck were as comfortable as any other conditions. There are those, to whom contentment seems synonymous with lack of ambition or desire; the death of appetite and passion; the indisposition to remedy existing ills. In this view of it, the one way in which a man suffering with poverty, can manifest his contentment, is to neglect all labor requisite to its removal. I am sure that I need not stop to show, that this is far removed from the contentment, which the New Testament exalts to a position among the Christian graces; and which, with godliness, it declares to be great gain. It never eulogizes sluggishness or indolence.

Nor, if we study the life of Paul, can we confound his spirit with that hard, severe control of his lower nature, which he knew as the outcome of Stoicism. There was something sublime in that silent, uncomplaining suffering; in that stern indifference to pain and affliction of every kind, which was the highest practical lesson of Greek philosophy. There was none of it in the man, who, tortured with the thorn in his flesh, cried out to God in agony for relief. Stoicism would have commended silence; and, had it taught the power of prayer, would still have forbidden its exercise to escape the pain, which, it instructed its disciples, man should bear without a protest.

Christian contentment, then, is neither satisfaction, nor indolent resignation, nor stoical indifference. The first is impossible, the second is sinful, and the third is hard and forbidding. "I have learned," said the Apostle, "in whatever state I am, therein to be self-sufficing." A life of contentment is a life superior to externals, to surroundings. It is a life in which one stands above the world, and all that it can do for or against him. We must be the masters or the slaves of circumstance. We must depend upon them; or, self-sufficing, we must rise above them. The former condition is the condition of most men. Paul was one of the few who attained the latter.

Let us look into our lives and hearts, friends, that we may understand the exalted state of the man who could make these words his own: "I have learned, in whatsoever state I am, therewith to be content. Everywhere, and in all things, I am instructed, both to abound and to suffer need." Mark the force of the declaration: "everywhere and in all things," I am content. How far he is in advance of every one of us! What an absolutely controlling influence outward circumstances exert on most of us! Who of us could face sickness, hunger, bankruptcy, the pestilence, with unquailing spirits? Yet, just this is the power which the Apostle affirmed of himself when he wrote the words: "I can do all things through Christ, which strengtheneth me." It is, as if he had said: "My happiness is dependent on nothing in the world around me. No burden that the world can lay upon me; no bereavement that I can suffer; no pain which can be inflicted; no disappointment that I can experience can disturb the central and supreme joy of my spirit. The sources of my highest happiness are beyond the reach of all of them. In whatever state I am, I find these remaining. I am self-sufficing. I have learned to be content."

How far any one of us is from this condition, can be easily ascertained. Each can make suppositions for himself. You are enjoying a competence to-day; suppose that to-morrow it should be swept away. In its removal you would learn how much of the happiness of your life was dependent on wealth. The despair and bitterness of your soul would teach you your distance from the Apostle. Or look forward to the time when the home, in which you now delight, shall be entered by death; and one whom you love shall be suddenly removed to another world. The difficulty which you will then experience in saying: "Thy will, O God, be done," will reveal to you how hard the lesson is which Paul dares to say that he has learned. Or your life is one of contined activity. You rejoice in labor, in enterprises which demand the forth-putting of all your powers. Suppose your powers blasted by disease in the midst of labors which seem to you as life itself; and ask yourself: "Could I say, I am content; I am still self-sufficing?"

Suppositions like these will serve to show us, how far almost every one is, from having attained the height, on which the man stood, who wrote this Epistle to the Philippians. The oftener I read this declaration, the more I marvel at its boldness. It seems rather the unthinking outburst of youthful confidence, than the sober statement of one, who had learned by bitter experience, how much the world can do to invade and destroy the sources of human happiness. And the statement is the more remarkable when we notice—what is very plain—that there is no bitterness in it. It is not the statement of one who, like Solomon, had tasted the joys of life and found them vanity, and cried out bitterly in disappointment—all is vanity and vexation of spirit. There is a spurious contentment, which is the result of disappointment only; which undervalues the power of surroundings to bestow happiness. There is a cynicism which would find a hovel and palace alike in this, that neither would give joy. And there is a morbid asceticism which turns from all worldly joys as from sin. There is not the least taint of either in the words of Paul. The text is an echo neither of Jacob's "Few and evil have the days of my life been," nor of the Preacher's "Vanity of vanities, all is vanity." Nor the expression of one who has forsworn the joys of this world. The words are cheerful. Moreover, they are connected with an expression of grateful joy for relief from impending physical want, which the Philippian Christians had sent to him in his captivity. The contentment, then, of which St. Paul is an example, is the contentment neither of bitterness, nor of morbid asceticism, nor of disappointment. It is the positive power of finding, in one's self, the happiness which most men find in things around them; so that, when sickness, or sorrow, or bereavement comes, the soul rises superior to its power.

I need not stop to show how much we need this contentment. Each day reveals its absolute necessity, in order to real joy. The world changes hour by hour, and our relations to it change; and, resting as we do in these relations, happiness and misery alternate perpetually. We are the victims of circumstances, which are inevitable. And as we suffer from their coming, we cry out for power to say with the Apostle: "I have learned, in whatsoever state I am, therewith to be content." That such a power is possible, is evident from the fact that Paul possessed it. Nay, we ourselves have witnessed approaches to it. I have seen men and women—calm and self-sustained in the midst of the most violent and terrible transitions, in change of fortune, in fatal sickness, in bereavement, in the hour of death itself—content that the will of God be done.

II. And this brings us to the second part of the subject, namely, the source of Paul's contentment; of his superiority to the changes of his changeful life. He himself attributes it to his religious life. "I can do all things through Christ, which strengtheneth me." The elements of that life were the fountain of his spiritual power. In proportion to the vigor of his religion, was his ability to rise above all surroundings. And so it is with us. Doubtless, without a real Christian faith, it is possible successfully to cultivate a hard, forbidding, stoical indifference to the violent, disappointing changes of life. The spirit, which leads one, without hope for the future, to say: "I have learned to accept the inevitable without cursing fate. I have been taught, both by what I have seen and by what I have felt, to be content in whatever state I am"—this spirit has more than once found expression in an ethical system. There is possible, therefore, a fortitude born of despair; a superiority to change, which owes nothing to faith. "The waves of mutation," accursed or adored by most men, as they come freighted with burdens or blessings, beat upon a few who stand and receive the shock impassive as granite. But even if this state were one which all could attain, it is to be doubted whether it is a desirable condition. The man who, for this reason, is insensible to woe, will be just as insensible to the happiness which comes from surroundings. There is no cheerfulness, no hope, no joy, in such contentment. This is not the joyful resignation of the Apostle Paul. It is at the greatest possible remove from it. And it is not what we need to make this life more blessed. You do not increase joy by dulling sensibility, in order to make yourself indifferent to affliction. We want a contentment that will enable us, as Paul did, to *rejoice* in tribulation. And therefore, I repeat, we must look for its source in the elements of a Christian life. Here Paul found the fountain of contentment; and here, friends, must we find it.

I have said that Paul's contentment was a self-sufficiency. And it may seem inconsistent with this statement to say, that the source of his sufficiency was his religion; something outside of himself. But the harmony of the two statements will be evident if we remember that Paul's religion was not so much a possession, as a part of his being. His Christianity was his habit of mind, his view of life, his faith in God the Father and in the Son of God his Saviour. It was because this faith was thoroughly his, because his life—his views and hopes and activities—were molded by it, that he was self-sufficient; finding his supreme joy in what he was and felt, whatever he lacked or possessed of worldly good. And, if we study this Christian life, which was so thoroughly Paul's life, examining its elements, our wonder that he was able to make the remarkable declaration: "I have learned, in whatsoever state I am, therewith to be content," will soon abate.

For first, Paul's religious life, so far as the element of belief was concerned, included an *unfaltering faith*, that his surroundings were appointed for the purpose of securing his eternal blessedness. This, in Paul's view, was their God-appointed mission; and, therefore, their profoundest significance. No one can read his life or his Epistles, without recognizing the fact that this faith was as much a part of himself, as his belief in his own existence. Indeed, he is always intent on discovering, if possible, and on declaring the gracious meaning of God's dealings with him. It was this habit of mind that led him, when writing of his imprisonment, to justify the providence of God which permitted him to become a captive at Rome. In the same faith, he writes of that lacerating thorn, whose painfulness had called forth the thrice-repeated prayer for its removal: "Most gladly will I glory in mine infirmities, therefore, that the power of God and of glory may rest upon me." His faith that God directs all events to contribute to this beneficent result, is so strong, that he writes of it, as though it were a matter, not of belief, but of knowledge. "We *know* that all things work together for good to them that love God." Can we wonder that a man with a faith so overmastering in a truth so inspiring could say: "I have learned, in whatsoever state I am, therewith to be content"? It had been impossible for him not to be content. In abasement as in abundance, in shipwreck, in captivity at Rome, under the rod of the executioner, or in persecution from his countrymen, he was contented, because of his conviction, that these were necessary disciplines in the education of his soul for the far more exceeding and eternal weight of glory.

Christian friends, if you and I have not attained this contentment; if we are still the slaves of change and circumstance; if our highest happiness is dependent on what we possess;—we may not irrationally charge our enslavement to this want of vivid faith in God, and in what he has most clearly taught us concerning his gracious government. Contentment may be a very exceptional Christian grace; but if it is, the reason is not far to seek or hard to find. Most often we need go no farther than to the primal Christian grace. We disbelieve; or, if we do not disbelieve, we doubt; or, if we do not doubt, our faith is dormant, and therefore powerless. I am quite well aware that I am uttering the veriest commonplaces of religion. But it is just these commonplaces that we need most often to ponder. We need to hold them distinctly before us until we are awake to their meaning. And this is one of them: that contentment—the nobility of soul that makes man superior to surroundings—the triumph of the spirit over matter and time and change and death—is the fruit of faith in God. Holding this truth before us, let us offer, with fervor and importunity, the prayer that always befits disciples: "Lord, increase our faith."

To this faith in God, let us add, as a second source of the Apostle's contentment, the fact that Paul's most earnest labors as a Christian were labors for objects, which the changes of life could not affect. This labor was another element of the Apostle's religious life. Because his trust was in the eternal God, he gave himself to the eternal Kingdom of God. The disappointments and consequent discontent of men are not seldom born of the futility of their forth-puttings. Men are as often embittered by failures, following earnest and sustained effort, as by any cause. But here is a man who subordinates all lower labors to the endeavor to build up the kingdom of righteousness. Why should he not have little concern for outward surroundings? Why should not the Apostle, burning with this one holy ambition, intent upon this one great work, know how to be abased and how to abound? And may not some of us find in Christian activity for the spiritual welfare of our fellow-men, the one power we need in order to rise above the circumstances that now depress or embitter us? The soul, engaged in work for other souls, is always superior to lower wants. What a lesson for us all is that taught by the story of Christ at the well at Sychar! So absorbed was He in seeking the salvation of a fallen woman, that the wants of his body were forgotten. "My meat and drink," said He, "is to do the will of Him that sent me, and to finish his work." Thus the spiritual labors, which laid under tribute all his powers, enabled Paul to say: "I have learned, in whatsoever state I am, therewith to be content."

Let us notice, as another element of Paul's Christianity, the fact that his life, so far as it was contemplative, was the contemplation of great spiritual verities. It was not only true that he had faith in God, and labored for the redemption of his fellowmen, but his *meditations were unworldly.* He lived in the atmosphere of heaven; he looked at the unseen and eternal. His daily thoughts were closely related to the great truths of holiness, of mercy, of the revelation of God's grace to the world. There is a habit of mind, called spiritual mindedness, which the Word of God assures us is itself "life and peace." The man who possesses "the mind of the spirit" easily turns away from other subjects to the contemplation of God's great revelation of mercy. Such a man was Paul. And because the changes of this life were secondary and subordinate subjects of thought, it was easy for him to be content in the midst of them. The thoughts of truths that never change sustained him, and made him superior to them all.

Consider, finally, the *emotional element* of Paul's religious life. As his faith was in the eternal God, as his labors were given to God's eternal Kingdom, as his thoughts were employed on spiritual and eternal truth, so, also, his affections were called out most powerfully by the spiritual and eternal world. His profoundest love was the love of holiness, and his deepest hate was the hatred of sin. His sorrow for the sinner was his greatest sorrow, his joy in reappearing holiness was his highest joy. His outgoing love sought, as its chief objects, the spiritual God, and the immortal spirits of his fellow-men. It was chiefly, because of this habit of spiritual affection, that Paul was able to say: "In whatsoever state I am, I am content." For, apart from the satisfying character of their objects, there is a calmness in spiritual emotions—regarded simply as movements of the soul—which is in the highest degree favorable to the cultivation of contentment. Imaginative emotions—that is to say, emotions called out by material images—are so closely connected with the bodily life, that they are attended by physical excitements, strong in the ratio of the emotions' intensity; and they are followed by proportionate depressions. But, to quote the words of another:* "The emotions which strictly attach to the *moral sense*, and which have no connection with the imagination or the selfish passions—though they do affect the physical frame when they are intense—do so in a manner that is tranquil and safe, both to the body and the mind. Indeed, the agitation of the body is greater in the first movements of the moral emotion, than it is afterwards; and though, on a sudden occasion of spiritual feeling, the pulse may be accelerated, this movement subsides even while the spiritual feeling is becoming more and more acute." If this is true—and only slight reflection is needed to make its truth obvious—the habit of spiritual emotion will inevitably produce tranquillity of temper; will diminish the liability to weak and feverish excitements, and,—so far as it is a habit,—confer what Paul calls a "a self-sufficing," a contentment of the spirit in the midst of all surroundings.

But the close relation between the spiritual affec-

---

* Isaac Taylor: "Saturday Evening," the paper on the "Dissolution of Human Nature."

tions and contentment is seen, only when we contrast their *objects* with the objects of the lower affections—the physical appetites and desires—which the world at large labors most unweariedly to gratify. The spiritual world is not only the eternal world; it is also the world of eternal objects; of objects of which it has been well said: "time wasteth them not; but improveth the sense of their unfading beauty and indefectible sweetness." So have all its lovers found the spiritual world; and, therefore, in proportion to their spiritual affection, they have attained contentment. But what of men who have loved with their deepest love, the seen and the temporal? Has not the present world revealed itself to its most ardent worshipers, at last, as the vanity of vanities? "This," says Isaac Barrow, "according to continual experience, is the nature of all things, pleasant only to the sense or fancy—*presently to satiate*. No beauty can long please the eye; no melody the ear; no delicacy the palate; no curiosity the fancy. A little time doth waste away, a small use doth wear out the pleasure, which at first they afford. Novelty commendeth and ingratiateth them; distance representeth them fair and lovely; the want or absence of them rendereth them desirable. But the presence of them dulleth their grace, the possession of them deadeneth the appetite to them."

There are subordinate sources of contentment, of which I might have spoken; as, for example, the consideration of our general mercies; or the contemplation of the special gifts of God. But I have thought it better to dwell rather on its *primal* source; namely, the Christian life, which, above all else, is spiritual in thought, in labor, in faith, and love. Contentment, born of this Christian life, is the highest triumph, possible in this world, of spirit over the lower life. For the triumph is due to the spirit's concord with the law and the life of the spiritual God. This was the contentment of Paul. No other is worth possessing; no other is worthy of the name.

Dear friends, we wonder that we are the sport of time and change; that happiness and misery alternate in such rapid succession. To-day we are raised to heights of ecstatic joy; to-morrow we cry out of the depths of woe. We read of one who said: "I have learned, in whatsoever state I am, therewith to be content." We marvel at his triumph over all surroundings. We behold him overflowing with joy, though a prisoner in chains. We turn to ourselves. Each disappointment conquers us. Affliction buries us in despair. Why should we marvel at all? We are but eating of the fruit of our own way; we are but filled with our own devices. Shall I give my soul to that which is fleeting, and wonder that I sigh when it has vanished? Shall I live for the world, and not be affected by its mutations? Shall I give my life to riches, and not be afflicted when they fly towards heaven? Contentment in this world! There can be no such thing to any one who makes the world his god. Why should we be amazed at our weakness, our grief, our despair, our forebodings, when disaster comes? The cause is apparent as the sun at noonday. And the remedy is just as clear. We can not live this Christian life of ours in any half-hearted way, and still be strong in the day of trouble. Paul's contentment was real, because his faith in God was abiding; because his devotion to souls was entire; because he lived for the unseen and eternal; because his deepest affections were spiritual. And whenever our faith and devotion and spiritual mindedness and love shall be what his were, we too shall be able to stand serene and strong, in the presence of whatever desolation shall surround us, and say, not bitterly but cheerfully, rejoicing in tribulation: "I have learned, in whatsoever state I am, therewith to be content. I know how to be abased and how to abound. I can do all things through Christ, which strengtheneth me."

"A man's life consisteth not in the abundance of the things which he possesseth." Man, under the influence of indwelling sin and the tempting world, labors hard to persuade himself that these words of the Master are not true. The Earth—which Wordsworth aptly calls the nurse and foster-mother of man made in the image of the Highest—strives hard and, alas! strives successfully, by "filling her lap with pleasures of her own," to turn his affections to herself, and away from the God from whom, "trailing clouds of glory," he has come.

> "The homely nurse doth all she can
> To make her foster-child, her inmate, man,
> Forget the glories he hath known,
> And that imperial palace whence he came."

But Earth can neither satisfy nor stifle the longings of man's spiritual nature; though she may deceive him, for the time, into the belief that she can endow him with contentment. But contented he is not and can not be, until his spirit rests in God. And he can not rest in God the Father, until he believes in Jesus Christ the Son.

XIV.
THE EARTHLY LIFE VIEWED FROM HEAVEN.

"Thy prayers and thine alms are come up for a memorial before God."—ACTS x, 4.

The subject which these words suggest, is the earthly life as viewed from heaven. The person speaking is a celestial being; and his words reveal both the fact and the character of the interest which man's career on earth awakens in the heavenly world. " Thy prayers and thine alms are come up for a memorial before God." This subject, we shall best consider by taking up the words themselves, and answering the three questions: Who uttered them; to whom were they addressed; and, what is their significance?

I. Who uttered them? In Cæsarea on the coast of Palestine, an Italian centurion named Cornelius commanded a company of the Italian Legion. He was not a Jewish proselyte. But he was devout and God-fearing; and his religious life found expression in alms, and in prayer. Profoundly dissatisfied with heathenism, and seeking an outward revelation of the God, of whose existence his own conscience informed him, he was at this time rejoicing in a knowledge of

Jehovah; but, as we infer from the narrative, without conforming to the Hebrew ceremonial. He had found God; and, leaping the bounds of the ritual, he worshiped Him directly. His gratitude for this knowledge of God, he manifested in his gifts to the poor; and his soul's needs and longings he poured forth in habitual prayer. No longer a heathen, but not yet either a Jew or a Christian, he was ready for the clear revelation of God in Jesus Christ. To Cornelius, there appeared, not in a dream at night, when the understanding is the slave of the imagination, but in a vision of the day; not dimly and uncertainly, but as the writer is careful to emphasize, "evidently"—to Cornelius there appeared *an angel*, who addressed to him these words: "Thy prayers and thine alms are come up for a memorial before God."

With this narrative before us, we can not question the fact, that the Bible reveals the existence of a higher order of beings than ourselves, who are interested in our spiritual welfare. And, indeed, if we close the Bible, we may read in the stars another record, well-fitted to predispose us to a belief in their existence. It were the climax of egotism, to suppose that the suns and systems, that roll in infinite space, exist for the benefit of man alone. Thus predisposed to believe the assertions of the Word of God on this subject, we open it, and find clearly announced the existence, not of one order alone, but of orders of superior intelligences; of thrones and dominions and principalities and powers. We learn that their number accords with the vastness of the universe; and that their power and wisdom far transcend those of man. We learn, also, that sin has appeared among them; that on not a few has fallen the righteous wrath of God; and that for them, as for the incorrigibly wicked among men, awaits the judgment of the last day.

But, as more deeply interesting to us, and as the great truth illustrated by the text, the Scriptures teach, distinctly and repeatedly, the active interest of these high intelligences in the spiritual life of men and women. What else can mean the affirmations, that the angels desire to look into the outworking of the redemption of the world by Christ; that they are sent forth as ministering spirits to minister to those who shall be heirs of salvation; that there is joy in the presence of the angels of God over one sinner that repenteth? Moreover, these statements are vividly illustrated in the recorded lives of God's servants. The experience of Abraham on the plain of Mamre, of Jacob at Mahanaim, of Peter in the prison, of John on Patmos, and of Jesus in the desert and the garden, all testify to the profound interest of the angels of God in the spiritual conflicts and triumphs of men; an interest not only real, but helpful; manifested in ministries at crises, when dangers and temptations demanded the exercise of special vigilance and power. Nor is this all. As we read the inspired volume, we can almost hear the thunderings of an awful war, between those angels who are holy, and those who have fallen; a war, whose object is the dominion of the souls of men; a war, which shall cease only at the consummation of all things. As that war advances, you and I are subject to angelic and satanic influences and suggestions; and our Christian life becomes a struggle, not against flesh and blood indeed, but against principalities, against powers, against the rulers of the darkness of this world, against spiritual wickedness in high places.* With this revelation of angelic life before us, we are not surprised to read, that to this devout and prayerful Centurion, longing for a clearer vision of duty, and a deeper knowledge of God, there appeared an angel, who said: "Cornelius, thy prayers and thine alms are come up for a memorial before God."

I have referred to the character and offices of the class of beings, to which the one here speaking belongs, not to gratify curiosity; but because this is one of the many side-lights which the Bible throws on the redemption of Christ, for the purpose of better revealing its character. That must be a profoundly serious subject, on which the highest intelligences of the universe employ themselves, in anxious thought. That can be a crisis of no ordinary character in the career of a man or woman, which evokes the joy or the grief of the angels of God. And the warfare, in which you and I as Christians are engaged, can issue in none other than results of lasting and tremendous interest, since, in its progress, we are aided or attacked by thrones and principalities of the spiritual world.

Oh! friends, how grievously mistaken is our ordinary estimate of what is really great in life! Tomorrow and through all the week, you will vex your souls and weary your bodies, in order to attain temporary and incidental happiness. Thoughts and anxieties and toils, whose highest objects are described by terms like money, fame and leisure, will occupy you from Monday morning until Saturday night. Occasionally you may be surprised into spiritual hopes

---

*As an exposition of the teachings of Scripture on the relation of angels to the life of man, the astronomical discourses of Chalmers have never been excelled.

or fears. But these will probably be soon overborne by the rushing tide of your worldly life. Could your spiritual sight be quickened, like that of Elisha's servant, you would behold far loftier beings than yourselves, anxiously watching your movements through the week. But their interest rests not on your attainment of wealth and fame and ease; save as these are related to other and higher objects. Not these, but your relations to God and his righteousness, the issues of your life in the world to come, fill them with hope or dread. As Paul writing to Timothy—so I charge you before the elect angels. Is redemption or destruction a subject for mere casual reflection on your part; if, as God teaches us, our relations to both call down to earth and to man's aid, the morning stars, the ancients of heaven? Would that we might awake to an appreciation of the paramount importance of our spiritual relations and condition. Would you learn how transcendently important they are? Think of the motives with which the Bible appeals to us to consider them. At one time it tells us of a love too great for man to conceive; at another, of a sacrifice too costly to be computed; at another, of a redemption too glorious to be imagined; and again, of a destruction too fearful to be described. And again, as in the text, it reveals the deep and active, the joyful or sorrowful interest in our daily lives, of the loftiest and the holiest creatures in the universe. O, friends, if angels stoop to aid men to redemption; if the crisis of our souls calls forth in our behalf the might of these sons of God, how shall we escape if we neglect so great salvation?

II. Let us not be surprised or skeptical, therefore, as we read, that, to a man seeking God and light, an angel appeared and said: "Thy prayers and thine alms are come up for a memorial before God." And thus we are brought to the second question I purpose to answer: To whom were these words addressed? This is a profoundly interesting question. Here is a man in communion with heaven. I state what I shall repeat, when I add that he is blessed with a message of heaven's approval, and is promised new light from God. We may well ask the character and life of a man so highly honored and so greatly blessed. What were the traits that called down this spiritual benediction from heaven?

First. He gave heed to the promptings of his spiritual nature. It is evident from the narrative, that though brought up under the influence of a false religion, he was religiously an earnest man. He did not stifle, he nourished what religious life was possible under heathenism. Such a man, brought under the influence of the true religion, will be prepared to rejoice in the clear revelation of God which it contains. So always, up to the light he had, he feared God, and wrought righteousness. Doubtless, he was often enveloped in darkness. Oftener, perhaps, he was beset by doubts. But ever and loyally did he search after the God, whom he ignorantly worshiped. That this was his character, we learn from Peter's address to him, in answer to Cornelius' description of the vision of the angel. "Of a truth," said Peter, "I perceive that God is no respecter of persons; but in every nation, he that feareth God and worketh righteousness, is accepted of him."

My friends, God looks upon the heart. The honor of heaven's regard is for the man who is not unmindful of the claims of his higher nature. The difficulty with most men is, that they are carefully unmindful of these claims. It is not that they have doubts. Doubts must often have perplexed the soul of this Centurion. It is not that they are ignorant. Small must have been his knowledge of the true God. But neither doubt nor ignorance was able to build a wall of separation between heaven and his soul. The difficulty with most men is, that they are disloyal to the light they have; that they willfully ignore their religious promptings. Thoughts of God trouble them, and they drive the thoughts away. Questionings concerning duty are harassing, and these questionings are banished. It is a habit of sinful men to narrow their spiritual vision, and to weaken their religious powers, until, to quote the language of another, "religious talents are extirpated." Over against this habit, I place the conduct of this loyal Centurion. As I have already said, I must believe that his soul was often perplexed by the conflicting claims of heathenism and Judaism. But he heard the voice of conscience, and obeyed; he strained his spiritual vision in every direction from which he thought light might come; and, in response to this longing, heaven opened, and the angelic messenger was sent to him by God. I do not fear the honest doubts that attack our souls, half so much as I fear the worldliness that makes men ignore religious doubt and belief alike. Our perplexities are by no means so dangerous as our carelessness. Would that we were bravely looking toward the light, and were ready to welcome it! This is the attitude of soul that God honors. It is to such men and women that He sends the messengers of his grace.

Secondly. Add to this serious loyalty to his religious nature, his cordial reception of the light he had already received. There is an interest in religion, which postpones action, and awaits more light.

There are men who pray for the revelation of God and duty; but who, when answered, refuse the guidance of the revelation because it does not solve all problems. A study of this Centurion's character reveals a far different habit of mind. The light vouchsafed him, he used in the performance of his duty. The light given him did not, indeed, destroy his religious ignorance But his ignorance did not silence his prayers or prevent his charities. He knew enough of God to cry to God; and he knew duty well enough to seek the welfare of his fellows. And so he prayed, and practiced charity.

Can you, who parade your doubts on this and on that high doctrine, suppose that God will make these doctrines plain until you do the things you know? Prayer you can offer, even if you can not explain the presence of sin and suffering in the world. And you can give alms, even if you can not define the mode of God's existence. The divinely appointed method of learning is fidelity to truth already known. If you are unfaithful to your little knowledge, God will not trust you with more. It was because Cornelius was faithful to the light he had, that God sent an angel to prepare him for the knowledge of the truth in Christ. And our Lord has taught us that he that will do his will—and by fair inference he alone—shall know of his doctrine.

It often happens, that men and women complain that they are not the subjects of deep religious feeling. I suppose that there are some here, who wonder why others are stirred to their souls' depths by religious emotions, while the current of their own lives is scarcely ruffled. "It is not my fault," one such remarked to me—"It is not my fault that I am not more deeply religious. I am not so constituted, I suppose." It *is* your fault, and a grievous fault it is. The difficulty is, that you are not loyal to your religious nature. Instead of taking time to think earnestly of your relations to God, you take care to suppress all thought of them. Instead of looking for duty, you busy yourselves in looking for doubts. Instead of crying: "Lord, what wilt thou have me to do?" you perplex yourselves with the unrevealed truth concerning sin or predestination. The fault is yours. And for whatever woe shall follow the fault— and a grievous woe will follow it—the responsibility will be yours. God sent his angel to the Centurion, because he was in earnest search for duty, and gladly received what light was given him; and to such God sends his Spirit now. If you are earnest in asking, you will not fail to receive. If you pray, God will answer. If bravely and devotedly you live up to the light you now have, fear not the darkness that envelops you. New light will break upon your soul. If you cherish the religious longings you feel now, fear not their weakness. Only cherish them; and if God's Word be true, they will be deepened and satisfied, until your soul is made perfect in Christ Jesus.

III. And now, having considered the being who uttered these words, and the person to whom they were addressed; let us turn to the words themselves, and endeavor to seize the truths which they are intended to teach us. And, first, they teach the truth, that God looks not only upon mankind, but upon individual men. "*Thy* prayers and *thine* alms are come up for a memorial before God." Here is a personal God, regarding the peculiar acts and habits of an individual man. If we think of it for a moment, we shall see that just this regard for individuals, as individuals, is the great truth, which the Gospel reveals concerning God. Nature gives us no intimation of this truth. The sun shines, the rain falls, attraction operates everywhere in nature, in obedience to laws that are permanent and uniform. On the whole, and to the world at large, their operation is beneficent. But they move on relentlessly and swerve not, however you or I may be injured by them. If they are our servants, they are our masters also. Your little child, walking on a cliff, ignorant of the law of gravitation, moves heedlessly toward the edge. It knows nothing of its danger. But it moves toward the edge; and, so surely as it shall lose its balance, the relentless law of gravitation will act, and it will be killed. The child, with all other material beings, comes under this universal law,—a law that does not regard our individual loves or hopes. And, as nature reveals God through law, this is nature's revelation of God.

It is the Word of God *alone* that tells us that God regards not mankind alone, but individual men. Here only is found the revelation of a divine regard for men severally, like that expressed in the message of the angel: "Thy prayers and thine alms are come up for a memorial before God." This is the glory of Christ's revelation of the Father. His love is individual. His redemption is for each man, as well as all men. How beautifully our Lord announces it! "Not a sparrow falleth to the ground without your Father." It is to such a God that the Gospel invites you.

But the text not only teaches God's regard for individuals. It selects that part of their lives which He specially values: "Thy *prayers* and thine *alms* are come up for a memorial before God." I repeat it: how false is our estimate of what is truly great and important! If I should be called to describe what is merely incidental in our daily lives, what requires the least time, what engages our thought the least, I should do the most of us no wrong in answering: "Our prayers and our alms." How hurried are the former, how contracted the latter! A few minutes of formal devotion each day; and a few gifts thrown thoughtlessly away from the mere overflow of God's bounty to us;—do not these describe our prayers and our alms? And yet these are the stones with which we are building our memorials before God! The achievements of talent will perish. The riches of earth will be scattered by our death. Our social differences will be leveled by the last conqueror. And nothing will remain, save our communion with God, and the memory of our love to our fellows. Our prayers and our alms alone come up as a memorial before God. O, friends, in view of this truth, and in view of our lives, and in view of the fact that we shall soon stand alone with God, and be compelled to gaze upon the memorial that we are building now—is it hard to believe that in that hour some of us will awake to shame and everlasting contempt? Men and brethren, let us hasten to Him, who is the Life, and learn of Him how we should live.

We may learn again, from this *union* of prayers and alms, the character of the religion which God honors. The Gospel, like the law which it fulfills, influences man in two directions—toward God, and toward his fellows. As, in the Law, there are two great commandments of love to God and to man, so, in the Gospel, there are two distinct expressions of the religious life commended. Religion toward God exists in the heart as faith: it is nourished by the truths of God's Word, and its highest expression is prayer. Religion towards man exists in the life as good works. Thus, supplementing each other, do we find in the New Testament, faith and works, doctrine and precept, prayers and alms.

But such is the perversity of man, that he is continually fixing his attention on one of these departments of the Christian life, to the exclusion of the other. It is by no means an unusual experience for a minister to hear, even from members of his congregation, statements that imply the belief that there are two kinds of Christianity—a Christianity of faith and doctrine and prayer, and a Christianity of works and precepts and alms. But this is not the teaching of the text. "Thy prayers *and* thine alms," said the angel to Cornelius, "are come up for a memorial before God." The two are interdependent; and the two unite to constitute a single memorial. The spirit of prayer can not live and thrive, save as it is aided by the spirit which expresses itself in alms. "Faith without works is dead," said an Apostle. And no one who has carefully studied the religious life, has failed to notice that prayer, unless joined to active and self-sacrificing charities, ends at last in "vague aspiration and tearful sensibility;" and that almsgiving, unless the giver is made humble by continual prayer, ministers to pride and self-righteousness. No, friends, God has joined prayer and alms, and man may not put them asunder. Each lives by the other. Each grows in beauty by its union with its companion. Your prayers will become more fervent as your charities increase. Your charities will enlarge as your prayers become more frequent and more earnest. Let us learn to associate the two in our thoughts of either. Let every prayer that we offer to God, awaken a thought of the needs of our fellows. Let every labor for our fellow-men lead us to the throne of God. Thus each will aid the other, and our memorial before God will continue to increase in celestial beauty until we shall see God face to face.

We have thus learned from the text, that God's regard is for individual men; that this regard fastens distinctly on their spiritual life; and that this spiritual life is honored by Him, only when it reveals itself, in accord with his law and Gospel, in both prayers and charities, in both faith and works. And now let us notice the character of the *reward* which He bestows. How does God reward Cornelius? I answer: He appoints him to more important work, and blesses him with new and clearer views of truth. He sends him to Peter, to teach an Apostle the great truth that God is no respecter of persons; and when there, He reveals to him, by Peter, the truth as it is in Jesus. Larger activity on the one hand; new revelations of truth on the other; these are the rewards which God bestows on his faithful servants. In these, I doubt not, will consist the bliss of heaven. For activity is the soul's happiness, and truth is the soul's appropriate food. Fidelity in duty here will lead to larger duties there. And this will be our joy. "Because thou hast been faithful over a few things, I will make thee ruler over many things. Enter, then, into the *joy* of your Lord." So is it with a profounder knowledge of truth. Truth, as I have said, is the appropriate food of the soul. With what evident rapture does the Apostle write the words: "Now I know in part, then shall I know even as also I am known."

Thus, without any attempt formally to unite them in a single subject, I have endeavored to present the truths and lessons suggested by the text. And yet there is unity here. Cornelius does his part on the earth; but we see him, in the narrative, visited by an angel, and honored by God. It is *the heavenly view of man's earthly life*, that we have been studying. I have endeavored to shut out from your minds, for a time, earthly interests and earthly standards; and to show you the character of the interest which the heavenly intelligences take in your career, and the principles which determine God's estimate of your daily life. I wish that you might carry into the life of the week some slight impression, if not of these separate lessons, still of the great truth that unites them; the truth that others, besides your fellow-men, are interested in your life; that your daily acts are growing not only into a memorial which men will recall when you shall have passed away, but, also, into a memorial before God. I pray that you may go down from these meditations into active life, with the profound conviction to which Paul gave utterance, when he wrote: "With me it is a small thing to be judged of man's judgment; He that judgeth is the Lord!"

The things that are seen are temporal; the pleasures, the honors, the self-sacrifices of this life, will soon fade, "like the baseless fabric of a vision." The fashion of this world passeth away. Meanwhile, the life beyond, with its fearful or glorious destiny, approaches. The memorial of this life, which shall meet you there, will determine whether that destiny shall be unspeakably blessed or unspeakably wretched. And spiritual intelligences bend over you, in sympathy or hate, and war for you in angelic and satanic contest. And God himself regards you with infinite affection. And, lo! One comes—the Son of God—and speaks in tones of unfathomed love, and bids you listen to his words, and give to Him your heart. And still you live your life, careless, for the most part, of its relations to the life to come. Will nothing startle you? Hear, then, the truth which the Bible plainly declares. Heaven is interested in your earthly life because you are in imminent peril of spiritual destruction. "Awake, thou that sleepest, and arise from the dead, and Christ shall give thee light!"

XV.

THE HEAVENLY LIFE VIEWED FROM EARTH.

"Giving thanks unto the Father, which hath made us meet to be partakers of the inheritance of the saints in light."—Colossians i, 12.

There are two main aspects of the Christian life. We may regard it as a career of labor for our fellow-men; a career, terminated by the advent of death; or we may regard it as a career of exercise and discipline, in view of another condition to which death introduces us, as the redeemed of God. It is this latter aspect that the Apostle had in view when he wrote to the Colossian Christians the words which constitute the text.

It is important, Christian friends, often to hold before the mind the view here presented, of the life that we now live in the flesh. It is hard, I know, to do so. The business of the world so obtrudes itself upon us, and the beckoning pleasures of life so attract us, that we are prone to think of our present career, as one solely of labor and of enjoyment. But let us be sure, that whatever is our prevalent habit of mind, the view of life presented in the text will, not long hence, be pressed on our attention with an urgency that will utterly forbid distraction. If the experience of loss and sickness and bereavement fail to impress the truth, and to produce in us its proper impression; each of us, standing face to face with God, will feel, with an intensity that we can not now conceive, that death is not merely a departure from one world; that its supreme significance lies in the fact that it is an entrance upon another. Happy are we, if, as we anticipate that most solemn crisis of our being, we can repeat the joyous and grateful words of the Apostle: "Giving thanks unto the Father, which hath made us meet to be partakers of the inheritance of the saints in light."

The text presents for our meditation two related subjects: the first, the inheritance for which we are here made meet; and the second, God's method of making us meet for the inheritance.

I. And, first, the *inheritance* itself demands our study. These words bring vividly before us the truth, often taught in the New Testament, that heaven is *a place* as well as a state; a home as well as a condition of the soul. There is a sense in which heaven is begun on earth. It is not impossible, in some degree, to imbibe its spirit even while here. So long ago as before the flood, when Enoch walked with God, the world was permitted to see and know one, in whom the spirit of heaven so shone, that at last, without the pain of death, God removed him from the world in which he was so utterly a stranger. In this sense, so soon as one, by faith in Christ, is reconciled to God; so soon as the peace which passeth knowledge stills the agitations of the unrestful heart; so soon as prayer, instead of being recognized simply as a duty, becomes a delight, and the heart rejoices in the privilege of unhindered communion with the Father of us all; heaven is begun in the soul. The eternal spiritual life, in virtue of which the spirits of the just enjoy the companionship of the unfallen angels, is one with the life now to be affirmed of every Christian—the life implanted by the divine Spirit at the soul's new birth. The new creation, spoken into being at the new birth, is not destroyed at death, and another life substituted. The Christian life is eternal; and the thoughts and emotions, which characterize it here, will characterize it hereafter. Heaven, I say, so far as it is an inward condition, is begun on earth. But the happiness of heaven is not ours; the fullness of joy has not yet entranced us; the satisfaction that we are to know has not yet blessed us. Nor can it, until to this inward state there are added surroundings in perfect harmony with it. These surroundings are the inheritance to which the Apostle refers. The word of God does not reveal where or what they are. But in Gospel and Epistle alike, they are held forth by Christ and his Apostles to strengthen the faith, and animate the hope of the Christian.

I can not dwell on this truth at length, nor is it necessary to do so. I suppose that it is not difficult to believe it, if we believe the Bible. Indeed, it were difficult not to believe it. Christ's own words are: "I go to prepare a place for you." And when we remember that He ascended in a glorified human body, and that the glory of the life of the redeemed is to consist chiefly in their likeness to and communion with Him, it is almost impossible not to believe that the Scriptures teach that heaven is a locality as well as an inward state. This is the obvious teaching of one, at least, of the parables of Christ;

and this truth is certainly implied in the text. If heaven is not an outward state, there is not an *inheritance* for which we are made meet. In that case, the soul is its own inheritance. No! brethren, though where it is we can not tell; there is a place—the throne and center of this vast material universe—where is Christ in his glorified humanity. Thence issue his decrees, on whose shoulder is the government. There are gathered the unfallen angels. There dwell, delighting in his presence, and joyfully engaged in his worship and service, our friends, who have fallen asleep in Jesus. And there, by God's grace, we shall meet and be reunited with them, and join our voices with theirs in the new song of praise unto God and the Lamb. I can not tell what are the forms of its material beauty and sublimity. I can not catalogue the new powers with which the redeemed and glorified spirits have been endowed. I can not describe the engagements in which they are now employed. But we are within the limits of revelation, when we affirm and rejoice in the blessed truth; that, when at last death shall remove us from this world, we shall not only be made perfectly holy, but shall also be admitted to a home; we shall not only be free from sin, but shall enter a house not made with hands, eternal in the heavens. Let us take the comfort, friends, which God so lovingly offers to us. Let us not fail, as we anticipate our future state, to anticipate also the blessedness of our future home. As we think of those who have gone before us, let us not think of them as merely perfect in holiness, but as rejoicing also in material surroundings, formed by Him who has made all things beautiful, to be the residence of his redeemed.

The text describes this outward heaven, as an

inheritance: "Giving thanks to the Father, which hath made us meet to be partakers of the inheritance of the saints in light." And thus is brought before us the method by which it becomes ours. This word, inheritance, is intended to exclude the belief that heaven is ours by right of purchase; and to express and emphasize the truth, that it belongs to us as the adopted children of our Heavenly Father. And when we recall the fact that this adoption is possible only because of the death of Christ, we see this highest, this final bestowment of God's grace associated as a result with the gift of his Son. It is true that every gift of God is related to the death of our Lord. There is no mercy of his common and daily providence that is not ours because of the sacrifice of Christ. We recognize this, when praying for our daily bread in the name and for the sake of Jesus Christ our Redeemer. So, to Israel of old, came the manna from the hand of a merciful God. The manna, not less than Canaan itself, was the gift of his love. But the manna was a mere temporary expedient, bestowed by the way. Canaan was the inheritance; Canaan was the ultimate bestowment. And so, though there is no gift which was not made ours through the atonement of Christ, that, which his atonement especially purchased, is the final and blessed home, for which, by God's providence and grace, we are now becoming meet. And thus, dear friends, we gain a new and vivid impression of its glory. The perfect God, because of his perfectness, sees to it that there is ever in his government a due proportion between the price paid and the object gained; between the sacrifice and the reward; between the sufferings of Christ and the glory that shall follow. And if this be true, who shall tell what is the exceeding and eternal glory of that final home, to obtain which for us, the Son of God consented to a life so painful and death so terrible! No wonder that the Apostle says: "Eye hath not seen, ear hath not heard, neither have entered into the heart of man to conceive the things which God hath prepared for them that love him." No wonder that the beloved disciple exhausted all the wealth in the chambers of his imagery, to symbolize the new city of God. But is it not a continual wonder, and an awful commentary on our earthliness, that we, who are heirs to all this glory, should not bear with us continually a spiritual habit, becoming those to whom God has promised, and whom He is now preparing, for an inheritance incorruptible, undefiled, and that fadeth not away?

The Apostle describes heaven further as the inheritance of the *saints*. And thus is not merely suggested, but distinctly stated, the great and inspiring truth, that heaven—that the inheritance for which we are now being made meet—is a place of blessed and eternal human companionships. The saints in light are those followers of God who have gone before us—the people of God, redeemed in every age, and out of every kindred and nation. More than this, the word translated saints means the holy ones; and thus calls to mind the truth, that, with the redeemed spirits, shall be associated those unfallen beings, who live in the presence of God.

There is no word more mournful than the word loneliness. There is no view of the suffering Saviour more affecting, than the view which presents Him as solitary, forsaken of men and heaven, crying: "I have trodden the wine-press alone, and of the people there was none with me." How important an element of the terribleness of death is the solitude in which the soul must pass out of the world. The hand refuses to obey the will, and no longer grasps the hand of affection. At last, the spirit, unclothed of its earthly habitation, goes alone into the world beyond. Inevitably we ask the question: And shall the spirit remain in this solitude forever? It is in view of this inevitable question especially, that we appreciate the revelation of heaven as the inheritance of the saints. The spirits of those, whose bodies sleep in Christ, are not separated from each other. The solitude of death is not perpetuated in the life of the redeemed. The personality, which survives the wreck of the material frame, and which carries with it human desires—and of these the love of companionship is by no means the weakest—among the other joys of heaven, finds there a social life. They who, through the riches of God's grace, are admitted to the city of the living God, are brought into the society of the innumerable company of angels, and the general assembly of the church of the first-born, and the spirits of the just made perfect, and Jesus himself, the Mediator of the New Covenant.

I can do no more than barely state this blessed truth. But with what joy and gratitude should we anticipate the life, in which we shall have escaped forever the jealousies and bickerings and gossipings and littlenesses, which do so much to make our social life a burden instead of a blessing! Great and precious, indeed, is the promise that you and I shall sit down with Abraham and Moses and Paul and John, and hold great converse with them and with angels, and with One who is far above all angels, and who still is our Elder Brother. If you have ever longed for a perfect social life, for the interchange of highest thoughts, for communion with the great and good; if you have ever longed to learn from great intelligences, or to catch from converse, the spirit of those whose devotion burns like the seraphim—behold, in this revelation of the social life of the saints in light, the promised fulfillment of your souls' desires.

Once more, the Apostle describes heaven as the inheritance of the saints in *light*. The dissipation of mystery; the illumination of the soul; the increase, now unimagined, of the spirit's knowledge;—this is the truth conveyed by the word light, as here employed by the Apostle. And this truth is often insisted upon by the Psalmists, and by our Lord and his Apostles. Death, as we are distinctly taught, is not the coming on of darkness; it is the dawn of an eternal day. At the close of life the order of events is just what it was at the beginning of the world. Not the morning first, and afterwards the night; but the evening and the morning were the first day. You will find intimations of this truth scattered throughout the Scriptures. "I shall behold thy face," said David; "I shall know even as I am known," wrote Paul; "In thy light I shall see light." This increase of knowledge is the expectation of every disciple of Christ, and it is grounded in the promise of a perfect immortality.

Of course, we can say but little with regard to the *contents* of our knowledge hereafter. That would be to anticipate heaven. But we do know that in one respect it will differ from knowledge here. We are told by the Preacher, that "in much wisdom is much grief," and "he that increaseth knowledge increaseth sorrow." It can not be so in the world of light;

for side by side with this revelation of increased knowledge, is the revelation of perfect happiness. And this compels the belief that it will be such an increase of knowledge as will contribute to the soul's highest enjoyment. Now, if I were called to describe a knowledge that will inevitably exert this influence; if I were called to answer the question: "What knowledge is it that will itself be the highest benediction to the soul?"—I should reply, as you would reply, that it is a knowledge of the way in which God is bringing eternal joy out of the sufferings of the good. We could endure affliction, if only we could see the issue of it in perpetual and unspeakable happiness. It would not be so hard to bear the pain of parting, if we could have distinctly before us the joyful reunion in our Father's house of many mansions. It would not be so hard to contemplate the want and wretchedness and sin of this lower world, if, standing by the throne of God, we could behold the progressive execution of that plan, by which these become the ministers of a higher and a happier life. But then to ask again and again the question, without receiving an answer, "How can these sighs, and pains, and wants, and death be made to consist with the revelation of the infinite love of the Father of us all?" This is hard. And the knowledge of this question's answer is the knowledge that we need, in order to attain a joy whose song no earthly choir may sing. And just this is the knowledge of heaven. It is the inheritance of the saints in light. There we shall see, what now we can only believe; that this awful movement of events, that these griefs that embitter and these burdens that crush us are the servants of God, laboring to bless man with the far more exceeding and eternal weight of glory. There we shall know, that what seem woes are blessings. There, it may be, we shall recall with joy the fact, that we had faith enough, at least tremblingly to sing the lines: —

> "Blind unbelief is sure to err,
> And scan his work in vain;
> God is his own interpreter,
> And He will make it plain."

What a knowledge will be ours, when God, in the light of heaven, shall interpret to us the events that now appear inexplicable; when he shall reveal to our illumined souls, that what seems most terrible in his judgments is not only consistent with, but is the most appropriate instrument of that love whose depth no finite mind can fathom! If this be the knowledge of heaven, wonder not that its joy is past imagining. If this be the light that makes resplendent the inheritance of the saints, wonder not at the ceaseless song: "Worship, and honor, and riches, and glory, and blessing be unto Him that sitteth upon the throne, and unto the Lamb forever."

So much then do we gather from these words of the Apostle, concerning the heaven that lies before us; "the inheritance of the saints in light." It is not merely an inward state; it is an outward home. It is a home worth the price paid for it. Its glories must be such as to compensate the Redeemer for his sufferings, else he shall not see of the travail of his soul, and be satisfied. It is a home indeed, for its social life is perfect; it is the inheritance of saints; and a communion and high companionships await us, of whose blessedness our earthly lives, however they may prepare us for it, afford us only the imperfect symbols. It is the inheritance of saints in light; and that light will dissipate all darkness that now oppresses us, and solve all painful problems; and we shall know, what sin and suffering so often make us doubt, that God is love—is infinite and eternal love. This much I say we gather concerning heaven from these words of the Apostle. It may not satisfy our longings. It gives us no intimation of the material glories that shall surround us. But has not enough been said to enable us patiently to endure, and earnestly to labor, and cheerfully to give and sacrifice, until the Prince of Life shall call us to Himself, and speak the words of welcome: "Enter into the joy of your Lord"?

II. The Apostle not only brings before us our inheritance; he also teaches us that we are here made *meet* to be partakers of it. And this is the second truth to which, I said, I would call your attention. I must do so very briefly.

And here I desire, first of all, to say with emphasis, that this house of God, these songs of praise, the written Word and the whole round of Christian ordinances have their final cause, not in themselves, not in any thing connected with this earthly life, but in the life to come. Not, at last, to enable us to bear the burdens of the week, to do the work and fulfill the duties of our secular life, but to fit us for the life and the joys of our Father's house on high, was the Church established. And only as we remember this truth in all our prayers and songs and studies of the Word of God, shall we be blessed by them as God intends that we shall be blessed. We are here, to-day, not only in view of the week to come, but also and especially in view of the life to come. God is by these means of grace making us meet not only for the burdens of the wilderness, but also for the glories of Canaan. Let us never forget the meaning and the mission of the Church with its ordinances. It is no earthly expedient, designed to serve an earthly purpose, however lofty that purpose may be. It is a celestial revelation, intended to fit us for our celestial dwelling-place; "the house not made with hands, eternal in the heavens." Brethren, could we ever come to the house of God with this truth in our hearts; could we sing and hear and pray with our home in clear view; could we more often use the Lord's day as a preparation for the eternal Sabbath; and enter God's earthly house in view of our eternal home; and sing these hymns, thinking of the new song of the redeemed; and offer our prayers, remembering that one day we shall commune with Him face to face,—how would our engagements in this holy time enable us to do and bear and undergo and overcome, until the promise is fulfilled, and the inheritance is ours!

And what is true of the means of grace, is true. also, of grace which they bring to us. The Gospel itself is not to be explained by any thing that it does for us on earth. The character which it bestows, is indeed the loftiest known to man. The fortitude which it vouchsafes, is nobler than ever Stoic achieved. The graces which it makes possible, are more beautiful than those which heathen art portrayed. The life which it legitimates and secures is more symmetrical than, apart from it, man had imagined. But these do not explain the Gospel. These are not its last end. That is to be found only in the life to come. Our Lord did not die that this life alone might be saved and beautified. He gave Himself an offering for sin, that we might be made meet for the inheritance of the saints in light. If there is no immortality for man the cross was erected in vain. But it was not erected in vain. There is a heaven in which all ills are compensated, all wrongs redressed, all sorrows transformed into eternal blessings; and when we call you to believe in Christ, we call you to give yourself to Him who came to purchase it; and who now offers Himself to you, in order to make you meet to be partakers of its unspeakable and eternal joys.

But once more, not only by the means of grace, and by the Gospel, but by every event which He permits to occur, is our Father making us meet for this inheritance. This is a truth which ought never to sink below consciousness. All events that occur are making us meet for glory everlasting. All objects are our ministers. "All things," says the Apostle, "are yours." All things work together for good. Think of the sweeping character of the declaration. All things, whether death or life. In this view of truth, how utterly fades away the distinction between secular and sacred! In this view of it no object is trivial; no event is unimportant. Every thing is an angel of God. He who has made all things beautiful, in this great and gracious assurance, reveals to us the secret of their celestial beauty. These events, so dark, so painful; these objects, so unlovely to our earthly vision, are all God's servants and are our servants. The stars above us, and the dust below us; the joys that thrill us, and the pain that bows us are all his ministers; and their one work is, to make us meet to be partakers of the inheritance of the saints in light.

In view of these great and blessed truths, so clearly revealed to us in the Word of God; in view of such an inheritance, and of such a discipline—the one so glorious, the other so gracious—let us go forth to our weekly lives with increased faith in God, with strengthened hope and deepened love. Troubles and trials are ours; but so is the inheritance. Troubles and trials are ours; but if they were not, the inheritance could not be. They are ours; but they are sent forth to minister to us as heirs of this salvation. Can we not believe this; and, believing it, is it not possible even to glory in infirmity and rejoice in tribulation, because through them alone we can be made meet for the inheritance?

And to you who have not accepted Christ, let me say, that this inheritance is ours only through Christ. Through Him alone do its glories belong to us. Through Him alone do all events become our servants. Apart from Him, the future world is full of gloom. Apart from Him, nature and outward events are our foes. Therefore, we call you to come to Him, and to come now.

XVI.
THE TRANSFORMATION OF THE OUTWARD LIFE.

"Be ye transformed by the renewing of your mind."—Romans xii, 2.

I am confident that all of us who have professed the Christian faith, and who are in any degree conscious of that change in the governing motive of life which the Bible denominates a "birth" or a "new creation," have pondered, and perhaps have been troubled by, the questions: what exactly is this new birth or this "renewing of the mind," and what are its relations to the outward life? It is because this exhortation of the Apostle to the Roman Christians suggests the answer to the latter question, that I have selected it as my text. The particular subject which it invites us to study is the transformation of the outward life. "Be ye transformed by the renewing of your mind." This subject, I shall endeavor to unfold by considering, first, the law of transformation, and, secondly, the elements of the outward life as thus transformed.

I. Fixing our attention, in the first place, on the law or method of this outward change, it is obvious that underlying the exhortation is the general truth, that every one of our lives is undergoing a transformation. That which transforms us outwardly is that which dominates the spirit. The transforming power is that which has taken possession of the center of our being. This is the law of transformation. Here is a young man who discovers in early life any special taste or talent; for business let us say, or for mechanical pursuits. His taste or talent will soon master him. It will regulate all of his activities. It will determine the plays of his childhood, the books that he reads in youth, his boon companions and his amusements. Life will possess relish for him just in the proportion in which this governing talent is given appropriate food to feed upon. Right before your eyes you shall see a transformation going forward, until at last he becomes a skillful mechanic, or a great inventor, or a successful merchant. If, at its conclusion, you should be asked to describe the process, you would reply: "The man has been transformed by what has been dominant within him. That vital seed, which we call a taste or gift, has in its growth assimilated all the elements of the man's power; it has subordinated to itself all his faculties and other talents. He has been transformed by his mightiest endowment."

I count among my valued friends one who, at a very early age, revealed his possession of distinct musical gifts. He inherited them from both father and mother. At an age when other boys find their chief delight in outdoor sports, he was accustomed to steal into the parlor and to thrum the piano. He conquered by himself the difficulties of the instrument, and soon compelled it to reveal its locked up treasures of melody. Most of his friends predicted his future career with great confidence. His father, a large manufacturer, found a place for him in his business; but the boy, though he displayed capacity, refused to yield himself to what he considered the drudgery of its details. In business hours, his mind wandered into the region of musical ideas; he neglected the tasks assigned to him; he scribbled clefs and bars and notes on the bill-heads and letter-paper of the counting-room; nor was he happy until the day of his release from business toils—the day that permitted him to revel in the enjoyments to which his mastering passion determined him. His life was transformed by his dominant love and talent for music. Thus the inner man transforms the outward life.

These examples will help us to grasp the meaning of this exhortation of the Apostle to the Church at Rome. All of us, who have read the first chapter of this Epistle and have shuddered at its description of the character of man, can form some conception of the outward life of the people out from whom had come the members of this Roman Church. From Cæsar on the throne—for the Cæsar was Nero—to the slaves, who found food in the public feasts and recreation in the circus and the theater, the people were degraded and wretched almost beyond comparison; save a few who had inherited the spirit of the heroic age of the republic; and these could only contemplate with despair a society which they were utterly powerless to reform.

But some men and women in Rome had heard and accepted the Gospel of Christ. To them had come Apostles of the crucified Jesus of Nazareth, with tidings of a love that passeth knowledge; of the Father ready to forgive sin, of the Son who had given Himself a sacrifice, of the Spirit by whom men might be born again and their minds be renewed. They had accepted this Son as their Saviour; they had bowed their souls in adoring worship of this all-loving Father, and they had felt the throbbing of the new life imparted by the renewing Spirit. They had formed themselves into a congregation of Christians; and they were strengthening each other by their common faith and hope and love. And now comes to them the message of the Apostle: "You do not live for yourselves alone. The Master has taught his disciples that they are to be the salt of the earth, the light of the world. You are to preserve what is salvable in this fast-decaying Roman society. You are to illumine with your new hope the darkness that covers the noblest of your people; let your light shine in the midst of the darkness. Live your lives before men. But do not live lives like theirs; do not conform yourself to their conduct. 'Be not conformed to this world.' But since the Spirit has renewed you, let that renewal transform you outwardly. Let that new life be the dominant, the mastering, the transfiguring principle and passion. *'Be ye transformed by the renewal of your minds.'*" Such, historically interpreted, seems to me the significance of the Apostle's exhortation. The truth that it teaches therefore is the truth that our outward life, the life that we live in the world and before men, is to be transformed by our regeneration. In other words, that our regeneration—the renewing of our mind by the Holy Spirit—is to yield the elements of our outward life.

That there is such a regeneration, the Bible clearly teaches. There is no discourse on a spiritual subject to be found in the Word of God, more profound and fruitful, than that in which our Lord sets forth this fundamental but mysterious truth to the ruler who came to him by night. Nicodemus, it would seem, had been intellectually impressed by the miracles wrought by Jesus. Indeed, that this impression had already wrought a conviction of the divine mission of Jesus, is evident from the statement with which he introduces himself to the Master: "Rabbi, we know that thou art a teacher sent from God, for no man can do the miracles which thou doest, except God be with him." He was convinced, I say, that the mighty works wrought by Jesus attested his divine mission; and he therefore approached Jesus in a docile, reverent spirit, seeking further information. The Lord never did, nor does He now turn the teachable away, even though like Nicodemus they come secretly, because fearful of incurring the enmity of the world. And, therefore, He does not turn away Nicodemus, but teaches him the fundamental truths concerning Christian discipleship. And these are the first words of the great discourse: "Except a man be born again, he can not see the Kingdom of God." It is as if He had said: "My religion is not merely a new party with which you as a ruler may ally yourself. My religion is a *new life;* a life so thoroughly new as to involve a revolution in your heart, your disposition; a life in its spirit so different from and opposed to that which men naturally live, that men are not competent to begin it themselves. The vital seed of that life must be implanted by Divine power. You must be born again, not of the flesh, not of the will of man, but of God. By this regeneration—by this new birth alone—can you become a subject of the Kingdom, which I have come from heaven to establish in the world."

Just at the point at which Christ closed his dis-

THE TRANSFORMATION OF THE OUTWARD LIFE. 249

course to Nicodemus, the Apostle Paul takes up the subject in this exhortation to the Roman Christians. "You"—such is the substance of his statement—"*have* been regenerated; you have been born again by the Spirit of God; you have been renewed in your mind. It now becomes your duty to let that 'renewing of your mind' transfigure your outward careers. You are bound to let it determine your whole walk and conversation. If you desire to know what kind of lives you ought to live; go back to your regeneration and study its elements; those elements will yield the outward, the distinctive traits of the life appropriate to you as subjects of the Kingdom of God. 'Be ye transformed' by the renewing of your mind.'"

By its imperative form, the exhortation implies the possession by Christians of the power to transform their outward lives. But it implies also that this transformation will not take place unless the new spiritual energy of the Christian is purposely exerted to effect it. The inward spiritual life bestowed by the indwelling God, and which the Apostle here denominates "the renewing of the mind," is not a force which will transform conduct apart from the will. Indeed, it may be said that the transformation is thorough, exactly in proportion to voluntary activity of the Christian. There is much that is mysterious in the inter-relations of divine and human power in the redemption of man. But this we know: that in the renewal of man the Agent is the living God, and that man is given power adequate to the transformation of his conduct. Transformation, therefore, is a duty of the Christian. Because it is a duty, it is possible to neglect it. And because it may be neglected, the exhortation which constitutes the text is addressed to the Christians at Rome. Moreover—and this is the truth to which I desire especially to direct your attention—a method of transformation is prescribed to the Christian. The elements of the transformed life must be sought in the elements of the renewal. The conduct of the Christian must be determined by the character of his regeneration. We must be "transformed by the renewing of our mind." This is the inspired law of transformation.

II. And thus we are led to consider the *elements* of the outward life as thus transformed. What should be the traits of the outward Christian life? I know no more fruitful method of answering this question than just this method of looking for them in the traits of our regeneration.

Without further preface, therefore, let me mention as the first trait of our regeneration, the distinctively *spiritual character* of the life implanted at the new birth. It is spiritual in every sense in which that word is used in the New Testament. The author of the new life is the Spirit of God. It is the spiritual portion of our being that is immediately affected; and the design of the new life thus implanted, is to make our spiritual nature regnant, to release it from slavery to our lower life. Thus in every sense of the terms, is it true, that "that which is born of the Spirit is spirit." This is the first trait of our regeneration; the life implanted is a spiritual life, and its end is to make our spiritual nature regnant. By this trait of the renewing of our mind, our *outward* life should be transformed. In that outward life our spiritual nature, with its spiritual motives and aims and emotions, should reign.

This is a radically important statement. Man is

a creature of two worlds. He is formed out of the dust of the earth; but God has breathed into him the breath of life. We are allied by our animal nature, including our understanding—for brute animals understand—to this lower world. We are allied by our spiritual nature to the angels and to God. Both can not rule. A man must be guided by the one nature or the other. He must be ruled either by the nature which allies him to the seen and the temporal, or by the nature which allies him to the unseen or eternal world. Spiritual motives, on the one hand, or fleshly and worldly motives on the other, must determine the form of his outward life. As Christ finds men, as the Gospel finds them, they are ruled by the latter. I do not mean that they are all mere sensual brutes; that they are all given up to eating and drinking, to the gratification of physical appetites in their grosser forms; not at all. It has often been shown that the animals below us possess the rudiments of the love of beauty, which in the higher animal man, reveals itself in the love of fine art. It has been shown, also, that brutes possess hope and fear, that they reason about things which they see, and that thus they possess the rudiments of that very understanding which men exercise in buying and selling, in making bargains, in seeking wealth, and building homes. All this belongs to the lower and animal life of man. And if a man's outward life is formed by motives drawn simply from his business or his pleasures, though these pleasures are the result of the most cultivated artistic taste, it is scientifically true to say that he is governed by his lower, his animal nature; that he is living for the seen and the temporal; that he is dominated by the fashion of this world that passeth away, and that whatever else is true of him, this certainly is true: "Except the man be born again, he shall not see the kingdom of God."

But we are conscious of another nature; a nature of which something more than the mere understanding and the love of beauty may be affirmed; a nature that recognizes God; a nature that sees the beauty of holiness and appreciates the singular force of moral motives; a nature by which we discern the final cause of the universe to be God's glory; a nature by which we pray and worship with the rapture of the burning seraphim. No mere animal possesses the rudiments of this nature. This is the image of God in man. This is his crown and scepter; and thus he has dominion over the fowls of the air, and the beasts of the field, and the fish of the sea. This is his *spiritual nature*. And as I have said, this is the nature which was made regnant when the Christian was regenerated; at the renewing of his mind. And it is in view of this re-instatement of the spiritual nature as ruler, that the Apostle presses the exhortation: Let this renewing of your mind transfigure your outward life. "Be ye transformed by the renewing of your mind."

Thus, dear friends, by the method prescribed by the Apostle we reach the first essential trait of the outward life of Christians. Our outward life, so far as it is Christian, is a life ruled by our spiritual nature. It is a life governed by spiritual motives, a life determined by spiritual aims. Let us test our conduct of life by this great truth. From what region of our being, let us ask ourselves, do we draw the ruling motives of our daily careers? Observe that I am uttering no rules to bind your consciences. I am but proceeding in a straight line from our regeneration to its logical consequences in our life before the world. Let us not dare to conceal these from our minds. Certainly I may not hide them from you, when I speak as a teacher in things pertaining to godliness. And, therefore, I repeat, let us ask ourselves—since there is a transformation going on in us—by what part of our being is that transformation effected; by that which associates us with God, or by that which allies us to this lower world? No question more important could be asked concerning us, than the question: Is it true that we are transformed by this trait of the renewing of our mind?

But this is not all. Did I stop here, I might seem to be teaching that sin is a mere physical defect, and that the moment we are removed from this world and from this animal nature, sin will of course cease. This is not true. Every man, as I have already said, has a spiritual nature; but though that spiritual nature be dominant within him, and though he draw his reigning motives from it, he may still be an incorrigibly wicked man. Herein lies the danger of eternal sin. Was it by a physical sin that the angels fell? Does the Bible teach us that the hosts that kept not their first estate forfeited it by lifting their animal nature into the position of rule? Not at all. So far as we know, they do not possess such a nature. And thus is brought to view the awful truth—a truth not often enough and not distinctly enough insisted on—that the terrible thing in sin is that it is a perversion of the spiritual nature itself. And therefore—and this is the second essential trait of our regeneration—not only is the spiritual nature in man made dominant, but the *spiritual nature itself is renewed*, and made to find its proper end in the living and the holy God. This is the second trait of the life that was born within us at the new birth. Thus it is, that our new life finds its highest expression in obedience to the great commandment: "Thou shalt love with all thy heart, and soul, and mind, and strength the Lord thy God." It is into the Kingdom of God that as Christians we were born. As Christ said to Nicodemus: "Except a man be born again, he can not see *God's* Kingdom." Observe the distinction. It is not only true that our spiritual nature reigns, but it reigns to the end, that we may glorify not ourselves, but God.

As we hold clearly before our minds this second essential element of our regeneration we understand how purely spiritual beings may sin. They can not murder or steal or commit adultery; but they can turn from God and live each for self. Ambition—self as opposed to God—this is the essence of sin, and the existence of it therefore is not limited by this physical life. It may be eternal. Now, the Spirit of God, in the renewing of the mind, revolutionizes man in this second respect. The spirit of man lives no longer for *self* as the chief end, but for *God*. And the first cry of every renewed heart is the cry of converted Saul of Tarsus: "Lord, what wilt *thou* have me to do?" So were we renewed in our mind.

And now recall the exhortation of the Apostle. Let this renewing transfigure your outward life: "Be ye transformed by the renewing of your mind." Is our outward life thus transfigured? Is it true that, in our business, in our pleasure, in our home life, in all the places and relations in which we meet and touch our fellow-men, we are living for God?

Are the motives—I mean the supreme motives—that actuate us, drawn from our relations to Him who is our King and Father and Judge? I do not mean that these must always be our "most conscious" motives. I do not mean that they must take the place of all other motives. But I do mean that they must underlie all others and like the foundation of a temple must be the fundamental support of all the rest. I say again that I am binding your consciences by no rules. I am proceeding with logical precision from your inward to your outward life.

Once more—going back to our regeneration—it is not only true that the Spirit of God makes our spiritual nature dominant, and that our spiritual nature itself is so renewed that it finds its end in God; it is also true that it is renewed after *an example;* and this example is Jesus Christ. This is the third essential element of our regeneration. Our spiritual nature rules; we live for God; we live after the example of Christ. Thus is He the first-born among many brethren. And therefore you find in the New Testament such exhortations as: "Let this mind be in you which was also in Christ;" and such assertions as: "If any man have not the Spirit of Christ, he is none of his;" and such confessions as: "For me to live is Christ." Thus by his word and his life does Christ show our spirits how to live to God. Thus is He the Light that lighteth every man; the Way, the Truth and the Life. When therefore the Apostle says: "Be ye transformed by the renewing of your mind," his words have the force of the exhortation: Let the Spirit of Christ's life be reproduced in your lives before men; and, since you have been renewed in Him, be conformed to Him. Have we obeyed this injunction, brethren? Did we obey it last week? In honoring God, in living for men, in subordinating our lower life to our higher, has it been true of us that we have walked as Christ would have walked, had He been placed on the path which we have been called to tread? Again I say, I am binding your consciences by no arbitrary rules. I am but asking you to apply to your daily lives the essential elements of that life into which you profess as Christians to have been born.

And now, to sum up what I have said in a single sentence: the outward life that becomes a Christian, is one in which the lower nature is subordinated to the higher and spiritual nature, one in which our spirits live for God, and one in loving imitation of the example of our Lord Jesus Christ. I do not see what less I could have said on this subject. I do not see how, by stripping Christianity of all its accidental accretions and reducing it to its essential traits, I could have made it less than this. If regeneration is intended to affect our outward life at all, this is the outward life that it must secure. This is the transformation effected by the renewing of our minds:—the spirit dominating the flesh; God in place of self; Christ, the example, in place of the world. When these three traits appear in a man's outward life, that man is a Christian, judged by the essential elements of regeneration.

But there may arise in some minds the question: Who, then, can be saved? Was Paul, who confessed that often his spirit was subjugated by the flesh? Was Paul saved, who cried: "O! wretched that I am, carnal, and sold under sin, who shall deliver me from the body of this death?" And I reply: It is true, indeed, that a Christian may fall. It is true that he may be surprised into sin. But it is not true that he will abandon himself to its rule. This same Paul said also: "With my mind, I serve the law of God." And of this same Paul, it was also true that never until God released him from the body did he cease to fight; to beat his body, to war against his selfishness, to press on that he might win Christ. The difference between a Christian and one who is not a Christian is not that one does not fall into sin and the other does; but that the Christian, though he falls, still fights and prays and longs until he is thoroughly transformed.

We shall see how a man can be a Christian without being perfect, if we keep in view the difference between the two terms of the text: "transformation" and "renewal." The renewal is complete; the transformation is incomplete. The renewal is instantaneous; the transformation is a life-long work. The renewal is the planting of the seed; the transformation is the growth of the tree. The renewal is the work of the Spirit of God; the transformation is our work. The renewal of the mind is without degree; the transformation is a work of degrees. The renewal is of our inward life; the transformation is of our outward life. The renewal is the cause, of which the transformation is the effect. Hence we may be thoroughly renewed and only partially transformed. The dominion over our lower life may not be complete; God may not always be distinctly before us as the chief end of our souls; Christ may still be followed only afar off. But this is true: that the transformation will always follow and be like the renewal. And by the power of the new life the transformation will go forward from grace to grace until, made perfect in holiness, we shall pass into glory. I do not say, therefore, that in order to be Christians you must never sin. But I do say, the Word of God compels me to say, that you must never have a lower ideal than that I have described; and that against your lower nature, against your selfishness and against the world, by fighting, by tears, by agonizing struggle and by prayer, you must seek to make the ideal actual in yourselves. This is Christianity, and nothing less is Christianity. This is transformation by the renewing of your mind. Can this be said of us? If it can, eternal life is ours, and all the bliss of an inheritance that is incorruptible and that fadeth not away.

In conclusion, let me say, that the transformation, which I have so imperfectly described is possible in Christ alone. If you are not transformed by his life implanted by the renewing Spirit, you will be transformed by the power of the indwelling sin. And sin transforms the human into the satanic. And the satanic soul can see naught before it, and can hope for naught but wickedness and wretchedness for evermore. God help us and save us from *ourselves*, through Jesus Christ our Lord.

XVII.
THE CHRISTIAN NAME.

"And the disciples were called Christians first at Antioch."—
Acts xi, 26.

I shall speak first of the origin, and secondly of the meaning of the Christian name.

I. Antioch was to Syria what Jerusalem was to Palestine, at once the metropolis and the capital. No city in the whole empire—Rome alone excepted—equaled it in beauty of situation and wealth of adornment. Upon the plain on which it stood, between the river Orontes which flowed before it and Mount Silphius which stood in its rear, were gathered at this time scarcely less than four hundred thousand inhabitants. The patronage of the king who founded it assured it a speedy growth. Its position soon made it a great commercial emporium. When the kingdom was made a province of Rome, Antioch was endowed with the privileges of a free city. The glories of its climate attracted to it the inhabitants of the capital. It outgrew its bounds and spread itself over an exquisite island in the river. What art associated with pagan religion could do to adorn a city for which nature had done so much was done, not only by its inhabitants, but by successive emperors. A citadel crowned one and a temple to Jupiter crowned another of the summits of the mountain; "a glorious street extended for four miles across the length of the city, where sheltered crowds could walk through continuous colonnades, from the eastern to the western suburb." Its baths were scarcely less luxurious than those of Rome, and helped the citizen of the imperial capital to regret the less his distance from the center and mistress of the world. While its gardens and walls and statues and aqueducts and basilicas, the gifts of Roman benevolence and the monuments of Roman conquest, continually stimulated his pride by the reflection which they awakened, that his country conquered only to strengthen and adorn.

Not more than five miles from the city stood one of the most elegant shrines in the world. "A magnificent temple was built in honor of Apollo, and his figure almost filled the capacious sanctuary. Around this sanctuary grew the village of Daphne." Gibbon, from whose description I am quoting, has told us, that "the temple and the village alike were deeply bosomed in a thick grove of laurels and cypresses, which formed, in sultry summers, a cool and impenetrable shade. A thousand streams of purest water, issuing from every hill, preserved the verdure of the earth and the temperature of the air; the senses were gratified with harmonious sounds and aromatic odors." But the rites practiced and the pleasures pursued attested only too well the fact, that the religion which consecrated, and the art which adorned the shrine, had become the instruments of the grossest immorality.

The city was almost as cosmopolitan as Rome itself. There was, indeed, no Pantheon, which held within its ample walls the gods of all the provinces, but nearly all the gods were represented by their various worshipers. It had been easy, during this period, to have gathered in Antioch a group representing as many nationalities, as were represented by those who, a little while before in Jerusalem, had heard the fishermen of secluded Galilee declare in their several tongues, the wonderful works of God. Parthians and Medes and Elamites and dwellers in Mesopotamia and in Judea and Cappadocia, in Pontus and Asia, Phrygia and Pamphylia, in Epypt and Libya, and strangers of Rome, Jews, Cretes and Arabians beheld each other's strange attire, and heard each other's languages on the sheltered walk of its central colonnade. What London is to-day, and what New York is fast becoming, Antioch was when Luke wrote the Acts of the Apostles.

Though thus cosmopolitan, Antioch was by no means without a character peculiarly its own. It was, indeed, a great commercial center; but a large class of the population—the class which gave character to its social life—were not engaged in commercial pursuits; they were the wards of the government, made rich by the plunder of provinces. These, with the lower classes, divided their time between devotions and amusements. We are told that both Jewish impostors and Chaldean astrologers found the citizens of Antioch an easy prey, and that the alarm, which these produced, they sought to dissipate in the enjoyments of the theater. It was doubtless from their devotion to this latter amusement that they attained the facility, noticed by contemporaneous historians, of stigmatizing what they disliked with a name of derision—a facility to which the disciples of Christ are probably indebted for the name by which they have since that time been known.

Holding in our minds the character and position of Antioch, it is not difficult to understand why it was selected, after the persecution in Jerusalem had driven them from the capital of Palestine, as the center of the disciples' operations. Its cosmopolitan character made it hospitable to the new sect; its commercial character fitted it to become a starting point of the great missionary journey soon to be begun by the lately converted Saul of Tarsus; while the diversity of population, sojourning within its walls, aided the Apostles in spreading through every quarter of the Empire the tidings that a new religion had been given, that could be monopolized by no one nation or age, but would be for all men and all time alike. Thus it was that Antioch became what Jerusalem had been to the disciples. Thither came Paul. There the hand of the Lord was with them, and a great number believed and turned unto the Lord. And there, inspired and encouraged by tokens of their Master's approval, a whole year was passed in forming and maturing new and larger plans for the propagation of the faith of Calvary.

Up to this time the disciples had been without a distinctive name. The Jews indeed had called them Nazarenes. But the Gentiles had failed to distinguish them from other Jews, so long as they remained in Jerusalem. Not long since there was said to be an extended revival, and, what usually follows such a revival, a division among the disciples of Mohammed. The enthusiasm, which during the Crusades enabled the infidel to drive back the Christian Templar from the tomb of the Saviour, has been reawakened in countries of which we know scarcely more than their boundaries. However fierce may be the hostility between the sects thus created, we are unable to appreciate it. Islam is one to us. We discern no difference between the Mussulman of Constantinople and the Mussulman of Mecca. Of like character was the ignorance of the heathen world as to the difference between the Jews who accepted and the Jews who rejected Jesus of Nazareth, so long as the former remained in Jerusalem. Their internal quarrels had little interest for the Gentile, and were scarcely understood by him. To the Roman and the Greek they were subjects of one province, devotees of one religion and sharers in the same hope.

But when the Church came to Antioch, all this was changed. It could not fail to impress the most casual observer that the difference between them was radical. A name which one pronounced with bitterest animosity, the other never uttered save in reverence and love. A life which one party held up for execration, the other held up for admiration and faith. A death which one Jew proclaimed the deserved death of a criminal, the other announced as the appointed sacrifice of the Son of God. The Gentile living or sojourning in Antioch could no longer call the new party Jews, for it was evident that this word did not sufficiently describe or distinguish them. The necessity for a name became more and more apparent. Converts were multiplying. Those who a short time since were but an aggregation of disciples were rapidly crystallizing into a compact body, and were becoming a power both in the city and the province. Who first gave the name it is idle to conjecture; as idle indeed as to inquire who first said Puritan or Methodist. That the name came from the Jews is improbable, for they would scarcely have called the disciples by a name which acknowledged the Nazarene as the Christ. That it came from the disciples themselves is scarcely less probable, for we do not find any one of them using it except Peter, and he only once, and that twenty years after it had been bestowed. That it came from the inhabitants of the city it seems reasonable to suppose; for their facility in designation was almost a proverb. That it was given as a term of reproach we can not but believe, for that was the feeling with which the disciples were regarded. At any rate, the name came, was repeated from lip to lip, the association was soon complete, and once completed it remained, and remains to this day, the universally accepted designation of the successors of those disciples, who were called Christians first at Antioch.

I have been thus particular in narrating the origin of the Christian name, because it were unreasonable to suppose that any Christian can be uninterested in the subject. We may often repeat to ourselves the question: "What's in a name?" and affect an indifference to the designation by which our family is known; but I have never yet met the man who was without interest in the origin of the patronymic which he had received from his ancestors, and would transmit to his children. And because we are a household of faith, every one of us should have the same interest in kind, in the name by which all the children of our mother, dear Jerusalem, are known among men.

II. But the subject has an interest quite other than historical. It suggests, or should suggest, lessons of personal and immediate interest to every one of us. And it is for the purpose of setting these forth that I ask your attention to the *import* of the name first given the disciples at Antioch—the import of the Christian name.

You will be prepared, by what has already been said to be told, first of all, that it was a sign of the disciples' separation from other men. Mark what I say: It was a *sign* of their separation. The name did not cause, it was the effect of the separation. The inhabitants of Antioch discerned, as has been remarked already, a wide, indeed, a radical difference between the Jews who maintained the old worship of the synagogue and obeyed the traditions of their elders, and the other Jews, the Nazarenes, who cried: "The time is fulfilled, the law has been abrogated and the Kingdom of heaven is among men." There was that which they believed in common. Neither bowed down before a statue of their Divinity, and both declared his omnipresence. They sang many of the same hymns, and used many of the same forms of devotion. But there was a hope shared by one set of Jews in which the other had no part, and with which they had no sympathy. There was a name continually upon the lips of one, which the other uttered only to denounce. The one looked backward to a deliverer already come; the other looked forward to a deliverer who had not appeared. They might both indeed be Jews, as the inhabitants of Gaul and the inhabitants of Bithynia were alike subjects of the Empire; but between their religions was a difference as wide as the difference between the garb of the trader who had come from the south shore of the Euxine, and the garb of the trader who had sailed from the western shore of the Mediterranean. Separated thus from those to whom they were allied; separated in hope, in belief, in rite and conduct,—the name was given as a sign of separation. Henceforth they were a peculiar people; they stood alone, and apart from all others.

And not less now than then, Christian friends, should this name be regarded as a sign of separation from other men. Not, indeed, that the name separates us in any other sense than that of indicating a separation already made. Our acceptance of it is the acknowledgment of an accomplished fact. If we are indeed Christians, we are separated men and women; separated by the new hopes we cherish, by the new obligations we have taken upon ourselves, by the new privileges we enjoy, by the new example we profess to follow, by the new spirit which consecrates our lives. We can not afford to lose sight of this truth. I would not hide for one moment the other great truth, of which Christianity is the only revelation, that all men are the children of God, and have a right to say, "Our Father." But if "Christian" means any thing, those who are Christ's are children in virtue of an adoption which others have not received, and in virtue of a new birth which others have not experienced. I would not deny or depress the truth, that all men are brethren; but there is a household of faith to which the world does not belong. We are too prone, in these days, to shrink from the stigma of separation. But if we are Christians, we are a peculiar people; and the fact should call forth the question from every professed disciple: "If I am thus separated, how do I make my separation manifest among men?"

But this is only a negative view of the meaning of the name. It is to be remarked, more positively, that the name reveals the fact that the world at once seized the important and radical truth, that the Christian religion is intensely *individual*. The name

given them was not a collective name. They did not
describe these disciples as the Church. The name is
indeed the name of a class, but it is not the name of
a *body*. It described individuals as individuals—as
possessing each a character, and as holding each a
belief. It is important to recall this fact. The name
was evidently given them because of something
distinctive in the conduct and attitude of these disciples. It is scarcely to be doubted, that had Christianity, as represented by its disciples, first made itself
known as an institution—as a definitely organized
Church—this would have appeared in the name by
which they were designated. Because it did not so
make itself known, but as a Gospel to be received
and believed by individuals, the people of Antioch
gave its believers a name to be applied to individuals.
It was far from the purpose of the Apostles to establish an organic body which should seem more important than its several members. They were sent
to individual men. And the Church, the outward
organization, was intended to be no more complex
than would be necessary most efficiently to bring the
souls of men into harmonious relation with Christ.
When Church organization becomes so important or
is so emphasized, as to impress the world more than
the Christianity of its members, a large interval has
been traveled from the position occupied by the disciples at Antioch. I have not time to dwell at length
on this branch of the subject. Let me say, however,
that there is in all communions—in some the tendency is stronger and more evident than in others—
there is in all communions a tendency to emphasize
the Church at the expense of individual Christianity.
There is an "ism" which we may fitly describe as
churchism, which exalts the institutions of religion

above personal religion; in the view of which the organization and its canons are of more importance than the character and life of the individual. Had the first disciples been disposed, in those formative days, to establish a hierarchy which should itself startle or impress those to whom they proclaimed the Gospel, we may be sure that this fact would have appeared in the name which was first given them. Had they busied themselves most of all about councils or synods or successions or ordinations, it is not to be doubted that the citizens of Antioch would have incorporated that tendency in their designation. On the contrary, let it be noticed, they gave the disciples a name which is intensely individual. Not a word of the Church do we hear. The disciples were called Christians first at Antioch.

But not to dwell further on this, I remark thirdly, that the name given by the people of Antioch at least suggests, if it does not directly teach the truth, that the interests of the disciple and the interests of Christ *are one*. This is the truth at the root of this word Christian. If I am a Christian, then in a high and important sense Christ's life and my life are one. He is all and in all to me. If, languishing and in despair, I look for hope, I must if I would find it look to Christ; Christ in me is the hope of glory. If ignorant and needing spiritual wisdom, I must repair to Christ in whom are hid all the treasures of divine knowledge. If cast down and needing inspiration, I must consider Him who endured the contradiction of sinners against Himself, lest I grow weary and faint in mind. If I desire an example, I can find one that is perfect in Him alone who was holy, harmless, undefiled and separate from sinners. If in the hour of temptation, and ready to yield, I require support, He alone can bestow it whose strength is perfected in our weakness. More than this, Christ is the glory of his disciples, as his disciples are the glory of Christ. More than this, the path of their lives is the path of his own. Because He lives they shall live also. Such is the intimacy of this union that the Church has called it the "mystical" union between Christ and his people, and the language used to describe it in the Word of God fully justifies the designation. Christ and his people are the Vine and its branches. They are the Corner-stone and living stones of the temple which is the habitation of God. They are the Body and its members. And they are to be one with Him as He is one with the Father. Let us confess, friends, that there is much here that we can not now fully comprehend. The fact and the promise are all that we know. This truth the disciples proclaimed in Antioch;—the oneness of Christ and his people. Is it any wonder that those who heard them, called them by his name, that they were called Christians at Antioch? Looking back now upon their gatherings in that city, we can hardly think of them as known by any other designation, so all and in all was Christ to them.

And now let us ask ourselves, who call ourselves Christians, whether this oneness with Christ is an element of our experience? What is the meaning of this name as we apply it to ourselves? Do we indeed look to Him at all times for hope, strength, inspiration, example? We have no right to the name if we can not answer these questions aright. It often happens that the meanings of words in the course of centuries suffer no inconsiderable change. Often they lose the intensity of significance once possessed by them. Is not this somewhat the case with this word Christian as made use of by us? Let each one of us think of the depth of meaning the word possessed when it was first bestowed, and seek the spirit of these first disciples whose devotion to Christ earned for them the high honor of being called by his name.

In addition to what has been said it is to be remarked fourthly, that the word indicates the disciples' belief in the divine appointment of Christ to the work He did for them. They were called not after Jesus as a man, but Jesus as *the Christ*, the anointed and appointed Messenger of God. I refer to this because, as we are all aware, it is not uncommon nowadays while eulogizing the character of Jesus of Nazareth, to put out of view the divine origin and special character of his mission, and to resolve his redemptive work into his living an exceptionally holy life. And personal Christianity is reduced to an earnest endeavor to reproduce his life in one's own. It is undoubtedly true that following the example of Christ is no small part of discipleship. But that this is all of discipleship is far from being true. Certainly this does not describe the Christianity of these disciples at Antioch, whose name we bear and whose successors we profess to be. And this is evident not only from their whole history, but also from the name that was given them. The name Christ had in those days a distinct meaning. It described one promised and sent and consecrated to his work by God. In recognizing Jesus of Nazareth as the Christ, they confessed their faith in the prophecies of Israel as the Word of God. They not only professed an admiration of the lofty and holy character of Jesus, but they recognized in Him that Messiah in whom were to be fulfilled all the Old Testament predictions of a future deliverer. There may have been in Jerusalem, and doubtless were, many devout Greeks and Jews who could not fail to see in the teacher from Galilee a beauty of character and loftiness of aim that wonderfully contrasted with the character of the rulers of the people. But such recognition, even joined to admiration and earnest striving to emulate his virtues, would not have entitled such Greeks or Jews to the Christian name. And had they been in Antioch at the time the disciples were gathered there, the inhabitants of Antioch would not have made the mistake of confounding the two.

Christian friends, discipleship is more than admiration of the character of Jesus; more than following his example. He is not only Jesus but the promised Messiah of God. "Whom do men say that I am?" And the answer of the Apostles clearly indicated that there were many of his own nation not wanting in admiration of Him. "Some say that thou art Elias, and some John the Baptist?" "But whom say ye that I am?" Then Simon Peter answered: "Thou art the Christ, the Son of the living God." And it was to this confession of faith in his divine character and special mission, that Jesus made the reply: " Upon this rock I will build my Church."

Let us not be deceived. This name, taken in connection with the circumstances of its bestowal, shows clearly that, in the view of the disciples and of the world among whom they moved, more than admiration of Jesus was necessary to Christianity. Belief of his words, a recognition of his supreme claims as the Son of the living God, as the Redeemer who came from heaven in obedience to God, are no mere instruments, no mere means of grace, which may or may not be dispensed with; they are essential elements of discipleship, without which one has no right to assume the Christian name.

Once more, the name suggests the truth, that the *person* of Christ was the distinctive object of their Christian faith and hope. They were called, not after what He said, not after what He did, but after Him. This fact is not without its meaning. These disciples, you may remember, dwelt in these early days, with peculiar emphasis upon the last great miracle performed by Christ—his resurrection from the dead. They preached Jesus and the resurrection. So prominently did they hold forth the fact of Christ's and the promise of man's resurrection, that it seems strange that they were not called by a name derived from this fact. That they should believe in such a consummation must have seemed more singular to the men of Antioch, than that they were the disciples of a man of singular purity of life, and not less singular claims. And as names are given to describe peculiarities, it is to be wondered at, that we find in their designation no reference to what must have seemed to the Greeks of Antioch a most singularly foolish belief. And the only way to account for the fact that they received the name which they did, instead of a name derived from their belief in the resurrection, was that they made the personal, the living Christ so much more prominent, both in all they said of their religion, and in all their lives. We see the outworking of the same law nowadays. There are many to whom men instinctively refer by the name of the special communion to which they belong. The peculiarities of their sects stand out so prominently that it is hard, when speaking of them as religionists, not to say Presbyterian, or Baptist, or Congregationalist, or Episcopalian. There are others, however, to whom men just as instinctively refer, not by the names of their denominations, but by that name which is above every other name, the name of Christ himself. We may well ask ourselves, brethren, how men refer to us; what is most prominent in our lives as disciples of the Lord. Do men most often take knowledge of us that we have been with Him, or that we are most deeply interested in the peculiarities which, important as we believe them to be, do still divide us from our brethren in Christ?

So have I tried to set forth the meaning of the Christian name, as made known by the circumstances of its bestowment at Antioch. What a responsibility is ours who bear it! What a legacy is ours! When we remember these disciples at Antioch, and the faith and zeal and courage they exemplified in their labors for Him by whose name they were known among men, how should we be excited to more devoted labors for Him! To be a Christian then, to be known by this name—what consecration it involved; what love, what earnestness in living, what fearlessness of death, what hopes for the life to come! Brethren, as we bear their name, let us seek grace, that we may bear it not less faithfully than they. It was given to them as a reproach. But such was their life that it soon became honorable. It is honorable now. What a responsibility is ours! God forbid that any one of us should so wear it, as to make it in the view of any earnest soul a reproach once more!

Before I conclude, let me say to those before me, who do not bear this name, that in calling you to believe in Christ, we call you to bear the most honored name, by which a class of men has ever been known; a name, which, if it suggests great duties and sacrifices, suggests as well high hopes and eternal rewards. But we beg you to remember, that it is not only to a name that we call you; but to a union with Him whose name is above every other. We call you to become by faith the disciples of the Son of God, the Saviour of the world; in whom alone is eternal life. Give yourselves to Him in full and unhesitating trust; live in confiding communion with Him; make Him your all in all; and the honor of bearing his name here will be but the shadow of the unspeakable blessedness, that shall be yours in fellowship with Him for evermore.

XVIII.
CHRISTIANITY A RELIGION OF JOY.

"These things have I spoken unto you, that my joy might remain in you, and that your joy might be full."—John xv, 11.

The last discourse of our Lord to his disciples lacks the order of a studied address. In the freedom of conversation with intimate friends, at the table whereon is spread the Last Supper, He talks of the sublime truths that He came to reveal, the merciful mission that He came to fulfill, and the glorious triumph that He was about to achieve. Wedded, as most of these disciples were, to earthly views of the Messiah's kingdom, much that He said must at first have shocked their feelings and surprised their understanding. For this reason, "He repeats the same sentiments in order to impress them more deeply upon their unprepared minds." But, notwithstanding its lack of order, the discourse is unified by his desire, manifest in every part of it, for his disciples' release from distressing and dangerous sorrow, and their endowment with real and perfect joy. The discourse begins with the exhortation: "Let not your heart be troubled," and closes with the inspiring words: "Be of good cheer, I have overcome the world." And throughout the chapters which record it, are promises of peace that passeth knowledge, of the advent of a Divine Comforter, of the coming of the Father, and of a joy of which no man should rob them. That even as He was about to enter on his passion our Lord thought most lovingly of men, is thus made clear by his words as well as by his whole conduct. And we, to-day, would have known and felt it, even if the words of the text had been forgotten by his loving disciple.

"These things have I spoken unto you, that my joy might remain in you, and that your joy might be full." In these words, as you will observe, our Saviour connects the joy of his disciples with his Gospel: "*These things* have I spoken unto you," that you may be joyful. He connects it with Himself— "that *my* joy may remain in you." He describes the joy as permanent—"that it may *remain* in you." And He promises that it shall be perfect—"that your joy may be *full*." You know that there is in many a contrary impression; an undertone of feeling that Christianity is a gloomy religion, that Christians are melancholy in proportion to their sincerity, and that the millennium itself will be accompanied by a sensible diminution of human happiness. I shall not stop to inquire as to the source of this misconception. A pleasanter and I believe a more profitable task is that of presenting the considerations which show conclusively that this is a misconception; that if the world ever shall achieve ideal happiness, it will be when Christianity has attained its predicted supremacy, and that if you, my hearers, would know the blessedness of a joyful life, you must become one of these disciples to whom the Lord speaks to-day, as He spoke to those who ate with

Him the Last Supper, saying: "These things have I spoken unto you, that my joy might remain in you, and that your joy might be full."

Christianity, I say, is a religion of joy. This I shall endeavor to show, first from its constitution, and, secondly, from its contents.

I. In considering the *constitution* of Christianity—that is to say, the principles by which as a religion it is organized—let us notice, first, its relations to the idea of *duty*.

Christianity is not a system of duties as many mistakenly suppose. The remarks of many men when invited to become Christians would seem to indicate a belief on their part, that by becoming disciples of Jesus Christ they will assume new duties to God and to their fellow-men; that these new duties will be oppressive; and that the Christian, therefore, is exposed to if he does not actually suffer far more and far greater burdens than his fellow-men. Now even if Christianity were what these men suppose it to be—a system of duties—I doubt whether it could be charged with promoting the sorrow of humanity. For there are few pleasures more keen and few joys more noble than those which follow the recognition and the performance of duty. But Christianity is not a system of duties. Duty is not distinctively a Christian word, just as sin is not distinctively a Christian revelation. You do not ascertain that you are sinners by studying the declarations of the Bible. Neither do you learn what duties you owe to God or man or yourself, by studying the words of Christ. The great duties of life are revealed primarily, not by Christ, but by conscience. They are written on your hearts. Christ neither increases nor diminishes their number. They emerge, not out of your relations as members of the Church, but out of your relations as members of the human family. They do not begin to be duties on the day of your acceptance of Christ; you do not escape them if you refuse to accept Him.

Let me appeal to the testimony of your own hearts. What duty to God or to man or to yourself does Christianity impose, which was not imposed beforehand by conscience? Supreme love to God? Do you not owe it? Equal love to your fellow-man, with all that it includes? Who is there among you, that would *allow* me to say of him, that he is less bound than is the best Christian to do all in his power to promote the highest happiness of his fellow-men? "The sense of duty," which Emanuel Kant called one of the two sublime things in the universe, is an essential part of human nature. It can not be destroyed until the human constitution is destroyed. Christianity is not responsible for it. But this Christianity does; or this, let me rather say, Christ does. He reawakens the dormant sentiment of duty; He inspires us to perform it; He gives us divine aid; He holds out to us a good hope of ineffable reward; so far as we are one with Him, we are endowed with a boldness that enables us manfully to face it; out of his Word come the mightiest encouragements to its fulfillment. And therefore if there is any happiness in manliness, in the destruction of fear, in boldness that dares to look in the face whatever conscience commands; and if there is any joy in the reasonable hope that at last we shall succeed in the fulfillment of duty and be given an eternal reward,—so far as its relations to duty are concerned, Christianity deserves to be called by eminence a religion of joy.

Consider, again, the admitted fact that Christianity is silent on the subject of *amusements*. I do not say that it forbids this amusement or that amusement. But it provides none. This lack of provision has been made use of for the purpose of showing that Christianity is an enemy of pleasure. I need not take time to recall to your recollection the attacks made upon the Church, because she will not throw the weight of her influence on the side of the amusements of the world. Every resource has been exhausted to make it appear that this is clear proof of the melancholy of religion, or, at least, of evangelical Christianity. Who is not familiar with the caricatures intended to convey this impression— the solemn and long-faced preacher and the severe and angular elder or deacon? What Lord Macaulay said was true of the extreme Puritans of the days of Charles I. there is a disposition to attribute to Christianity itself: "They hated bear-baiting, not because it gave pain to the bear, but because it gave pleasure to the spectators." Were it worth while to do so, I could show without difficulty that there is abroad an easily recognized feeling, that in order to make good its claim to be a religion of joy, Christianity must either provide or cast its lot in with those who do provide amusements for the world.

But let me ask you this question: When you are happy in your home, when your family relations realize the ideal that floated before your mind, before you had a home of your own; when you can find *there* relief from the cares and consolation for the reversals of business; when conjugal and parental and filial love unite heart to heart, increasing joy and mitigating sorrow,—what need have you for public amusements and excitements? You are a joyful man without them. These excitements are for men and women who are not joyful, who have no resources in themselves, that will enable them to rise above or to drown the vexations of daily life. I am not declaiming against any set of men or any amusements. I am defending Christianity. And in doing so, I say that amusements are provided for men and women who need to forget themselves, to forget the present and the future, in order not to be overcome by their own wretchedness. In the days of degenerate Rome, when men were terror-stricken in view of the coming doom; when people were looking forward to a destruction which they could not avert; when the government was corrupt, and one Cæsar obtained the place of his predecessor by assassination,—how were the people held again and again from rebellion? Why, new baths were built; the spectacles in the Coliseum were multiplied; military pageants were more abundant; new public feasts were instituted; and bread and wine were given to the throngs of slaves. Why? That the sense of present danger and the fear of future destruction might be drowned in the excitement of the moment. Would you therefore call the Roman populace a joyful people? My friends, at that very time there was led to the imperial Capital a prisoner, to be tried before Cæsar for preaching a new religion. He was permitted to preach it, attended by a guard, while awaiting his trial. To this besotted populace this preacher offers no amusements; he scarcely mentions, except by way of illustration, the recreations of the Roman circus or the Roman theater. He does not indeed denounce them; but he speaks and writes as though they were not. But to this Roman populace he offers a hope that will enable them to rejoice in present tribulation, and to face without fear the advent of death. He expounds to them the life and labors and sacrifice of a Redeemer in whom there is no condemnation, and by whose power all things shall work together for their good. To this Gospel, thus preached, certain servants in the palace of the Emperor give joyful heed. I do not hesitate to put the joy of these Christian saints in Cæsar's household against the joy of the populace amused by Cæsar's shows and drunk with Cæsar's wine. And yet we are told, that Christianity is not a religion of joy because it does not provide amusements for the public. It is because Christianity touches man at the center of his life, because it Invests him—so far as it is accepted—with power calmly to face all possible disasters, that it does not need to provide opiates with which to dull man's sense of sorrow or foreboding. And because it invests him with this power, it has a right to call itself by eminence a religion of joy.

Consider again, in its relation to this subject, the *absolute liberty* with which the Gospel endows its disciples. I have already said that Christianity is not a system of duties. But I mean by its liberty something more than this. I mean the perfect confidence which it reposes in the individual Christian. If you contrast it with all other faiths in the world, you will not fail to notice the entire absence of what I may call ceremonial obligations. Take any one of these religions. Take indeed the Hebrew religion from which it sprang. The Hebrew was held to his religion by a detailed and splendid ritual, by a series of minute regulations, by ablutions and fasts and feasts and sacrifices—all carefully detailed and prescribed. The old economy was thus characterized by a severe and continuous superintendence of the daily life of the individual. There is not a position or set of circumstances possible, for which it does not make detailed provision. It was in this way that the pious Jew was held to communion with God and to preparation for death. But of this supervision there is an entire absence in the New Testament. The Christian is at liberty. He is held to his faith by no rules. He is compelled to walk along no narrow and prescribed line. Neither in work nor in praise nor in prayer, neither in being nor in doing does he find himself fettered by a single ceremonial obligation. Even as regards the Lord's day and the sacraments, the language of the New Testament is not so much that of law, as that of loving appeal. There is no command to do this or to forego that. The Son of God has made him a free man; and his inspired Apostles bid him, above all things else, stand fast in the liberty wherewith Christ has made him free. If there is one command in the New Testament more binding than another, it is that which forbids one Christian to judge another or to trespass upon another's freedom in the Christian life.

What is the meaning of this large liberty of the Christian disciple? Why is it, do you suppose, that you and I find ourselves so free in life and labor? There can be but one answer to the question; and that is, that the Gospel supposes its votaries to be held to a religious life by the joys of religion. It supposes that no rules are needed where happiness so abounds; and therefore no rules are prescribed. This is the religion of the New Testament; and this is the power by which it is moving forward to its supremacy in the world. It regulates, not by the rules which it imposes, but by the joy which it inspires.

It is the only faith in all the world—I will not say which has succeeded by—but which has dared to attempt this method. And yet we are told that it is a religion of melancholy; that "the tone of its pulpit is a whine, and that its psalm is a *miserere*." No more baseless statement has ever been uttered. No other proof that it is a religion of joy is needed than this liberty of the disciple. It succeeds by the reality and the abundance of its joys; and its mission can not better be described than it is by the statement, that Christ's joy may remain in men, and that their joy may be full.

II. Thus far, you will observe, I have not referred to the *contents* of Christianity. I have spoken simply of its constitution, of the principles of its organization. This examination shows us that it must be a religion of joy, if it possesses any power. Our confidence in it as a religion of joy will be deepened, if we advance to a consideration of the fundamental sorrow which it removes and the positive joys which it inspires. And here I can only touch a subject on which I might well dwell at length.

First, it removes absolutely the sorrow of the sense of *guilt*. The sense of guilt is an ultimate fact of human consciousness. Every thing has been done to explain it away; but there it remains. The awful shade, like the ghost of Banquo, will not down at human bidding. There it abides, the darkest shadow on the horizon of human consciousness, and awakening the most poignant agony that the human spirit can feel. "I am guilty before God. How dare I meet Him face to face, whom face to face I must behold!" This has been the cry of man in all ages and places. This it is that makes remorse possible and that makes death terrible. No other sorrow is like this sorrow;

for it is sorrow without hope. Now what but a religion of joy shall we call that religion, which can drive away this terrible specter and calm the agitation of the human spirit? What, to such a joy, are all the amusements and excitements, all the anodynes and recreations of the world? Show me a faith that will enable me to stand fearlessly before the living and the holy God, and I will show you a religion whose joy remains and whose joys are full. But is not this the characteristic triumph of the Gospel? What else but this victory is celebrated in the joyful cry of the Apostle: "There is, therefore, now no condemnation to them who are in Christ Jesus; who are sons of God, and heirs of God; whom nothing shall separate from his love"? And has it not proved in all its history its possession of power adequate to destroy this sense of guilt?

Next to the remorse that springs from a sense of guilt, the keenest agony of man is *despair* as to removal of sin. Man sees the perfect holiness in the distance, and though it attracts him by its beauty and invites him to accept its benediction, he knows he can not attain it. He is in despair; and all the voices in the universe, save that of Christianity, bid him despair; and thus in desperation he rushes headlong into new sin. O friends! how many men, how many women have ruined themselves through despair! How often has the drunkard sought again his cups with the cry on his lips: "I can not rise to a better life; therefore let me drown my griefs"! How often has the abandoned woman rushed back to unlawful life through dread of almost certain failure to reform! Now am I not justified in describing that as a religion of joy, which is the only power in the world that gives man good hope that he shall one day overcome, not this vice or that vice alone, but all sin; and shall stand complete in the beauty of holiness before God? And where is this power to be found, but in the religion of Jesus Christ which we are called so often to defend against the charge of being a religion of melancholy!

More than this, you know how large a proportion of the sorrow of life springs from untoward and painful *events*. Who can number them? The little vexations of daily life; the harassments of business; the disappointments of friendship; the hopes deferred that make the heart sick; the accidents and the diseases of life; the burdens of manhood; the weariness of age, when the grasshopper becomes a burden and fears are in the way! Then the great afflictions that lie like mountains on the sinking heart; as the awful sweep from wealth to poverty, or the sudden advent of death into the family! But why need I go on? "Man is born to trouble, as the sparks to fly upward." Now, I appeal to you, what but a religion of joy— of joy that remains, and of joy that is full—shall that religion be called, which can rationally assure the victim of these sorrows that they shall issue in a higher blessedness; that these are not his enemies but his friends, working for him a far more exceeding weight of glory? And is not just this the rational assurance of the Gospel of Christ? Is not the Gospel the only sufficient prediction to the world that every loss shall be a gain, and every woe the minister of a higher joy to those who trust through Christ in God?

Nor is this all. Who does not know, that deep in human nature is an abiding sorrow, growing out of the feeling that man can not *commune* with God; that the Creator and Father of all, hides Himself from his children? Could they only meet Him and commune with Him, believing that He wears the loving aspect of a parent, and assured that his heart beats with sympathy and love! Nature does not intimate the possibility of this communion, or the fact of this parental relation and regard. If this is so, shall I hesitate to call that a religion of joy which reveals to us his nearness; and bids us, sinners as we are, go boldly to Him and call Him, "Our Father which art in heaven"?

Again, the *inability* to do good in this world of evil—to overcome the woe and the wretchedness of humanity—is an awful sorrow whenever it is felt. Is not that a religion of joy, then, which bids me plow and sow for men in hope, which assures me that I am a co-worker with God and that no labor can be in vain in the Lord! And, finally, the *darkness* and mystery and solitude, that lie on the borders of this world, beget a terror, which all know who dare to contemplate death as the ushering of the spirit into another world. And what but a religion of unutterable joy shall I call that, which dissipates the mystery, and destroys the terror, and relieves the solitude of death; and illumines the dark under-world with the vision of a joy unspeakable and full of glory?

"These things," said Christ, "have I spoken unto you, that my joy might remain with you, and that your joy might be full." And is not the joy that springs from his Gospel abiding and perfect? Those who have brought against Christianity the charge against which I have been contending, and those who cherish the suspicion which I have attempted to destroy, do not possess either a true conception of Christianity or a true conception of human happiness. I am indulging in no mere declamation, but am giving utterance to words of soberness when I say, that you will never learn what joy is until in simple faith and penitence you become a disciple of Christ. The joy that is in Him and from Him is the only joy that remains, and the only joy that is full.

There are two or three inferences from this subject that I wish to press upon your attention. And first, Christian friends, if you are not joyful Christians, it is not the fault of the Gospel. If your lives are, in any true sense of the word, miserable, it is because there is some fault in your acceptance of the Gospel. I beg you to reflect on this statement. It is not your temperament that is at fault. The Gospel was not meant for this temperament or for that temperament, but for all mankind. It is not your adverse circumstances that are at fault. Like the stanch vessel that was built, not only for fair weather and for smooth seas, but to ride the tumult of the waves and to sail through the storm, the Gospel of God's grace was given us, not for health and wealth alone, but for days of sickness and poverty and affliction, and for the day of death. If we are not superior to them all and joyful in them all, the fault is in our lack of faith. We do not believe the things, which Christ has spoken in order that his joy may remain in us, and that our joy may be full.

The subject teaches us what is the spirit in which we should preach and live the Gospel that we profess to believe. It is not a sorrowful message that the Gospel announces. It is glad tidings of great joy. Nature and sickness and sin and death are sorrowful; but not the Gospel of forgiven sin, of God's fatherhood, of conquered death and of an opened heaven.

And therefore the Gospel should be proclaimed with joy. So it must be proclaimed by us, if we would win souls. And so must we live it, if we would have men led by the light of our lives to Him who is the Life and Light of men.

So would I preach it now to you, O men and women, who thus far have refused to accept the Gospel and the Saviour whom it reveals. I need not tell you—for you know too well already—that from no other source can you obtain this real, this abiding, this interior and strengthening joy of which I have spoken. I bid you recall the mission of Christ as He himself describes it. He came that your joy might remain and that your joy might be full. I will not say, you must be born again. Alas! your own ineffective struggles too well attest your need of a new life. But I will say that in Him you *can* be born again—born to a life, whose present peace nothing on earth can destroy, and whose eternal and unimagined joy nothing in heaven or in hell shall disturb. This is the promise of Christ. This is the joy that He offers you. Listen to Him and come to Him and rest in Him, as from his gracious lips fall the words, and from the gracious Spirit proceeds the almighty power, by which alone your spirit's joy shall conquer all sorrow here, and shall become hereafter, in the presence of God, fullness of joy and pleasure for evermore.

XIX.
KEEPING IN THE LOVE OF GOD.

"But ye, beloved, building up yourselves on your most holy faith, praying in the Holy Ghost, keep yourselves in the love of God, looking for the mercy of our Lord Jesus Christ unto eternal life."—JUDE 20, 21.

There are statements in the New Testament, which, taken by themselves, leave the impression that in the work of sanctification the Christian is simply passive and recipient, and God alone is active. We are told that we are kept by the power of God; that we are saved by the grace of God; that faith itself is his gift; that it is God who calls, who regenerates, who justifies and who at last glorifies the children of men. On the other hand, there are exhortations to activity addressed to Christians which seem to proceed upon the supposition that the disciple alone is active; or, at least, that the utmost done by God is to appoint for his people favorable conditions in which to become perfect as He is perfect. I shall not stop to show the harmony between the two classes of passages. Let me say, that it is not our business to perplex ourselves with the seeming contradiction, but rather to rejoice in the truth that both God and ourselves, if we are faithful, are active in the work of our redemption; that while we are working out our salvation with fear and trembling, we are not alone; for God is working within us to will and to do of his good pleasure.

Whenever a passage of the latter class is found in the Epistles; whenever an exhortation is addressed to Christians which seems to devolve the whole responsibility of their redemption upon themselves, we find associated with the exhortation, and often as a a part of it, a distinct reference to the means and agencies which they are to employ. When the duty is stated, the method of its fulfillment is brought clearly into view. We have an illustration of this in the words which I have chosen as my text. In language as vivid and vigorous as any to be found in the New Testament, Jude describes those who have turned the grace of God into licentiousness, who have made shipwreck of their faith. He depicts their character in terms that must have enabled the true disciple to detect these spots in their love feasts, and prophesies their destiny in the bold and striking metaphor; they are wandering stars for whom the blackness of darkness is reserved. From these he turns to the Christians to whom he is writing with an exhortation, in obedience to which they would find their rescue from this awful life and condemnation; and while exhorting them he states the method to be pursued in obeying the exhortation.

I shall not endeavor to show that the surroundings of Christians when this Epistle was written, were similar to our own; or that we have here a prophecy of the days in which we live. I simply insist that as our work is the same as theirs, as our aim is one with theirs, and as the same reward is to compensate us that compensated them, we may consider these words as though primarily written to us. The injunction is quite as appropriate to our circumstances as to theirs. The words of the text, therefore, are the words of God, addressed to you and me, and they should come to us with all the urgency with which they fell on the ears of the primitive disciples who first heard them: "But ye, beloved, building yourselves up on your most holy faith, praying in the Holy Ghost, keep yourselves in the love of God, looking for the mercy of Jesus Christ unto life eternal."

I shall speak, first, of the great duty to which we are here exhorted,—we are to " keep ourselves in the love of God;" and, secondly, of the aids which are furnished us, or the means we are to use,—we are to keep ourselves in the love of God, by "building ourselves up on our most holy faith;" by praying in the Holy Ghost;" and by "looking for the mercy of our Lord Jesus Christ unto life eternal."

I. And first, let us study the *duty* to which we are here called. " Keep yourselves in the love of God." This does not mean, "Keep ourselves loving God." It is not our affection for our Father in heaven to which the writer refers; it is the amazing, the infinite, the enduring, the individualizing love of God for us. As thus understood, it is obvious that the exhortation is not, "See to it that God loves you." That would be little short of impiety. God has charge of his own affection. It rests upon all who trust Him; and neither death, nor life, nor angels, nor principalities can separate them from his love. God's love goes forth from Him as the light and heat go forth from the sun, without waning and without intermission. But often between the earth and the orb which warms and illumines it clouds intervene, and the earth, so to speak, becomes unconscious of the sun's light and heat. In the same way, between the Christian and his Father in heaven, mists born of the Christian's life often arise and hide the Father's face; the disciple, unconscious of the love of God, grows cold, and graces droop, and Christian character is weakened and distorted. So common is this experience that all of us, doubtless, will acknowledge the need of this exhortation, and of its continual iteration: "Let nothing intervene to hide from you the face of your Father in heaven. See to it that you do not lose your consciousness of his affection for you. Keep yourselves, beloved, in the love of God."

You shall see, if you will think of it for a moment, the propriety of the language in which the exhortation is clothed. What is the great revelation of the Gospel, but the revelation of the love of God for individual and sinful men and women? This is the glad tidings of great joy. Outside of the Gospel, there is not the slightest hint that any thing properly to be termed love for men exists in God. If I question nature in any of its aspects as to the existence of this affection, I obtain no hopeful response. The most that nature tells me is that the procedure of the Governor of the universe is determined by laws, which were ordained in infinite wisdom and in infinite goodness, and which are executed by omnipotence with unerring precision. It assures me that, on the whole, the result of their execution is happiness, and that certainly wherever the beings under them are obedient, their bliss and harmony are perfect. This is the whole of the love of God that nature reveals or can reveal. And when I go to nature with the confession, that I have violated God's law; when I cry out of my sinfulness and misery: "I have sinned against heaven, and in the sight of God; has He any love for me, will He forgive my sin, will He avert the destruction which I have brought upon myself?" nature can make no other reply than "The soul that sinneth it shall die." If God has any affection for sinners, or entertains the purpose of releasing them from the condemnation in which they have involved themselves, nature knows nothing of it; she has no revelation to make, and she makes none. So far as her voice is concerned, man is without help and without hope, and so must remain forever.

Now if the Church has correctly interpreted the Gospel of Christ, the Gospel means that the revelation which nature has not made has been made in another way. The Gospel is thus a voice from heaven assuring us that God is love, and loves sinners; that the God who is a lawgiver is also a Father; that though we are sinners, in Jesus Christ we are God's children, and his love is ever active in our behalf; that nothing can harm us, and nothing will; that no labor of ours can be in vain; that no experience of ours can fail to minister to our highest well-being; that the Son of God is head over all things to his people, and will make all work together for their good. This is the truth on which the exhortation is based. So Jude writes to the Christians of the Apostolic Church: "Never let your perception of this great revelation be clouded. Never permit the consciousness of God's affection to be other than vivid. Carry it with you everywhere. See that nothing weakens or disturbs it. It is the great revelation of the Gospel. Losing your hold on this truth, you lose the one sure anchorage of your soul. Without it you must make shipwreck of every noble hope. Hold fast by it, therefore, beloved. Keep yourselves in the love of God." This is the meaning and force of the text; and so absolutely necessary to the Christian's peace does the habit which it contemplates reveal itself to be, that one wonders that any necessity for the appeal should ever have existed. Having once accepted the truth, having once had this love of God shed abroad in the heart, it would seem that we could never lose the thought of it, that it would be our contemplation all the day long, that the sense of it would make every hour an hour of prayer, and transmute every act into an act of praise.

But is this the case with us, brethren? Is it true that we obey the exhortation? Is it not rather true that it has become largely a dead letter to us? Do we not make nearly every act and habit of our lives an obstacle in the way of obeying it, instead of an occasion to bring it to our remembrance? One would suppose, for example, that the cares and engrossments of business would lead a Christian to hold the love of God for him in clear and constant view. For the worry and harassment of business life, what effective antidote is there save the consciousness of the divine affection which appoints our duties and fixes our circumstances, and which will one day make plain that they are the best that could have been appointed? If you were accustomed to go to your counting-rooms and shops and offices with the consciousness of the love of God for you dominating all thoughts and feeling, how less than now would losses seem; how far brighter would all times look; with how much more zest would you live your daily business lives! If toil would be no less severe, care would be less wearing; and if losses would be as frequent, your spirits would never break beneath the load of them. And have we not a right to expect, that this consciousness of God's love will be permanent and influential in a Christian's life? Have I not a right to prophesy, that the cares of business will render it more distinct; that they will become the occasion of its more vigorous life? But what is the fact? Is it not that these cares and labors become obstacles to faith in the divine affection? Instead of bringing God's love before us, they tempt us to forget or to ignore it; and thus life becomes more earthly, and we are surprised by our own doubts of the love's reality. Hence, I say, the need of the exhortation, and its constant and forceful repetition: "Keep yourselves in the love of God."

So is it also with the allurements of pleasure. To a Christian, one would suppose that all sources of enjoyment would appear more blessed because of this new revelation of God's love for him; and that, thus sanctified, they would become means of grace as real as the Church, the Word and the Sacraments. Am I a child of God, and does He love me? Then every pleasure should appear as the fruit of his affection; every appetite which finds gratification in the world He has created, every capacity which is ministered to by the forms of beauty and sublimity which He has spoken into being, every association with my fellows out of which springs happiness, ought at once to connect themselves in my mind with the divine love which has so enriched my life. But is this the fact? What is the temptation when pleasure allures but to sink the thought of God below the thought of the pleasure itself; to run riot, to become the slaves of appetite? So happiness tends to become unsanctified; so pleasure grows more sensual, and thought and life become defiled. Who does not see that we need to hear again and again the voice of the Spirit, calling us to "keep ourselves in the love of God"?

So, did time permit, I might speak of affliction; of intellectual engagements; of the entire earthly life of man. Did we not know what the fact is, we should prophesy with confidence that this great revelation of God's love having once been made and having been once a possession, we could give ourselves to no engagement that would not make the revelation appear more valuable, and the consciousness of the love of God a greater and more blessed power. Is the malign influence of indwelling sin more horridly conspicuous anywhere than it is in the lives of Christians, when, as we know it does, it changes these occasions of bringing the love of God more clearly before us, into clouds that hide it from our sight? Do you wonder that the New Testament is full of calls to vigilance, that it breathes the spirit of a solemn and a real fear that we shall lose this priceless possession? Need you be surprised that the exhortations most often uttered from the pulpit to Christians have just the force and meaning of the text: "Keep yourselves in the love of God"?

If you would know the importance of these words of Jude, ask yourselves what your lives would be, if there were *no* love of God in which to keep yourselves. Suppose this revelation blotted out. Suppose this Christian consciousness lost. Suppose that every loss in business, that every sickness which weakens you, that every death of a friend could be explained only as the precursor of that to which all material things seem tending; remediless disaster—

what would be their influence upon you? Could your character endure? In the absence of this revelation, could you maintain your purity and integrity? I hope I do my race no wrong. But if history teaches one truth more plainly than another, it is the truth that in the absence of hope for the future life men sink at last almost to the level of brutes; they fight with each other; they grasp at the lowest pleasures; they cry: "There is no help, no hope; let us eat and drink, for to-morrow we die." Or let us reverse the supposition; let us suppose this consciousness of the love of God to be now, what one day it shall become, permanent and uniform and universal—regnant in all the world, and in the whole of life. What event, in that case, could occur which it would not make a minister of grace? What circumstances could surround us, which it would not transfigure into aids to holiness?

I do not know that, as a minister of the Gospel, I could repeat a more needed exhortation than this of Jude: "But, ye beloved, keep yourselves in the love of God." If you who are Christian teachers could carry the consciousness of this love to your scholars, with what power and unction would you tell the story of the sacrifice of the Son of God! If I, as a preacher, could always be constrained by it in preaching, how soon would the Gospel prove itself here to be the power of God unto salvation! If this whole congregation were strong in the conviction of it, and uplifted by the constant realization of it, how soon would worship be adorned with the beauty of holiness, and gifts be multiplied, and self-sacrifice for men's highest well-being become like the sacrifice of Christ himself! I bring to you, therefore, Christian friends, this urgent exhortation. Let nothing rob you of the conviction, let nothing dim within you the consciousness, let no experience weaken your sense of your heavenly Father's affection for you. It is infinite as his own being. It rests not on men as a class, but on each one of you as individuals. It is mightier than angels, or affliction or death. It is enduring as eternity. See to it that it is ever shed abroad in your hearts. Keep yourselves, beloved, in the love of God.

II. At this point the question may well be asked: "But how shall I obey the injunction? If the difficulties are so many and so mighty, if the very occasions which should bring it into clear view become obstacles to its remembrance, what am I to do but resign myself to their baleful power? Are there no helps to obedience; no methods in adopting and pursuing which I shall be able to keep myself in the love of God?" The text clearly answers this question. We have here presented the three great aids which God offers all men who would keep themselves in his love. These are, first, spiritual nourishment;—"Building up yourselves on your most holy faith"; secondly, worship;—"Praying in the Holy Ghost"; and, finally, contemplation of the end of our Christian course;—"Looking for the mercy of our Lord Jesus Christ unto eternal life." No Christian man or woman, who shall faithfully and relying upon God make diligent use of these means of grace, will fail to keep himself in the love of God.

Let us dwell briefly upon each of these aids. The first is spiritual nourishment;—"Building up yourselves on your most holy faith."

The metaphor is drawn not from the erection of an edifice, but from the life of the body. We are to build up ourselves on appropriate food, and by appropriate exercise. We shall not be able to keep ourselves in the love of God, unless we nourish ourselves with the bread which God has given us, and by the activity which He appoints. This bread and this activity are designated by the comprehensive phrase—"your most holy faith." The word faith is employed in the sense of "that which is believed and accepted." So that the exhortation up to this point may be paraphrased as follows: "If you would keep undimmed your consciousness of your heavenly Father's affection, see to it that you regularly feed your soul upon the Bible, and then engage in the religious activity which that Bible commands. Make the Word of God the theme of contemplation, and the manual of your active career, and the clouds that hide your Father's face will soon be dissipated." Here we touch the secret of both the world's skepticism and the individual disciple's gloom and weakness. I desire to give distinct expression to my profound conviction, that the popular infidelity of which we hear so much is the product, not of knowledge, but of ignorance. Men doubt God because they do not know Him. They disbelieve the Scriptures because they have not studied them. Did they come to them with the reverence and the docility which their antiquity and their historical influence in the world ought to inspire, and earnestly study them, doubt not that much of the popular criticism and denial of the day would disappear, and the Bible would authenticate itself, as the special revelation of the love of God to sinful and dying men.

But I am addressing believers, not skeptics; and I appeal to your own Christian experience. You complain that the things of the world obscure your vision of the love of God; that the affection of God for you is not the mighty power in your career which you had been led to believe it would be—and you ask the reason. Let me reply by asking another question: Are you building up yourselves upon your most holy faith? Are you nourishing your souls upon this word of God—this bread of life eternal? Are you engaged actively and laboriously in work for the Kingdom of God? What a story would your Bibles tell of regular and habitual and devout study? What a story would the last week tell of labor for Christ and man's salvation? You do not expect the powers of your body to enjoy vigorous health unless you feed them with nourishing food and give them suitable exercise. Why should you wonder that the eye of faith is dimmed and the vigor of your soul is relaxed when your Bibles remain closed and your days pass without earnest engagement in Christian work? Depend upon it, brethren, God will be faithful if you are faithful. His promise will not fail if you neglect not his provisions for you. Here is his word; feed upon it. There is his work; engage in it. Your souls' meat and drink are given you, and the labor is appointed. You can not expect spiritual health without the nourishment afforded by the one or the exercise furnished in the other. When you shall make God's law your meditation, when you shall look out with something of the spirit of Christ upon souls dying in sin and misery around you, no outward surroundings, no enticements or threatenings, no positive disasters will disturb your souls' repose and your souls' strength in their consciousness of God's infinite and eternal love.

Besides this nourishment of the divine life by food and exercise, the text suggests as another means of keeping ourselves in the love of God, communion with God himself. We are to keep ourselves in his love, by "praying in the Holy Ghost."

How many of us esteem prayer a burdensome duty! How many of us engage in it as though it were nothing but a duty! But suppose the revelation of prayer destroyed; suppose that you did not know God as the rewarder of them that diligently seek Him,—how would you cry in darkness and agony: "O, that I knew where I might find Him!" Blessed be God, there is no need to utter this cry in despair! The announcement that God hears the prayers of men, that He longs for their communion with Him, that He will not fail to answer them, could not, by any possible use of human language, be made more clear than it is in the Word of God. The Old Testament and the New alike repeat the assurance. Invitation is joined to command; examples of answers are multiplied; the blessed influence of engagement in public and private devotion is clearly stated; the method of approach to the Most High is pointed out; the veil is rent from top to bottom, and the mercy-seat within the most holy place is accessible to all the people. Nothing is left undone to impel men to treat God as a Father ever near, always gracious—nay, scarcely waiting to hear his trusting children's cry, before He bestows his richest blessings.

Now, when a Christian complains that he finds it well-nigh impossible to maintain his consciousness of God's love for him, and with it to hold himself strong and steadfast in the Christian life, in engrossment and enticement and affliction; when he says that secular duties possess his being, or untoward events destroy his Christian comfort, or his appetites, appealed to by earthly enjoyments, make him unspiritual,—what more appropriate question could be put to him than: "My brother, do you pray? Do you pray earnestly? Do you pray in the spirit? Do you pray without ceasing! Is your daily life a constant praying in the Holy Ghost?" I come, dear friends, with these questions to you this morning. Have your prayers been real or perfunctory petitions? Have you, believing God's Word, gone to God and poured your real sins and actual wants into his open ear, and begged forgiveness and supply? Let us examine ourselves. The magnificent revelation, that the God of heaven attends our cry, has not been made that you and I may ceremoniously repeat from day to day set phrases without earnest request: it has been made that we may approach our God with the faith and the earnestness of children, remembering, "that if earthly parents, being evil, give good gifts to their children, much more our Father in heaven will give good things to them that ask Him." Do not suppose that you can keep yourselves in God's love if you do not pray to Him. It were folly to believe that you can carry with you an abiding sense of his affection while you neglect this great privilege of free and confiding communion. All conviction of his love will die, and all the strength which that conviction imparts will die; and faith and courage will droop, and your soul will be the sport of every changing circumstance,—unless, familiar with your own closets, and suffering often the strong agony of real supplication, your life is one of "praying in the Holy Ghost."

There is one other aid mentioned in the text, not less important than the two already dwelt upon. We shall find it impossible to keep ourselves in the love of God, unless we "look for the mercy of our Lord Jesus Christ unto eternal life."

I have already said that nature says nothing of the love of God for sinners. But nature and providence do reveal, and that in terms not indistinct, the wrath of God against unrighteousness. In the awful certainty with which the laws of nature inflict their sanction upon transgressors; in the hopeless career of men who trifle with the constitution of their physical frames; in the wrecks of cities and empires and civilizations that obeyed not the law written on the human heart; more than all, in the solemn monitions and forebodings of the consciences of men, is made clearly known the divine displeasure with the sin of man. Over against all this nature gives no hint of love and forgiveness; her single statement is: "As man has fallen, man must die." How, looking merely on the pages of this solemn volume that God has written in the stars, and in the life of man, can any one "keep himself in the love of God"?

But another revelation is yours, Christian friends. Immortality has been brought to life. Against the sufferings of the present is put the glory to be revealed hereafter. The death that has conquered the world, becomes your servant in Christ. The troubles and the joys of this mortal life are made the steps of your ascent to the throne whereon you shall reign with Him for evermore. Eternal life is yours by the love of God in Jesus Christ. And now comes the exhortation: "Keep yourself in the love of God by looking toward this eternal life." You complain that you lose the consciousness of this affection; at least that the consciousness of God's love is not a power in your daily life. But on what is your attention fixed? On earthly things; on trial and trouble; on sickness and death; on the awful retributions of nature, and on the predicted "wreck of matter and crush of worlds?"

These are not the revelation of God's love to you. And you can not keep yourself in his love by contemplating them. They will only make your gloom deeper. They will only multiply your temptations to doubt God's affection. They will make sin more easy and holiness more nearly an impossible attainment. Look beyond them. Look to eternal life. In the promise of eternal life is the revelation of God's infinite love! How full the New Testament is of passages which teach the truth that this contemplation of eternal life uplifts the soul! We are saved by the hope of its glories. It is the anticipation of them that makes us pure, as Christ is pure. It is when we are looking at its unseen and eternal blessings that affliction works for us a far more exceeding and eternal weight of glory. If, therefore, you would keep your consciousness of God's love, think often of the blessedness He has in store for you. Anticipate the undefiled inheritance. Live in expectation of your life in the heavenly city. "Look for the mercy of our Lord Jesus Christ unto life eternal."

Thus, in terms as plain as I can employ, I have tried to show the importance of the exhortation and the means which you are to use in obeying it. Day after day you will be assaulted by temptations to doubt God. In your business, in your homes, by means of vexation or pleasure or affliction, the untiring foe of your souls will seek to separate your life from God. If he can not allure you to commit open crime, he will endeavor to poison the springs of your spiritual life. And evil thoughts and unworthy suspicions will suggest themselves; and so by slow but sure gradations will you fall into captivity to sin; unless an effective antidote is yours. Such an antidote this Word has furnished us in its revelation of God's love for us. Am I indeed beloved by Him? Has He given his Son to die for me? Does his creation exist, and do the plans of his providence move forward to their fulfillment, that I may rise to fellowship with God? Could this thought be ever-present and powerful, how could I war with sin, how could I grow in grace, how would my light shine as the path of the just more and more unto the perfect day! But this thought can be always present, and always mighty. If it is not, it is your own fault. Build up yourself on your most holy faith; nourish your soul with God's Word, and exercise yourself in Christian work day by day. Pray in the Holy Ghost; never be satisfied with vain repetitions, but wrestle like Jacob, and plead like Abraham. Look for the mercy of Jesus Christ unto life eternal; keep in your mind the all-blessed consummation of your present life; and, if God be true, the sense of his love will never be absent; and by its power you will know what it is to be more than conquerors.through Him who loves you.

There are those here who do not know the love of God in Jesus Christ—who have not accepted Him. My friends, with what can you meet temptations to sin? What is your strength against the day of affliction? How do you propose to make or keep your lives lofty in the presence of so many and such mighty allurements to unhallowed lives? If you do not believe in Christ, you certainly can not believe in God's love of you. Estranged from the Son of God, you know God only as the unfailing executioner of his law, and you know yourselves only as sinners. Are you content with your condition? Do you dare to reflect on the hopeless and wretched issue of such a life as yours? I can not portray it. I can not tell the horrors which nature and your own conscience prophesy to be your doom. But I can lift my voice and say: In Jesus Christ, God is love, and He bids you come to Him by faith in his Son. Without Him you have no hope, and you know it; when you think of it you feel it and confess it. His is the only name given under heaven whereby you can be saved. To Him then come, and come now. A new light will glorify your life, a new power will nerve your spirit, a new hope will brighten the hour of your death, a new bliss will dissipate your forebodings of the life to come. For the love of God—the love that no time can diminish, and no created being can destroy—shall be shed abroad in your hearts by the Holy Ghost given unto you.

XX.

THE LIGHT GRANTED IN DARKNESS.

"But all the children of Israel had light in their dwellings."— Exodus x, 23.

This statement is taken from the narrative of the ninth plague sent upon the land of Egypt—the plague of darkness—a thick darkness which might be felt. It serves to show the determination of the haughty monarch not to be defeated in his contest with what he regarded as the national divinity of his bondmen; that after eight terrible calamities had befallen his people, he was still intractable and would not let the children of Israel go. How terrible these judgments must have been to Pharaoh and his nation, will in some measure be understood, when they are studied in connection with the country they befell. "It is not an ordinary river," says Dean Stanley, in his lecture on the Exodus, "that is turned into blood; it is the sacred, beneficent and solitary Nile, the very life of the state and of the people. It is not an ordinary land of which the flax and the barley, and every green thing in the trees, and every herb of the field are smitten by the two great calamities of the storm and the locust. It is the garden of the ancient

Eastern world, the long line of green meadow and grain-field, and groves of palm and sycamore and fig-tree from the Cataracts to the Delta, doubly refreshing from the desert which it intersects, doubly marvelous from the river whence it springs." And pursuing the line of remark thus suggested by the lecturer, it may be said concerning this ninth plague: It was not a land accustomed to the obscuration of the sun by day and the stars by night, through the intervention of fog and mist and rain-cloud, which a thick darkness that might be felt enveloped for three long days. Modern travelers have made us all familiar with the deep blue of the noonday sky, the brilliant heavens by night, and the perpetual dryness and clearness of its atmosphere. Such was the land of Egypt, over all of which when Moses stretched forth his hand toward heaven, there came a darkness, even a thick darkness, which might be felt. "Men," we are told, "saw not one another; neither rose any from his place for three days." The sudden gloom must not only have produced great positive misery, through the necessary cessation of all industries, but must also have been to the Egyptians ominous of a near and total destruction.

Residing in the land, and doubtless suffering in some measure both inconvenience and positive pain from this visitation, the children of Israel were still released not only from many of the greater miseries which it brought upon the Egyptians, but also from apprehension. Whether by physical miracle, or by previous information concerning the coming judgment that enabled them to make provision, we are not told;—but in some way God so intervened, that during the plague of darkness "all the children of Israel had light in their dwellings." Doubtless they suffered with the Egyptians; their intercourse with each other must have partially been suspended; and discomfort must have been universal among them. But they knew that the end would come; that the darkness had been sent by their Father's God and their God, and meanwhile, "all of them had light within their dwellings."

We hear a great deal said about the typical character of the life of the children of Israel. It is true that there is much in their career, and particularly in this portion of their career, that is typical of the life of the children of God, his spiritual Israel, in this world. But it is easy to believe that many things are types which are not types; and I am disposed to think that many Christian students of the Bible have erred on this side. It is essential to a type that it be preordained as such. If this treatment of the children of Israel is *typical* of God's treatment of his people now, then was it ordained to be typical. But this we do not know; this we can not know. I do not therefore insist upon it. It is enough to say that it is strikingly illustrative of God's treatment of his children in these last days; that there are marked resemblances between the two on which we may dwell with interest and profit. And why should we not expect just such resemblances? It is the same God who is the actor. They were his children, and we are his children. He had a high mission for them to fulfill, and He has a high mission for us to fulfill. So, I say, we ought to expect resemblances, and with this expectation we ought to study the Old Testament. In its narrative of the career of his chosen people, we may, if we search for them, find the same principles of gracious administration, and at last the same infinite and enduring love which shine so conspicuous in the New Testament of our Lord and Saviour. So let us study the older volume; so let us study this statement: "But all the children of Israel had light in their dwellings." We shall find it full of suggestion as to God's treatment of his people in affliction.

I. And first I ask you to notice that in his great providential judgments *God treats his people, and those not his people, exactly alike.* In this respect we discern no difference between the most devoted Christian and the most malignant foe of God; between the children of Israel and the Egyptians. The difference in their condition is not to be ascertained by a study of God's providential visitations. The children of Israel had light within their dwellings, but this was not providential; it was a gracious interference. It is true also, that like the Egyptians, they suffered from the plague. There was darkness over all the land of Egypt—and this includes the dwelling place of the Hebrews—a thick darkness which might be felt. If we could always in affliction, remember the truth thus illustrated, our murmurings at the providence of God would be fewer and less bitter. It is not the purpose of God to remove from the Christian while in this world the great causes of suffering which sin has created. The Christian, not less than the man of the world, is subjected to all the ills that flesh is heir to. I do not stop to explain or justify this appointment of God, to show its consistency with his infinite or his special love. I call your attention simply to the fact, and assert that it has always been so. When darkness came at the command of God over the land of the oppressor, there were not rifts of light over the habitations of Israel. Darkness settled over their homes just as it settled over the homes of their idolatrous foes. And so it is now. When the pestilence that walketh in darkness is abroad in the land, it is perfectly impartial in its blind obedience to the laws of nature. Other things being equal, it enters with the same eagerness and upon the same errand the houses of the good and of the bad. Because you are a Christian you are not freed from sickness, or losses, or bereavement, or death. And yet, who does not know, that the first impulse of every Christian when thus suffering, is to cry out against the Providence which selected him, a child of God, a devoted laborer in the Church, as the object of a terrible visitation. All of us are disposed, when a Christian man is stricken suddenly with sickness, or poverty, or perhaps is taken away in the midst of a useful life, to say: How mysterious the providence of God! How inexplicable the procedure!

Now, it ought to be remembered that God in his Gospel does not come to us with a promise to alter the course of his providential dealings, but with a promise to adjust our spiritual life to them. In other words, the Spirit of God in this world, effects not so much a change in nature, as a change in man's heart. I know that a time is coming when outward circumstances will be changed; when there will be no more darkness of any kind; when the former things will have passed away. But that time has not yet come. Sickness is here. The reign of death continues. "In the world ye shall have tribulation," are the words addressed by our Lord to his disciples. We may not, as Christians, expect exemption from it. When a great judgment is abroad in the land, God's people must anticipate suffering. To anticipate any thing else were to mistake the whole scope and purpose of the redemption which He has provided. That redemption, during our present life, is not distinctively a redemption from worldly ills, but distinctively it is a redemption in the midst of worldly ills. We may not expect to rejoice as freed from tribulation. It will be enough to rejoice in tribulation. When darkness is over all the land of Egypt, Israel must expect that the darkness will visit them, and they must not murmur when the cloud begins to obscure the sky. Let them rather rejoice and give thanks to their covenant God that, unlike the Egyptians, all of them have light in their dwellings.

II. And this brings me to the second truth suggested by the text; the truth, namely, that the comfort and light given to his people, is *individual in its application*. The darkness was over all the land of Egypt, over Israelites as well as over Egyptians; but to the Israelites, his children, God gave a special and gracious relief. And this relief was not a dissipation but a mitigation of the darkness. In some way, either miraculously, or by enabling them through prophecy of the coming disaster to provide for it, He gave them light in their dwellings. There was, at all events, a special and gracious interposition on the part of God to prepare them against the general catastrophe, in which, because dwelling in the same land with his enemies, they were necessarily involved.

And just this is the trait of the provision which God makes for us in his Gospel. Among the many contrasts between his law and his grace, there is no one more striking than this, namely, that the former does not and the latter does take note of individuals. You and I are under the laws by which God's government is administered and by which the operations of his Providence are determined. We can not escape them any more than we can escape his presence. They are executed upon us, just as they are executed upon his most malignant enemies. They know neither the good nor the bad. The fire which destroys so many lives, does not stop in its destructive course because a good man stands in its way. The movement of the accidental missile is not deflected by the presence of a Christian. When the earthquake engulfs a city, the pious and the impious alike are swallowed up. Death knows no distinctions. Just as in Egypt, the darkness is over all the land. But God's grace is always given to mitigate the disaster. There is light vouchsafed the Israelites. His grace does note individuals. It is not only for all mankind in its proffer, but for each man who accepts it at the hand of God. Thus the Gospel blesses separate persons with its gracious and powerful aid. This is a great truth, dear friends, commonplace as its announcement may appear to you. God does not change the course of his government for any man. His inexorable laws move forward like the stars, unhasting and unresting. But this He does, and this is the glory of his Gospel. Whoever becomes an Israelite indeed; whoever separates himself from God's enemies—the Egyptians—is from that moment under the most high God's special care. He may suffer, but God will give him light. He may be a victim, but God will see to it that he is not utterly destroyed. In tribulation he will know that he is not utterly forsaken. I do not now dwell upon the character of the provision which God makes. I only call your attention to the truth that He cares for you as individuals. This is the only comfort that the soul feels to be adequate when foreseeing or feeling disaster that visits all men impartially with misery. Does God know *me?* Does God care for my soul? Will He hear my cry? Will He give me light in the inevitable darkness of sickness and loss and death? With these questions, I turn to his Gospel, and there alone, among the voices of the universe, do I find the response that I desire. The Gospel, I repeat, is a personal Gospel. Its promises are for individuals. God notes the fall of each sparrow, and cares for the special wants of each Christian soul. As separate from all others, I pray and labor, am bereaved and die. In the great crises of my life I am in utter solitude; I tread the winepress alone. And God comes to me and makes provision for me and hears my prayers, just as though I were the only being in the universe. To my dwelling—not to the whole Church of God, but to my separate dwelling—the God of Israel brings light to mitigate the thick darkness. Brethren, if this personal application of the grace of God were not a truth, then were the Gospel no Gospel. What to me were the revelation that the Almighty is merciful in general, if I, as an individual, am not an object of his mercy? No, friends, the blessedness of his grace is that his light is in the humblest and most isolated dwelling where one of his people resides. The supreme comfort of his Gospel is, that no one who accepts Christ may say, my way is hid from the Lord. The consummate loveliness of the Shepherd of Israel is that, as He leadeth his flock, He knoweth and calleth and careth for each member of it by name. And therefore it is, that in calling you, who are not Christ's, to become his, we do not call you to place yourself under a general system of mercy, but we offer you a personal Saviour. He will be as much yours as He would be if you were the only redeemed soul in the universe. He will care for you as though He had no other care. The light of grace in your dwelling will be given you, just as though there were no other dwellings which He would illumine with his presence and his peace.

III. But, again, the text suggests that God's gracious interposition here is not only individual, but also a *partial mitigation of ill;* that is to say, He interposes only enough to enable us to trust Him and to perform the duties which his providence devolves. The darkness was over all the land. The gloom spread where both the Egyptians and the Israelites dwelt. To the latter, we are told, God gave light in their dwellings. The language, however, clearly conveys the fact that it was not an entire dissipation of the darkness. They were not flooded with the noonday light of a new sun. Just enough was given them to enable them to feel that God was their friend; just enough was vouchsafed to assure them that the gloom would not be perpetual; just enough to enable them to go about the necessary duties of life. This, as I read it, was the character of God's gracious interposition. It was not an utter overthrow of the empire of darkness; it was rather a mitigation of its tyranny. And thus the statement of the text pictures as in a parable the partial nature of God's gracious interposition now.

Death is over the land now, as darkness was over the land then; and so are sickness, and losses, and the sad agony of bereavement.

> "The air is full of farewells to the dying,
>   And mournings for the dead.
> The heart of Rachel for her children crying
>   Will not be comforted."

And now, in this darkness, God gives light to his people, to all who repose on his promises. But the light that He gives, like the light to Israel of old, is, it must be confessed, dim at best. Still do we see as through a glass, darkly. He does not open the heavens, and reveal to us the glory with which the sufferings of the present are not worthy to be compared. He does not enable us, in the case of each affliction, to foresee just how it will fulfill his promise of a higher blessedness. He does not permit us to behold those, whom He has taken from us, rejoicing in his presence. The light that He grants is dim; our hearts still suffer because of the mystery of affliction; still does He say to us: "What I do thou knowest not now, but thou shalt know hereafter."

It is true, that what He gives us is invaluable. It suffices to keep the bruised reed from breaking, and the smoking flax from becoming utterly quenched. It is an unspeakable relief in affliction, to possess the promise that He will never leave us nor forsake us; and to possess the assurance that all things work together for our good. But we want more; we cry like the dying German poet: "More light." How hard it is in the darkness to keep from murmuring, even at the mercy-seat! How difficult at times to preserve our faith; so dim is the light within our dwellings, while a thick darkness is all around them. Why is it—we ask ourselves—why is it that God does not dissipate the mystery that is incident to affliction? Why does He not pour down upon us a flood of celestial light, instead of giving us only enough to make the darkness more visible? I do not know that the question can be adequately answered. Indeed, to answer it would be to dissipate the darkness. But I think that it may be said, that God's conduct towards us in affliction, is determined by the reasons which led Him to deal with the Israelites in the same way. He was educating them for a great future; and it was requisite, above all things else, that they should learn to trust Him; and therefore He gave them only light enough to show them that He was their God; and for the rest He bade them trust implicitly to Him. Where had been the virtue of their faith had He not, after evoking, tried it? And so it is with us. He gives us only comfort enough to call forth our faith in Him as an ever-present and almighty Friend, and then calls us to believe Him. It is ours to respond: "Though He slay me, yet will I trust in Him."

IV. Let us notice, as another lesson of the text, the truth, that these mitigations of the darkness of affliction are evidence that *God is our friend*. We understand this, in the case of the children of Israel. When we read the statement that there was darkness over all the land, we describe the darkness as a terrible judgment of God on guilty Egypt; and when we read the statement: "But all the children of Israel had light in their dwellings," we at once say, with what gladness and thanksgiving must the light, faint though it was, have been welcomed by the people of Israel; since it was the evidence of God's friendship—the assurance that the Omnipotence, which had wrought on their foes an awful infliction, was working also in love to them. Of course they poured forth their gratitude in songs of praise; and why should not we also? God gives us light as He gave them light; promise after promise shines into our hearts from the pages of his Word; we do not walk in darkness unrelieved. The light that

God gives us is not all He might bestow; but it is enough to indicate his friendship. Does He not tell us that all things are ours? Does He not bid us cry: "If God be for us, who can be against us?" Now, how shall we treat his promises, when we suffer from sickness or loss or bereavement? Shall we complain because the light is not more brilliant; shall we murmur because these are promises only, and not their fulfillment; shall we return no love because God awakens hope instead of vouchsafing its fruition? This is too often our conduct. But how unworthy of the children of God! Let us seek grace to accept God's promises, not only uncomplainingly, but with gratitude to Him who thus makes us sure of his friendship; of his infinite and everlasting love.

V. But not to dwell further on this, I remark, finally, that the light in the dwellings of Israel was not only the proof of God's friendship; it was also—and this was its special mission—*the pledge of final triumph.* It was the earnest of deliverance from Egypt, and of a victorious entrance into Canaan. I can not stop to dwell on this truth. Indeed, there is needed only its simple statement. Let me say, however, that this is true also of the light which He gives to us. The comfort that we receive on earth is the pledge of heaven. Heaven will be filled with joyous surprises; but heaven itself will be no surprise; for, even here, God has prepared us for it, not only by the promise that it shall be ours, but by some token of his presence that makes it easy for the Christian to believe the promise. In the loneliness, in which He calls us at times to walk along the pathway of our pilgrimage, He permits us to feel the grasp of the hand of the Friend that sticketh closer than a brother. In the deepest grief He sheds abroad his love in our hearts. Why should we not believe in heaven? Why should we not feel sure that we shall survive all losses, and praise God for them? The light which God gives us now, is the pledge of his bestowment on his redeemed people of the city whose light is the Lamb, and in which there shall be no night for evermore.

These words will have been spoken in vain, if they shall not call into more vigorous activity our faith in God. I do not wonder that Christians lose, for the time, their faith and hope. The cares and the adverse occurrences of life are so many and we are so weak, that it would be strange if we did not sometimes doubt God's love. But if we have listened to these words in the right spirit, they can not fail to strengthen our faith in God. The Church of God was founded and the Word of God was written in order to reanimate our drooping graces. And with his Word in our heart, the method of God's dealings is not hard to understand. As we have seen, He does all, in order to lead us nearer to Him and prepare us for the perfect happiness of heaven. And yet, when affliction comes, we are tempted to doubt Him. Brethren, let us uproot these doubts, and let us urge the petition always befitting disciples: "Lord, increase our faith!"

Moreover, these truths should stimulate us to more earnest labor in behalf of the Kingdom of God. For they imply that God is always active in behalf of those who trust in Him. Doubt not, that when God calls you to work, you are called to be a co-worker with God himself. Be sure that nothing that you do for Him will fail to bless the world. "Be ye steadfast, immovable, always abounding in the work of the Lord, forasmuch as ye know that your labor can not be in vain in the Lord."

Finally, let me say, that the light which God gave in Egypt, was given only to his covenant people. It is so now. Until you make yourselves his, no light can fall from heaven on your pathway. Every sorrow's darkness will be unrelieved; for none of your disappointments or losses will you see compensation in a future life. Sickness will be dark; bereavement will be dark; and looking forward to death, how shall you be able to describe the experience which it prophesies, except by the words "a thick darkness that may be felt"—a blackness of darkness? Come, then, to Him who is the Light; who has brought life and immortality to light; and who will welcome all that become his covenant people, to the city of which it is written: "And there shall be no night there."

XXI.

PRAYING THE MORE BECAUSE DOUBTING.

"And the multitude rebuked them, because they should hold their peace; but they cried the more, saying, Have mercy on us, O Lord, thou Son of David."—MATTHEW xx, 31.

These words are found in Matthew's narrative of the healing by our Lord of two blind men at the gate of Jericho, when He was leaving that city on his last journey to Jerusalem. There is an apparent discrepancy between the three accounts of this miracle, which it may be well to explain before taking up our subject. According to Matthew, our Lord healed two blind men on leaving the city; according to Mark, He healed one blind man on leaving the city; according to Luke, one blind man cried for sight when Christ entered the city, and our Lord healed him; and but for Matthew's and Mark's accounts, we should have said that He healed him before He went into the city. The fact seems to be, that our Lord, when entering the city, was invoked by one of these blind men,—Bartimeus by name,—and that, without healing him, He went into the city; purposely postponing the miracle, in order to try his faith; that on the next day, Bartimeus, now joined by another blind man, made his way to the gate, out of which the Lord and his disciples would go on their journey to Jerusalem; that on the approach of Jesus, the two men united their cries for mercy; that Jesus stood still and called them and said: "What will ye that I shall do unto you?" that they answered: "Lord, that our eyes may be opened;" that the miracle of healing was performed, and the two men joined the company of his disciples and followed Him toward Jerusalem.

The incident which our text records occurred, then, at the gate through which our Lord and his company made their exit from Jericho. Advised of the approach of the great Prophet and Healer, the blind men cry out vehemently, in words of worship, of faith and of prayer: "Have mercy on us, O Lord, thou Son of David!" Whether the multitude were priests and Pharisees, who could not bear to hear the Nazarene addressed as the "Son of David," or whether they were disciples, who did not wish their Lord's triumphal procession disturbed by the cries of beggars, or whether they were both, I do not know. At any rate, the multitude rebuked the blind men, commanding them to hold their peace. Instead of obeying, the sightless beggars, we are told, *cried the more*, saying: "Have mercy on us, O Lord, thou Son of David!"

The miracles of our Lord and the record of them serve three purposes. In the first place, as evidences of his power over nature, they authenticate his claims as a Teacher sent from God. In the second place, since most of them are miracles of blessing, they are intended to reveal his mercy to men. And in the third place, they illustrate truths and facts and methods connected with his gracious dealings, and with the approach of men to Him for the mercy and the grace they need. In other words, they are enacted parables and discourses. It is in this third aspect of it, that I shall treat the incident from which I have taken my text. Thus regarded, the incident is full of interest, and we shall be instructed and strengthened, I trust, by making it the subject of this morning's study. There are three related topics on which I shall speak: man crying to God in prayer and tempted to desist; the proper conduct of man when thus tempted—he should cry the more; and the considerations which should make this conduct ours.

I. First, then, we have here a picture of man crying to God in prayer, and tempted to desist.

The blind men, having heard of Jesus, of his power to give sight, and of his willingness to exert this power, and having learned that this hope of the poor and needy was in the city, and would soon leave by a certain gate, of course hastened to it; and, as their quick ears caught the sound of footsteps which indicated his approach, they did the most natural thing in the world,—they cried out in prayer: "Have mercy on us, have mercy on us, O Lord, thou Son of David!" No doubt the words, "thou Son of David," grated harshly on the ears of the priests and the enemies of Christ. No doubt, also, the disciples of Christ felt that a procession like theirs should not be interrupted by the loud and anxious voices of the mendicants. And therefore, Bartimeus and his companion were told to hold their peace. Pharisees said: "This is no Son of David, but a Galilean peasant." And disciples said: "This is no time to trouble the Master; hinder Him not, with your private griefs, from hastening to the

Holy City to seize his rightful throne." One said: "He will not heal you, because He can not." And another said: "He will not heal you, because the hour is not propitious." And it would have been no wonder if the blind men, influenced by these calls to desist, had ceased their praying and remained in darkness all their lives.

So are all of us tempted to desist from crying to God, whenever we approach Him in the spirit of real prayer. I say the spirit of real prayer; for if, instead of praying, we only "say our prayers," we shall not thus be tempted to desist. The tempter does not esteem it worth his while to hold back a man from "using vain repetitions as the heathen do." Why should he? The man is doing the tempter's own work. But if we pray; if out of a sense of need like that felt by these blind beggars, and in faith and hope like those which drove them to the gate of Jericho, we cry from the depths of our hearts; then, let us be sure, we shall be told to hold our peace, not only by the devil, but by the world and flesh as well. Who does not know this? Who has not heard in his heart the suggestion not to pray, as clearly as if it had been audibly syllabled? It is these suggestions, springing out of our own hearts, pressed upon us by our association with the world, and inspired, some of them, as I verily believe, by another order of beings, that make real prayer so hard a spiritual exercise. For there is nothing hard in prayer, in itself considered. Prayer is not only rational; it is instinctive. Every man naturally cries to God in his extremity. Every man feels spiritual wants that he knows he can not himself supply. And whenever the word is spoken: "Pray to God," and he hears the assurance: "God is more willing to answer than earthly parents are to give good gifts unto their children," he must be something else than human if he does not feel a strong impulse to lift up his voice in earnest petition to his Father in heaven.

But let him act in accordance with this impulse, and he will find himself full of voices commanding or enticing him to desist. Why, he will be asked by himself, should he trouble himself with spiritual wants? Let him eat and drink; let him take what the world affords him, and leave his spirit to be cared for in the spiritual world. Or the thought will arise within him: "God does not hear me; I have no ground for believing that He answers prayer. Indeed, He is infinite and unchangeable, and my words can not alter his perfect plans, or change the movements of his invariable laws." Or he will be beset by suggestions of his own sinfulness, and the impossibility of his being regarded favorably by a God who is of purer eyes than to behold iniquity. Or, as often happens, in the midst of his earnest petition, he will be tempted to cease by the consideration that God is omniscient; that He knows man's wants without prayer. Why should man cry to Him? Is not prayer the veriest mockery in which one can engage? Who, that recalls his own spiritual history, does not know that by voices and suggestions, like these which I have named, the tempted man is at times brought to a state in which prayer is the hardest of spiritual exercises to carry forward in sincerity; a state in which God seems to be nothing, or, at least, nothing to him; a state in which the firmament is for him only a brazen and impenetrable vault? Then arises the terrible danger, that the human spirit will surrender in spiritual conflict, and renew allegiance to the world and sense and sin. I say, that it is no uncommon experience—this experience of temptation, made strong by a multitude of considerations, to desist from crying to God in prayer. From Jacob the wrestler onward, every earnest spiritual man has felt the temptation. Augustine, Luther, Baxter, Edwards and Payson all record it as part of their experience. It is just this experience, which, in our day, furnishes ground for the assertion, that Christian living is still the "good fight of faith." We do not wrestle now, as our predecessors did, with hostile governments and persecuting heathen. So far as exterior and conventional Christianity is concerned, nothing could be more respectable. It is the *cultus* of the times and the nation. One's standing in society and one's reputation among his associates are rather helped than hurt by his connection with the Church of God. But it is true, nevertheless, that there never was a time, when the movement of personal Christianity was more distinctly marked "by all the arduousness of a battle in its progress, and by all the glory of a victory in its termination." For never has there been a time when the seen has so obtrusively asserted itself as against the unseen, and the temporal so engrossed men to the exclusion of the eternal. Science, literature, civilization, language, art—all the interests and implements and employments of modern life—sometimes seem to me to be the selected instruments of the subtilest and evilest of created beings, to tempt men away from the belief that the living God is their Father, and to constrain them to desist from crying to God. And, therefore, for a man to live a life of real prayer, to bring his spiritual and temporal wants, habitually and sincerely and believingly, to his heavenly Father, is to engage in a veritable combat; and a combat, the more fierce and the more difficult to wage successful, just because he wrestles not against flesh and blood, but against enemies far more insidious, against doubts and habits of mind, which, I must believe, are the last resort and the consummate artifice of principalities and powers, of the rulers of the darkness of this world. O friends, if the temptation of which I am speaking has assailed you, believe me that you are in no slight danger. And if you have ever yielded to it, you have put yourselves in imminent peril of that awful condition, in which men are past all spiritual feeling, and are doomed to what the Bible calls the second death.

II. And, therefore, it becomes us seriously to ask, how, when it assails us, is the temptation to be met? How are we to resist these doubts and suggestions that induce us to cease from prayer? In order to answer this question, let us revert to the narrative. The two blind beggars were assaulted by this very temptation. The multitude interrupted them, and bade them hold their peace. How did they resist it? They cried the more. And this, brethren, is at once the Biblical and the only philosophical method of resisting the same temptation to-day. When tempted to desist, "let us cry the more."

You can easily imagine another mode of dealing with this temptation. You can imagine a man—borne down by the force of a habit that hinders his growth in holiness—bringing the habit to God in prayer, and asking for strength to enable him to conquer it. But as he cries to God, doubts as to the efficacy of prayer suggest themselves. The burdened soul thus tempted to desist, says: "I will postpone my praying until I shall have dissolved my doubts." The mode which I propose for your adoption is the mode adopted by these blind men; in spite of doubt and temptation of whatever kind, still to urge the petition; and because of the temptation itself, to cry so much the more. This I believe to be the only safety of the imperiled soul. At any rate, regarded as conduct, it is both Biblical and philosophical.

It is Biblical, I say. It is supported by the great promise of the Son of God: "He that will do the will of God shall know of the doctrine." What is the meaning of these words of the Master, but that obedience is the organ of spiritual knowledge; that the one divinely appointed method of dissipating doubts and of destroying the force of temptation, is bravely and persistently to continue walking on the path of revealed duty. It is as if the great Teacher had said: "Do not wait until duty has fully commended itself to your understanding, before practicing it; do not postpone its performance until you are able to answer all objections. Let it be enough to know that it is my will. Then while you are performing it the doubts will be dissipated; the objections will be answered in your experience; you will see the duty's reasonableness; you will know the doctrine, that it is of God." It was precisely in accordance with the spirit of these words of Christ, that the blind men acted. We can not doubt, that it would have been impossible for them to reply to all the reasons that Pharisee or disciple might have urged against praying to Christ at this time. Had they engaged in argument with the doubts thus raised, they would have desisted from praying, and would have failed to obtain the incalculable boon they sought. But instead of this, they persisted in their cries. To all argument, and to all command to be silent, they replied effectively with more vehement solicitation, until the Lord spake the word of power, and gave them the blessing that they sought.

And just this, if I rightly read his Word, is what God would have us do in respect to prayer. We can not prevent these temptations; we can not hinder these suggestions of doubt. If I may so say, they are in the atmosphere we breathe. The "times" are favorable to them; our own hearts are by nature hospitable to them; the engrossments of this world help to give them force; Christianity, as a personal experience, would not be the sore combat that it is but for them; we can not expect to be freed from the temptation of them, nor can we take time to answer them as they arise. Perhaps we have not the ability or the culture required for an adequate reply. But this we can do; and this, both the example of Bartimeus and the promise of Christ call us to do. We can oppose them with more vigorous prayer; we can lift up our voices in more earnest petition; the darker the clouds above us, the more piercing can become the voices of our longing souls. "We can cry the more." And unless the words of Christ be false we shall gain the victory. Prayer will not only be answered, but temptation will become innoxious, and doubt will die. Faith will revive, and God as our Father and answering Friend will manifest Himself anew to us, as He does not unto the world. I do not hesitate to say, that because of the use of this very weapon of persistent loyalty to duty, triumph has issued from many a spiritual conflict, which otherwise would have resulted in terrible defeat. Many a Jacob has thus come out of a night of prayer, "Israel, a prince of God." And be sure that if you are thus faithful when faith is attacked; if you continue to cry, even when you must cry out of the depths of doubt; if you pray so much the more, even when tempted to doubt prayer and God alike, you also will triumph, and your soul will be saved.

For observe, that not only is this the Biblical method of attacking doubt and temptation, but it is also the philosophical method. Loyalty to duty, even when its reason is not understood, is the surest and the swiftest method of reaching a comprehension of it. Is it not true, that in matters of education, for example, the one right method is to begin with practice and so to ascend to theory? You are teaching your little one the alphabet. Do you desist until you can satisfy your child's mind as to the usefulness of the characters whose configuration he is learning? You are not so irrational. On the contrary, in spite of his doubts you persist and you compel him to persist, knowing that the quickest way to dissipate his doubts is to hold him to what seems to him an unmeaning task. Or permit me to take an example from my own professional experience. There are times when I am physically well, and yet when, in preparing myself to speak from the pulpit, I find my mind infertile, my thoughts moving sluggishly, and the composition of a sermon the hardest and most distasteful of tasks. Now what is the one rational, the one philosophical method of overcoming the temptation to postpone my appropriate labor to a more convenient season? What, but in spite of all infertility and sluggishness, faithfully to engage in my appointed work. And I am telling what has been my experience scores of times, when I say that the one way to overcome obstacles to composition is, in spite of reluctance, to engage in the work with redoubled diligence. The same thing is true of moral actions. There is many a man who finds beneficence a terribly difficult duty. It is the easiest thing in the world to call up the most specious objections to its performance. It is hard not to postpone it indefinitely. Doubts as to its efficacy, the temptations of selfishness, and a host of other difficulties oppose one's Christian instinct to do good as he has opportunity. And over and above them all will come the suggestion: "Well, even if I do give against all these opposing feelings, my giving will not be the expression of benevolence." Now if, in spite of them, the man is simply loyal to duty; if, courageously and by a painful effort, he acts in accordance with his benevolent impulse, who does not know that these temptations will soon lose their force, and that what he began as a severe duty, will become a privilege, in whose exercise he will learn how far more blessed it is to give than to receive! Thus man learns that in the keeping of God's commands there is great reward. Thus he learns the law, which underlies Christ's words: "He that will do my will, shall know of the doctrine."

It is just this great law, operative in all departments of human life, that I would have you apply to the characteristic act and habit of the Christian life; the act and habit of earnest prayer to God. Of course there are temptations to desist from praying. They are many, and they are mighty. Your flesh, your business, your mind, your associations with the world, your sinfulness and the great enemy of your souls unite in bidding you hold your peace, just as Pharisees and disciples united to restrain blind Bartimeus and his friend from crying to the Great

Physician and Redeemer. What shall you do? O, friends, what but follow the example of these blind men, and on your bended knees, and out of your burdened souls, cry again and again—cry the more: "Lord, have mercy on us." There are repetitions that are not vain. And repetitions like these are by no means in vain. The Bible, Christian experience and the constitution of man unite in proclaiming this to be the one method of conquering doubt, and of cleaving a way to a position in which we shall find prayer a constant power, a never-failing delight.

III. And that I may further commend this habit to you, let me, finally, reinforce what I have said, by simply naming some other considerations which should lead you to adopt it.

Is not prayer, let me ask, an instinct of the soul? What is more natural to a human being, when all his own resources have failed, than to cry to God? Doubt as you will prayer's efficacy, you will never destroy the ineffaceable instinct which will at last drive you in extremity of body or spirit to the Most High. Is not prayer God's appointed means of obtaining aid from Him? What words could be more clear than the words of Christ: "Every one that asketh receiveth, and he that seeketh findeth, and to him that knocketh it shall be opened"? Is it not the one rational means? Speculate as we will, there can not be a more reasonable method of seeking the spiritual or temporal benefits we need but which we have not power to obtain for ourselves, than the method of asking them of Him who is Head over all things. Nay, rational or irrational, is it not the only means? What are we to do about the great facts of sin and death and the looking for of judgment, if we are not to pray to God? And, finally, has not Christ Himself indicated that He places the highest value on importunate prayer, on this "crying the more"? Is not just this the lesson of the story of these blind men? Is not just this the meaning of the miracle wrought for the Syrophœnician woman? And what but this is the great lesson that He would teach us in the parable of the importunate widow and the unjust judge?

My hearers, there is no more imminent or terrible danger than just this danger of desisting from prayer, when tempted to do so. There is but one way to resist temptation and to overcome doubt, and that is to pray the more. Our Christian life, so far as it is active, will become weak and ineffective unless we pray. That is an eloquent passage, in which the great Apostle to the Gentiles portrays the Christian, panoplied in the armor and bearing the weapons of a soldier of the Roman legion. How suggestive of the number and prowess of the foes of our spiritual life! How vividly it brings before us our danger! And yet, one would suppose that the armor of defense and the weapons of offense were in themselves sufficient. The shield of faith, the helmet of salvation, and the sword of the Spirit; are not these enough to obtain for us the victory? So thought not the great and inspired Apostle. He knew the foes. He had known doubt. He had been in the thickest of the fight against principalities and powers; and, therefore, he added to his exhortation to take the whole armor of God, this other exhortation, without obedience to which all else will be found to fail: "Praying always, with all prayer and supplication, in the spirit." I repeat his exhortation to-day. I bid you recall your past experience. What victories have you won over appetite and passion worth naming, that you did not win by the power of earnest prayer? What growth have you attained, that you did not attain by calling upon God? What temptations have you successfully resisted, what graces cultivated, what spiritual joy achieved, when not aided by earnest and importunate wrestling with God in solitude? And now, when tempted to give it up, by the devil or the world or the appetites of the flesh or the doubts that float before you, will you yield in the face of your experience; in opposition to God's word; in spite of the instincts of your soul, and against sound philosophy? What madness! O brethren, by the value of your immortal souls, by the glories of the righteousness you may achieve in Christ, dare not yield to these beguilements. Recall these blind men by the gate of Jericho, and when bidden to hold your peace, cry the more; cry the more! And you shall know that prayer is no mockery, that God hears and responds and blesses and saves.

It is because God reveals Himself as the prayer-hearing, the responsive God, that as a minister of his Word I dare to offer Him, as a Saviour, to individual men and women; to individual men and women, I say. This plan of redemption is no general system of salvation that regards masses only. If it were such a system, I could not speak to you, as individuals, in words of hope. You might reply to me: "What to me would be the redemption of the masses, if I were left out?" You will not be left out, if only you will cry to Him. The Redeemer is marching in triumphal procession to Jerusalem. Crowds attend Him. But suddenly two blind beggars seated by the gate of Jericho cry to Him in prayer: "Have mercy on us." Does He reply: "I must go on to Jerusalem, to fulfill my great work for the masses of humanity; I can not stop to attend to the wants of two poor beggars?" So thought the multitude. And they bid the blind men hold their peace. Not so the Son of God. His redemption is for individual souls; and, therefore, the blind are healed, and follow Him rejoicing. So is it now. Think not that in the vastness of his realm, He can not or will not regard you, if you cry to Him. Say not: "My way is hid from the Lord, and my judgment is passed over from my God." The government of the universe is, indeed, on his shoulder. He binds the sweet influences of the Pleiades and looses the bands of Orion:

> "His state
> Is kingly: thousands at his bidding speed,
> And post o'er land and ocean without rest."

But his consummate greatness is in his condescension. Not a sparrow falls without Him. There is no being so small that He will not heed him. Betake yourself, O wearied, blind, and sinful soul, to Him. Cry: "Lord, have mercy on me; have mercy on me!" And when doubts and temptations bid you hold your peace, cry the more. And you will hear his words: "What wilt thou that I shall do unto thee?" You will feel the touch of the hand that was pierced. A new sight will be given you. A new world will be open to you. And right before you, as before Bartimeus of old, in the glory of his infinite grace, you will behold your loving and healing Physician, your redeeming and omnipotent God.

XXII.

CASTING CARE ON GOD.

"Casting all your care upon Him; for He careth for you."—
I. Peter v, 7.

This Epistle was addressed not to any church or churches, but to individual Christians. When, therefore, the writer says: "God careth for you," the particular truth which he announces is not God's watchfulness over a mass of men, but his care for individuals. The writer of the Epistle is the Apostle Peter. As Peter is portrayed in the Gospels, he is most distinctly marked by his oscillation between the two extremes of rash self-confidence and timorous anxiety. It is Peter who is bold enough to attempt to walk on the water; but he has scarcely touched the yielding element, when he cries out in fear: "Lord, save me, I perish!" It is Peter who alone dares to follow Christ to the High Priest's palace; but he is no sooner accused of fellowship with Christ, than he denies Him with cursing. It is clear, however, from this exhortation, that his spiritual habit has undergone an entire revolution. Here is no timorous anxiety about the future, for he casts away all care.

At the same time there is no rash confidence in himself, for he casts his care on God.

It would be interesting and instructive to take up the life of Peter, and study the progress of this revolution, the causes which effected it, and the incidents by which it was marked. But this morning, I desire not so much to illustrate my theme by a reference to Peter's career, as to make it practical by referring to your own. Both the interest and importance of the subject on which I purpose to speak to-day, are due to the fact that our lives are such, and our minds are so constituted, that we are a prey to continual anxiety. I suppose that the unhappiness of men and women is due far more largely to what they fear than to what they experience. It is the evils which impend rather than the disasters which occur, that make the soul sorrowful and the countenance sad. When the worst has come and passed; when the financial panic has swept away property, or the loved one has been carried to his last resting place, the soul of man begins to regather its powers, and, though chastened and sad, looks to the future not without hope. This is neither so destructive in its influence on happiness, nor so continuous as that anxious look toward the future which we call by so many names. When I simply repeat the words; fear, foreboding, dread, anxiety, apprehension, solicitude, alarm, concern, care,—I make evident, that, by multiplying synonyms, we confess the universality and the misery of the feeling. It is not so much the present as it is the future—big with evils whose vastness we can not measure, with evils often exaggerated by excited imaginations—that depresses or distresses us. Are you parents? You would gladly endure far greater pain than that which you suffer now, if only you could be sure that your children's lives will be all that you desire. Are you in business? It is not mere work, mental or physical, that is breaking you down. If you are breaking, you know that you are succumbing to anxiety in view of dreaded contingencies that may arise; contingencies of which you have no certain knowledge, and over which you can exercise no certain control. Day after day, we live in suspense more or less painful. No man can say, I am wholly free from it. The future grows darker with multiplying ghosts of ill, while he is advancing from youth to manhood, or moving forward from manhood to old age. And, as for the future life, unless either by sheer skepticism or by faith in Christ he can sweep them away, it is filled with shapes of evil; for there is in every sinful soul "a fearful looking for of judgment and fiery indignation." And thus it is, that our forms are bent too early, and our faces are too soon corrugated, and we speak of ourselves as care-worn, and talk of the increasing burdens of life, and confess that, notwithstanding the blessings of God which are crowded on every side and into every moment of our lives, it is still true that "man is born to trouble as the sparks to fly upward.")

You will observe that I am speaking not of outward infliction, but of an inward state. It is a habit of mind that makes outward blessings powerless to bestow happiness, and that increases the power of affliction. If there were no remedy for this state of mind, I should not be justified in speaking of it. But the remedy I bring to-day, is the truth stated and the exhortation addressed to Christians by the Apostle Peter: "Casting all your care upon Him; for He careth for you."

The text, as I have said, is addressed to Christians. Let no one, who is not a Christian, complain that the comfort it contains is not for him. Christ is offered to all of us. If we will not accept Him, what right have we to complain that the consolations of his Gospel are denied us? The fountain of life is flowing; what right have we to complain that we are dying of thirst, if we will not drink? The way to life is open, plain and free; what right have we to cry out against God if, refusing to walk thereon, we do not reach the city of the great King? The comfort of these words is for all who will accept it in Christ, in whom alone God's promises are fulfilled. Remembering then, that though they are addressed to Christians, Christ is offered to all men; let us attend, first, to the truth announced in the text: "God careth for you;" and, secondly, to the exhortation: "Cast all your care upon Him."

I. If you have never read the astronomical discourses of Thomas Chalmers, I advise you to do so at once. I shall not soon forget the profound impression made on me, when, for the first time, I read the first of them, in which he endeavors to make real to the imagination the vastness of the visible universe, and our insignificance before the Creator; the discourse in which occurs the passage: "Though this earth were to be burned up, though the trumpet of its dissolution were sounded, though yon sky were to pass away as a scroll, and every visible glory which the finger of Divinity has inscribed on it were to be put out forever,—an event so awful to us and to every world in our vicinity, by which so many suns would be extinguished, and so many varied scenes of life and of population would rush into forgetfulness,— what is it in the high scale of the Almighty's workmanship? A mere shred, which, though scattered into nothing, would leave the universe of God one entire scene of greatness and of majesty." It was the same impression, made by a view of the same firmament—though his vision was unaided by the modern astronomy—that evoked from the Psalmist the mournful question: "When I consider the heavens the work of thy fingers, what is man that Thou art mindful of him?" All of us find it difficult to believe, that in the vastness of his realm the Ruler of the universe takes special note of individual men. Often arises the complaint now, as it arose of old: "My way is hid from the Lord, and my judgment is passed over from my God." The thought of his regard for each of us seldom serves to abate our wearing anxiety.

And yet, if Christianity is true, God does care for each man every moment of his life. Indeed, there is a hint of this in nature. I have quoted from one, permit me to quote from another of the discourses of the great Scottish divine. In the third astronomical discourse—the discourse on "The Extent of the Divine Condescension"—he says, that "it was the telescope which enabled us in some degree to realize the vastness of the universe. But about the time of its invention, another instrument was formed which rewarded the inquisitive spirit of man with a scene no less wonderful. This was the microscope. The one led me to see a system in every star, the other shows me a world in every atom. The one taught me that this mighty globe, with the whole burden of its people and its countries, is but a grain of sand on the high field of immensity. The other teaches me that every grain of sand may harbor within it the tribes and families of a busy population. The one tells me of the insignificance of the world I tread upon. The other redeems it from all its insignificance, for it tells me that in the leaves of every forest, and in the flowers of every garden, and in the waters of every rivulet there are worlds teeming with life and numberless as are the glories of the firmament." Thus if the observation of the universe in its vastness suggests the thought that God's Kingdom is too great to justify the belief that we are noticed by Him, the observation of any portion, however minute, indicates that there is nothing too small for his constant and superintending care. So if science makes faith in God's care difficult, science offers to faith abundant aid.

Moreover, the necessary laws of thought ought to help our faith. Our conception of God involves his knowledge of each of his creatures; though we too often think of Him as altogether like ourselves. How little we know of our fellows' lives! We observe an action, and at once, we begin to generalize from it about the character of the man who committed it; and we are tempted to suppose that a like process goes on in the mind of God. A little reflection, however, would impress upon our minds the truth, that if there is a God who designed and has created the universe, He must possess faculties so perfect as to discern all that it contains, and to foresee all the events which will occur in its career.

But much as faith is aided by science and the laws of thought,—it is, after all, the assertions of the Word of God which constitute faith's warrant. The Bible everywhere brings into view a God who notices not all only, but each of his creatures. His care of them is involved in the truths that He hears prayer, and that He will reward every man according to his work. In his first great address to his disciples, our Lord distinctly asserts, that not a sparrow falls without his Father's notice, and that the hairs of our heads are numbered. Each act, each event, each joy and sorrow, every plan for the future, every circumstance which aids in making up the history of the hour, are before Him. He knows all and directs all, in the fulfillment of his own wise and loving purposes.

You will notice again, that the statement is not, God careth *about* you, but God careth *for* you. If our littleness awakens doubt as to whether God notices us at all, that doubt is scarcely dissipated before another, arising from our sinfulness, springs into activity. When the sense of sin is vivid, we say inevitably: "God may indeed notice us, but that which a Holy Being must notice first and care about the most is our sinfulness." Whenever the human spirit is penetrated with the truth, so often insisted on in the Bible, that God can not look on sin with allowance, it is troubled. Sinful men fly from the thought of God. This explains the well-known, though not always confessed disinclination of men to pray. The hardest invitation to accept, is that to which is joined the most gracious assurance in the whole Bible—the assurance that our crimson sin will be made white as snow. It is hard to accept, because it is an invitation to solemn communion with a Holy God: "Come, now, and let us reason together." The sense of sin is the greatest foe to faith in God's love. But this is the assurance of the text: that God cares not only about us but for us. I would not make too much of a single preposition; but the word "for" translates a preposition which puts beyond all doubt not only God's thought of men, but his most favorable and loving thought. It is as if the Apostle had said: "Little though you are, God sees your individual life; and sinful though you are, his loving heart throbs still for you in infinite and personal affection." O, that we could grasp this truth most firmly when the thought of our iniquity threatens to overwhelm us;— the truth that perfect as God is, He looks on us as his children; that, wayward and unloving and uncaring as He often finds us, the eye, that slumbers not, regards us with more than parental fondness, and the arm, that wearies not, is always active in providing and protecting!

But we have not yet unfolded the whole truth stated in the text. It is not only true that God cares for us, *although* we are weak and sinful; He cares for us *because* of our weakness and sinfulness. The exact truth stated by the Apostle is brought out when the sentence is thus paraphrased: "Because you can not care for yourselves; because you are weak and sinful, you are one of your heavenly Father's anxieties." For the Greek verb, translated *careth*, expresses anxiety when used in the form in which it is found in the text. And the figure which forms the basis of this comforting declaration, is that of a Father who, not having to think anxiously of most of his children, has still one weak and wayward son, who fills his mind with anxious thoughts, towards whom his heart goes out in a kind of love that he can not feel for the rest; and for whose protection and guidance and defense and final welfare he is, therefore, continuously and actively employed. A mother, though she may love all her children equally, does not care for them equally, is not equally anxious about them all. For whom is it that her heart throbs with anxiety? For whom is it that with tears and sighs she pleads the promises of a covenant God? Is it not for the weak and tempted son—the one for whom enticements seem too strong? It is for him that her *care* is active; and it is active just because he is weak and sinful. When I think of the mighty and the holy Gabriel, obedient to all the laws which God has ordained, I do not think of God as anxiously caring for him. He is in harmony with the whole creation. But when I think of a man tempted by sinful passions, allured by the world's pleasures, perplexed by doubts, bowed in the dust by affliction, I easily believe that God is active in protecting and in guiding him, to the end that he may be glorified and beatified.

Instead then of letting our weakness and sinfulness lead us to doubt, the thought of them should deepen our faith in the declaration: "God careth for you." We are not orphans; we are the accepted children of God. The way before us is often dark. Our feet bleed on the rough pathway, that He compels us to tread. One and another of our loved companions vanish from our sight as we journey on our pilgrimage. Often we mistake mirage for flowers and palms and fountains. The fierce heat of the sun scorches us, and our burdens grow more heavy; or blinding storms sweep across the plain, and we fear that God has forsaken us altogether. No, friends! God cared for Israel in the wilderness, in a sense in which He never cared for the loftiest of the angels. And He cares for you as He cared for Israel in the desert. Because you need his watchfulness, He watches over you. Doubt Him not, but trust Him; believe his words: "I will never leave you or forsake you," and cast all your care upon Him; for He careth for you.

II. But if God cares for us, what have we to do? And the text makes specific reply: "Cast all your care upon Him."

Here, just as in studying the truth of God's care, we shall best ascertain our duty by studying the very words of the text. And first, you will notice that the Apostle advises not a mere *flinging away* of our cares to the winds, an indifference to our troubles and anxieties; but a most solemn and religious laying of them on the Most High. The meaning of the text is not, God careth for you, therefore fling care aside, and eat and drink and be merry; but God careth for you, therefore cast all your cares on *God*. There is a striking congruity between the truth and the exhortation which we must not fail to notice. Had Peter been a Stoic philosopher, he would not have said: "God careth for you," but, "You are in the hands of an awful system, of which physical evil is a part"; and his exhortation would not have been: "Cast your care on God," but, "Oppose to the inevitable evil the fortitude of an unbroken spirit." Had he been an Epicurean, he would not have said: "God careth for you," but, "Chance has sent these evils. Fight chance the only way in which you can, by drowning all forgetfulness in a sea of pleasures." But he was neither a Stoic nor an Epicurean, but a Christian, and as the truth he uttered was Christian, so is the exhortation. God is our Father; He loves us with an affection past understanding. If we are perplexed, and anxious, let us trust God just as a loving child trusts its parent. If our burdens are too heavy to bear, or their meaning too dark to discern, or their issue too far in the future to discover, let us cast them on God. He can bear them, and He will bear them. His heart beats with infinite affection; his power is omnipotence; his wisdom is perfect; his knowledge is omniscience. If we believe the truth, do we obey the injunction? What is our habit with reference to the things that wear, or pain, or weary us; the cares that seam our faces, and bend our forms? Where have we laid them? Have we confided them to friends? Vain is the help of man. Have we flung them to the winds, and said, in our impatience, we will not think of them? What comfort is there in that? They belong to God. He says to us, "Trust them to me. Confide in me." Have you done so? Have you cast your care *on God?*

Notice again, that the Apostle does not exhort us here to cast our *separate* cares upon God, but to cast our *whole care* on Him. The truth in the Apostle's mind, and the truth that should be in our own minds, is that our whole life is one. The cares with which we suffer to-day, and those with which we suffered yesterday, are not separate units, but are connected in that one plan of God which binds together all the events of life, just as one controlling purpose of our own dominates and reduces to unity all our separate acts. Now the Apostle says to us: "As God has a plan in your life, which in his providence He is fulfilling; as that plan was devised in infinite love; as He is thus not only overruling each separate bereavement and loss for your advantage, but is making all things work together for your good; do not deem it sufficient to take each care to Him as a separate experience, but in one mighty and blessed and all-including act of trust and self-surrender, cast all your care on God; the whole of life with all its troubles and joys and unknown issues." To translate these words by those of another Apostle, each of us is called to hide his whole life with Christ in God.

It is only when we have performed this all-including duty, that we are prepared to bring our separate cares to Him. I have no doubt that every man has special anxieties that he wishes God to dissipate. One is anxious for wealth, and another for power, and another for position. And each is quite ready to bring his special anxiety to God, and to ask Him to relieve it by bestowing the desired blessing. But, this is not the exhortation of the Apostle. He calls you, first of all, to bring your whole life to God, to cast the whole of it on Him, in full faith of his assurance, that whether wealth or poverty, sickness or health is yours, He is still caring for you, and is making all your experiences your servants. When you have done this, and then only, will you be in a frame of mind to bring to Him each separate anxiety that is wearing you. And, therefore, I put the question: Have you gone to Him with this whole life of yours, and trusting in his love revealed in Jesus Christ, have you said: "My life is too perplexing for me to understand. I am in thy hands, and Thou art infinite Love. I cast it all on Thee, for Thou carest for me." Only when you shall have thus rolled the burden of your whole life on Him, can you know the peace which passes understanding.

And this leads me to remark, finally, that the exhortation of the Apostle contemplates a distinct and conscious *co-operation* of the human spirit with God in labor. Obviously the text does not exhort us to any thing like indolence. The statement is not: "God careth for you; therefore do not take up the cares of life. Let them lie unnoticed and forgotten." The Apostle is very far from teaching that the Christian is to shrink from duties, because they involve anxieties. He says to us: "God cares for you; his heart throbs with infinite love. Therefore take up the duties of life; but, whatever anxiety may be involved in their performance, cast that on God. Do not be troubled while you work. Yours is the planting and the nurture; it is his to send the rain and sunshine, and at last to grant the harvest." Shall the farmer neglect to plow the ground or plant the seed because he knows the faithfulness of God? On the contrary, for this very reason he plows and plants; and as for the result, he commits it all to God, who has promised that seed-time and harvest shall not fail. Labor then in the lot in which God calls you to stand. But having exhausted all your own resources, do not perplex your soul about the results that belong to God. Cast all anxiety concerning them on Him, rejoicing in the promise: "He that goeth forth weeping, bearing precious seed, shall doubtless return again rejoicing, bearing his sheaves with him." For the promises of God provide for every contingency; and the history of the Church proves his fidelity in their fulfillment. What more, Christian parent, can you desire than his great covenant with parents; what more, Christian laborer, than the assurance that no labor in Him can be in vain; what more, O Church of God, than the promise: "Lo, I am with you alway, even unto the end of the world"? Let us not weary ourselves, therefore, with anxious thought about the results of our labors; but having done all and borne all, let us rejoice that our gifts will be supplemented from his infinite riches; that our sacrifices will be made blessed by the power of his sacrifice; that our poor speech will be followed by the demonstration of the Spirit, whom

He has promised who is over all God blessed for evermore.

Permit me to say, again, that the comfort of the truth that God cares for each of us, is for Christians alone. It is promised to you only on condition of your acceptance of it in Jesus Christ. In view of the anxieties of life that are wearing and breaking you; and the death in whose experience all your earthly ambitions will be destroyed, come to Him, in whom alone all anxieties can be dissipated, all afflictions become steps in the path to heaven, and death itself be made the minister of everlasting life. Cast your soul on Him, and with your soul all wasting care; and you will thank Him for the peace that passes all understanding; the peace which no man can know until his life is hid with Christ in God.

XXIII.

THE FOUNDATION AND THE BUILDING.

"For other foundation can no man lay than that is laid, which is Jesus Christ. Now if any man build upon this foundation gold, silver, precious stones, wood, hay, stubble; every man's work shall be made manifest: for the day shall declare it, because it shall be revealed by fire; and the fire shall try every man's work of what sort it is. If any man's work abide which he hath built thereupon, he shall receive a reward. If any man's work shall be burned, he shall suffer loss: but he himself shall be saved; yet so as by fire."—I. CORINTHIANS iii, 11–15.

There are some difficulties connected with the interpretation of this passage, but they are not of sufficient magnitude to hide the general meaning of the Apostle's language, or to obscure the practical lessons that he endeavored by means of it to impress on the members of the Church at Corinth. If we shall come to the study of the passage, earnestly seeking to know its relation to our own lives and duties, and hopes, we shall find no difficulty or obscurity whatever.

However difficult it may be to apply it to our lives, the figure is a familiar one, and the picture in the mind of the Apostle is easily called before us. We have presented to us a builder, erecting a structure on a foundation already laid and assigned to him, the only possible foundation, indeed, for a building like the one that he has been called to erect. He is aware, while engaged in his work, that a day is coming when it will be subjected to the test of fire; and wisdom dictates the choice of those materials alone that will outlast such an ordeal. The Apostle, however, suggests the possibility, indeed, the probability, that not having continually before his mind "the day that shall try and the fire that shall declare his work," the builder will be led to use materials that must be consumed, as "wood, hay and stubble;" instead of "gold, silver and precious stones." He points out the loss which the builder will suffer, and contrasts it with the reward which another builder, who holds distinctly before him the day of visitation, will enjoy. He closes the passage with the comforting assurance, that, because he has built upon a foundation which will abide, the man who builds with even perishable materials will not be consumed with his work, but will be saved; yet he adds: "Saved so as by fire."

If we keep in view the fact, that he is addressing those who profess to be Christians, we shall easily catch his meaning. As Christians, we are not only living, but building—building characters which shall one day be tested in the presence of God; and by means of an ordeal, which the Apostle teaches is so radical as to justify the figure which he here employs: "Every man's work shall be made manifest, for the day shall declare it, because it shall be revealed by *fire*." Every thing that we do or think or feel as Christian men and women is work done, so to speak, upon this character of ours that we are constructing, and which will one day be put to a trial so crucial that only that which is permanent and valuable, as "gold, silver and precious stones," will abide. I shall not occupy your time in endeavoring to fix the period of the trial—whether in this life, or immediately after death, or at some period in the life to come. Nor shall I endeavor to state the precise character of the trial—the methods which God will adopt. These have not been revealed, nor is it important that we should know them. It is enough to know that, as Christian men, we are building characters which one day are to be tried as gold is tried in the heated crucible, to make us serious in both the purpose and the method of our several lives.

Holding in our minds the general significance of the passage, as thus explained, let us attend to the special and very solemn truths which it announces.

I. Of these, no one is more solemn and important than that which stands at the very beginning of the statement, namely, that it is impossible to build a character which God will approve—a character whose elements shall be in his sight as "gold and silver and precious stones," unless it rests upon Christ. "Other foundation can no man lay than that is laid, which is Christ Jesus." I do not at this point explain just what is meant by this building upon Christ Jesus. But, taking the words as they stand, and speaking to those who are rejoicing in their native or self-cultivated goodness, I beg them to take heed to these solemn words of the Apostle: "Other foundation can no man lay than that is laid, Christ Jesus." The Bible freely and often admits, that there is much that is amiable and graceful in the temperament and deportment of those who will have nothing to do with the Saviour of men. And observation compels us often to admit, that they know the joys of benevolence, and illustrate the power of self-sacrifice in the home for the the family, and on the field of battle for the commonwealth. But if these words of the Apostle are to be believed, these do not constitute, nor are they distinguishing traits of that character, which will save a man in the day of the thorough testing and final arbitrament of God.

It is not to be doubted—it were cruel so to soften the statement of the truth that it shall lose the power of a constraining motive—that this word does teach with wonderful clearness, the absolute necessity of the connection of the soul with the Redeemer, in order to the soul's salvation. "There is none other name given under heaven among men whereby they can be saved," but the name of Jesus. "Other foundation can no man lay than that is laid, which is Jesus Christ." To ascertain what this connection is and to complete it, and that without delay—this, it would seem, is the plainest dictate of prudence. And, blessed be God, its character has been revealed in terms that none need mistake. God does not mock his creatures in the exercise of his mercy, by establishing a condition of its bestowment, either unintelligible in its announcement, or in itself hard to be fulfilled. His greatness is most clearly proved by his condescension and by the adaptation of his grace to the character of those to whom He reveals it. So, when He tells us that the only character which He will approve is that built on Christ, He very clearly explains what building on Christ means. It is believing on Him, resting on Him, looking to Him; connecting our life with Him, as the object of faith, the ground of hope and the end of labor.

Let each of us ask himself whether he has complied with this first and all-including condition. Do we believe in the Son of God? Do we indeed accept Him as the all-needed and all-sufficient redeemer of our souls, the one foundation upon which character that shall abide forever can be builded? And let us who profess that we have accepted Him, examine ourselves anew, in order to ascertain whether we accept Him as He is here presented;—a foundation to build character upon. Ah! friends, there is not a little accepting of Christ as a shield, that will ward off from us the just judgment of a holy Lawgiver; as one who will stand between us and destruction. But this other accepting of Him, as the foundation on which to rest character not only, but as the foundation that reveals to us the form and that kind of character that we ought to build; this accepting of Him as the rule of all active life here, as well as the ground and reason of all that we hope for in the world to come;—it becomes us to ask ourselves whether we have so received Him, whenever we read these solemn words: "Other foundation can no man lay, than that is laid, which is Christ Jesus."

II. The Apostle, in the second place, brings into view the truth that one may build a very perishable, and for that reason a very *valueless structure* upon this one right foundation. "Now if any man build upon this foundation gold, silver, precious stones on the one hand, or wood, hay, stubble on the other, every man's work shall be made manifest."

This is a truth of which we need constantly to remind ourselves. We are accustomed to place all Christians in one category, and to class all work done for Christ and his Church together. When we say of one man that he is a Christian, and of another that he is not a Christian, we sometimes feel that we have exhausted the subject of religious differences. It is well, therefore, to be reminded that there are differences, and very important differences, within the limits of personal Christianity—differences too, that do not arise from mere variations of individual temperament, for, for differences of this kind Christians can hardly be held responsible—but differences in the habit of the Christian life, in the character of the work done and of the objects on which the highest regard is fixed. There are those who so live their Christianity, that it may be said of them, that they are building of "gold, and silver, and precious stones," and however fierce the ordeal that shall try them at last, its fire will only purify that which it can not destroy. While of others it may just as truthfully be said, that they are building of "wood, and hay, and stubble," which the same fire must consume. Both are Christians indeed; both trust in Christ; both build upon the foundation than which no other can be laid; and both, therefore, shall at the last be saved. But in the preservation and the value of the work and character of the one, he shall receive a reward; while the other shall suffer loss, and shall himself be saved with such difficulty as to justify the expression, "saved so as by fire."

We are personally and deeply interested, therefore, in the endeavor to distinguish between the two classes here so sharply discriminated. Notice then, what, as as it seems to me, the Apostle clearly teaches; that the one fixes his regards upon, and devotes his energies to building that which is essentially permanent in Christian life; the "gold and silver and precious stones;" while the other gives himself to that which, however useful and important it may be for the time, is essentially temporary, and which at all events must perish in the day of testing. It is as if, of two builders, the one labors for the completion of the monument itself; and the other gives himself solely to the perishable scaffolding that surrounds it, and has little interest in that which will abide a thing of beauty for ages after the scaffolding shall have been removed. It is as if, of two members of a Church, one gives himself wholly to the interests of the outward house and the other gives himself to labor for the Church which gathers within its walls, each living stone of which is an immortal soul, and precious beyond all computation in the view of God. It is as if some of us gave ourselves to the enjoyment of the means of grace which shall only continue with the Church on earth, and others of us to the cultivation of that grace of which we have in this world the means;—that righteousness, and peace, and joy in the Holy Ghost, which shall endure forever.

I am confident, Christian friends, that I am pointing out a difference which exists not only, but which is obvious to every observing and intelligent believer. There are those—and many of them are earnest and zealous, and, I may add, most useful here on earth—whose whole life and labor seem to be exhausted by the outward business of the house of God, by things connected with Christ's Church and Kingdom, which are seen and temporal; who stop there; who, if I may be permitted to speak plainly, seem to be more deeply interested in religious affairs that have but a passing interest, and are of a quasi-business character, than in those high and eternal interests, the development in others and themselves of that lofty spiritual habit, that interior holiness, which will bear all trials in this world and the world to come, and will abide while immortality endures. And there are other Christians—and I bless God for the belief that they are multiplying, and for the assurance that they will multiply more and more—who look beyond the outward and the temporal to the inward and eternal; who rejoice in the means of grace for the grace itself which they are thereby enabled to secure, who value all outward institutions and churches and associations and conventions, just in the proportion in which they advance the interests of that Kingdom whose mere ministering servants they are, that Kingdom which "cometh not with observation," which "is not in word but in power," that Kingdom of God, which is "righteousness, and peace, and joy in the Holy Ghost."

The Apostle does not intimate of these two classes, that one is Christian, and the other is not—and God forbid that, in attempting to interpret him, I should dare to intimate it—but he does say of those of one class, that they are building into the characters which they are rearing against the day of God's trial, "gold, silver, precious stones," which can not perish; and of the others, that they are building "wood, hay, and stubble," which in the day that shall try every man's work, of what sort it is, must be consumed.

I have said enough, I trust, on this subject, to enable us all to ask and intelligently to answer the question: How much of our labor stops at that which is merely temporary in our religion, and how much goes beyond it, to that which is permanent and eternal? Do we value the means of grace, as we rightly term them—churches and associations—for their own sakes, or for that inward grace which they are so well fitted by God's blessing to develop within us? Does our love find its most cherished objects in the earthly organizations with which we are connected, or in that spiritual Church which Christ loved and for which He gave Himself, that he might present it to his Father without spot or wrinkle or any such thing? I simply suggest the various subjects, with regard to which questions like these may be asked. To every thing connected with Christianity as related to man, belongs something that is outward and temporal, and something that is inward and eternal. In every sacrament there is the outward and visible sign and the inward and spiritual grace. To every sermon belongs the adornment of mere rhetoric and the religious lesson which it is intended to convey, to every song of praise the beauty of rhythm and the adoration which is syllabled. And it is as our attention or our love or our labor rests upon that which is outward, or upon that which is inward, that we are building with "wood and hay and stubble," or with "gold and silver and precious stones" which can not be consumed.

III. The Apostle having dwelt upon the one foundation on which Christian character can rest, and the radical, or at least the very important difference in the materials of which Christians may make use in building on it, calls the attention of the Corinthian Christians to the fact, that a day is coming which shall, as by fire, try and declare the permanence or the temporary character of their building. "Every man's work shall be made manifest, for the day shall declare it; because it shall be revealed by fire, and the fire shall try every man's work of what sort it is."

The Church has always believed in the judgment of God to be pronounced on each soul hereafter— a judgment in respect to that soul's relations to the law of God, and to the Saviour whom He has sent to redeem the world. Upon that judgment, the Church believes the soul's destiny in the world to come to be suspended. But Christians have not possessed a very distinct faith in the coming of a day in which their lives as Christians are to be tested, and by which the permanent or merely temporary value of their labors here is to be determined. We hear a great deal said about the final discernment between the righteous and the wicked, and the division of men on the right hand and the left. But we hear comparatively little about the final determination of the relative value of the lives, and the relative goodness of the character of those who have accepted Christ. And yet it must be clear to every student of the passage, that such a trial and such a judgment are in these words most clearly taught. There has been appointed a judgment which shall finally decide whether the materials, that we have used in the construction of our life-work, are abiding or perishable. I do not say that there will be all the accessories of a court of justice; and that before its bar the soul will be arraigned, and evidence will be sifted, and judgment be solemnly recorded. But that all the work of our Christian life-time will be tested, and its value and character for eternity be determined—of this I think there can be no doubt in the mind of any thoughtful Christian man or woman. It may be, that the day of one's departure from this world will be the day of his trial, and the very article of his death, and his entrance upon the scenes and occupations of his new life will be the trial—the test of all that he has done or has been here. Indeed, I do not see how we can escape the conviction, that the experience of death and of God's presence must of necessity try and declare the value of the earthly life. Is it not the plainest truth in the world, that a man's entrance into any position is a test of his fitness for that position; that the trial of one's fitness for the chief magistracy of the Republic begins on the day on which he begins the performance of its duties? And is it hard to believe that a Christian, entering heaven with all the character and experience he has accumulated during his religious life on earth, will on that day behold his character tested as it has never been on earth; tried, "so as by fire"? And if he has busied himself about merely worldly affairs connected with the Church of God and the religion of Christ, will he not find all his labor and experience burn and shrivel into ashes, in the blaze of the celestial light in which he shall see God face to face, and know Him even as He is known.

I do not affirm that, having said this, I have exhausted the meaning of these words of the Apostle: "The fire shall try every man's work of what sort it is;" but what I have said, makes it easy to believe, that such an ordeal is awaiting us; and that it lies within the power of natural events to cause it; and the truth should make us careful to live in view of its approach.

IV. But, not to dwell longer upon this part of the passage, the Apostle next states the important truth, that the rewards of heaven are determined always by the character of our work and life here. In other words, he announces the great principle that God is never arbitrary in his bestowments. These are his words: "If any man's work abide which he hath built thereupon, he shall receive a reward. If any man's work shall be burned, he shall suffer a loss." The Christian's labor here determines his reward hereafter. In a high and important sense, he is the author of his own heaven. The principle thus announced is clearly taught in the Word of God. In parable, in prophecy and in direct statement, we are informed that what are obedience and reward in the moral government of God are obedience and reward in the natural government of God; that they are cause and effect; that the natural and moral constitutions of his kingdom coincide; that if, in the moral government of God, the soul that sinneth shall die, in the natural government of God to be carnally minded is death. God always proportions his rewards and punishments to character. So the future world will be to us just what we shall make it by the character of our lives here. Each man goes to his own place. The sinner, by a law of his own nature as well as by the judgment of God, will gravitate to the hopeless abode of evil, and the righteous will rise to the abode of the righteous God. That is an instructive picture in the Book of Revelation, in which we behold the wicked, not driven from the presence of God, but themselves calling upon the rocks and mountains to fall and cover them and hide them from his face. God, I repeat, is never capricious in his bestowments. Those, who shall be lost, will be compelled to confess themselves suicides. They shall eat of the fruit of their own way, and be filled with their own devices. So it is with the Christian in heaven; his reward there, the greatness and glory of it, his very capacity of enjoyment will be determined exactly by the character of his life and labor here. He who builds in such a way and with such materials that his work shall abide, will receive a corresponding reward. Those whose labors shall be destroyed, will suffer corresponding loss.

Let us live and labor therefore, brethren, as those who know that we shall reap in the hereafter the natural fruit of our labors here. "There are distinctions in the condition of the redeemed in eternity; harps of a more amazing power; scepters of a wider sway; stations nearer in honor to the throne of our God." These may be ours, but only on condition that we labor for them. These are not for those who build with "wood and hay and stubble," but for those who, laboring for that which shall abide the consummation of all perishable things, build with "gold and silver and precious stones."

So, brethren, I have tried to make plain the meaning of these words of the Apostle. The lesson that they teach is solemn and urgent. How simple, yet how hard to learn; how easily remembered, but how easily forgotten! To live and labor and endure for those truths and graces in the Kingdom of God that will live beyond the world that now is. To seek a character that will fit us for the enjoyments of heaven as well as for the labors of earth. In all labor, worship, and study, to look beyond that which is seen and temporal to the unseen and eternal. So shall we build with gold and silver and precious stones, and so receive a reward in the day when many shall suffer loss of hopes they cherish now, and be saved so as by fire.

The passage is a very solemn one, and yet a very comforting one as well. How unspeakably blessed it is to be assured that though we may suffer loss, and be saved so as by fire; we shall still be saved, if we but build upon the one foundation that is laid, which is Christ Jesus. Our sins, our mistakes, our worldliness, our vices, our follies, our errors of judgment, these and their results will all be burned; and though many hopes and brilliant visions will be destroyed in their destruction, we shall be saved, if, amid the wreck about us, we still stand upon the one foundation—the Rock Christ Jesus. May God help us all to build on Him, and so be safe in the day when all things shall be tried as by fire!

XXIV.

THE REWARD OF LOVE.

"She hath done what she could."—MARK xiv, 8.

The words of the text were spoken by our Lord. The circumstances of their utterance were the following. Jesus was accustomed, during the last week of his life, to retire towards evening from the crowded city of Jerusalem to Bethany, the home of Martha and Mary and Lazarus. On Wednesday—as it seems to me, and not on the Saturday previous, as some suppose—two days before his crucifixion, a supper was made for Him in the house of Simon the leper; probably one on whom the healing hand of the great Physician had been laid, and not improbably a kinsman of the family which gave to Jesus three of his most faithful disciples. Lazarus was there—the living evidence of the Divine power residing in the Master—and with him were gathered many of the disciples, who for three years had accompanied Jesus and beheld the miracles He performed, and heard the wondrous words with which he announced the Kingdom of God. Martha served at the table, acting in perfect harmony with the disposition which she is elsewhere described as possessing. We do not catch sight of the other sister, however, until near the close of the meal; but before its conclusion Mary enters—unobserved, it would appear—and approaches the couch at which Jesus sits reclining before the table. As one has said in describing the scene, "She can not now, as in the privacy of her own dwelling, sit down at his feet to listen to the gracious words coming from his lips. But she has an alabaster phial of fragrant ointment;—her costliest possession—one treasured up for some unknown but great occasion. She is here because the occasion has arrived. Having approached Jesus, she pours part of its contents upon his head, and resolves that the whole shall be spent in his anointing. She compresses the yielding material of which the phial is composed, breaks it, and pours the last drop of it upon his feet, flinging away the relics of the broken vessel, and wiping his feet with her hair. Kingly guest at royal banquet could not have had a costlier homage of the kind rendered to Him. It was the final expression of the fullness and intensity of her gratitude, her loyalty and her love."

As the fragrant perfume pervades the apartment in which the guests are gathered, the disciples catch sight of the kneeling Mary, and wonder at the Master's acceptance of her homage. Heretofore their loyalty had not forbidden their protests against some of his actions, and they are not silent now. They break out in lamentation at the waste of the costly ointment. The voice of the treasurer of the company is louder and more angry than the rest. "Why," he cries, rebuking both the Master and the humble disciple who is bending to wipe his feet with the hair of her head—"Why," cries Judas, "was not this ointment sold for three hundred pence, and given to the poor?" And in reply the Master pronounces the eulogy that I have selected as my text, and utters this memorable prophecy: "Verily I say unto you, Wheresoever this Gospel shall be preached throughout the whole world, this also that she hath done shall be told for a memorial of her."

"She hath done what she could." No greater praise could have been spoken by any one, and this was spoken by the One whose praise is the highest honor mortals can receive. It is the praise of Him whose plaudit all of us at last shall covet, when to some he will say, "Depart, ye workers of iniquity;" and to others, "Well done, good and faithful servants; enter into the joy of your Lord." I am sure that I have a right to expect your attention, while briefly and familiarly I endeavor to state the truths and lessons in respect to *Christian work*, which these words of Christ to his disciples are meant to teach us.

I. You will remark that Christ pronounced this eulogy upon Mary's act, although it did not immediately advance his Kingdom, or bless mankind. It is at this point that our Lord's estimate of Mary's conduct antagonizes that of the disciples. Those disciples felt that they had a right to judge Mary, by referring to certain obvious needs and wants which existed and obtruded themselves on their minds, and which Mary's act of homage to Christ did not in the least meet and supply. They supposed that their indignation was righteous and appropriate, and that while the poor were perishing for lack of food, it did not become a disciple of Him who went about doing good to engage in so useless and costly an expenditure. Now, what does the eulogy of our Lord mean, when we study it in connection with the circumstances in which it was thus spoken? Does He mean to say to his whole Church: "You need not be troubled with the poor and suffering around you. You may pour out the treasures of your wealth in what seem to you mere unuseful and costly ceremonies"? Does He mean to announce as a law, that every expenditure by his people, whether or not it appears to them to serve the purposes for which his Kingdom was established, will receive his approbation? Not at all. There is no volume in which mere ceremony and adornment are made to appear at such a disadvantage as they are in the New Testament. And no religious teacher that has lived demanded so little ceremonious worship from his followers, either for Himself or for the Father whom He revealed. What, then, does He mean? I doubt very much whether this eulogy of the Saviour upon Mary's anointing would have been uttered, had it not been called out by the indignation and judgment of the disciples. If we would understand it—and here we see the first lesson the record of it is meant to teach—we must remember that it was spoken to rebuke the disciples for their attempt to estimate the moral quality of the conduct of a fellow disciple. We shall not learn the first of the important lessons it contains, unless we consider this element of reproof.

Here comes the sister of Lazarus, her heart overflowing with gratitude for the recovery of her brother from the power of the grave. What can she do for the Prince of Life, who wept with her in her desolate grief, and then pronounced the words which transmuted her grief into joy? She can not aid the omnipotence which He displayed at the open tomb. All that she can do, is in some signal way to reveal her gratitude; and so the alabaster box is broken, and the feet of Jesus are wiped with the hair of her head. Now the disciples presume to pass judgment upon this act of Mary, and to condemn it by a reference to labors in which they would naturally have engaged, and Christ praises Mary first of all in order to rebuke the disciples.

And they needed the rebuke, and we need it now, my friends. I suppose that there is no disposition more difficult to eradicate than the disposition to judge the Christian work of others, by referring to what we would have done in the same circumstances. Only a few years have passed, since it was no unusual thing for some Christians to apply harsh epithets to other Christians—who felt it to be their duty to send the Gospel to distant lands—because there were languishing in ignorance so many heathen within the limits of Christendom. Many of us remember that a great English novelist, calling himself Christian, felt justified in holding up to the scorn of the world, by means of caricature, the work of Foreign Missions, because of the poverty that blighted the lives of millions in his own country. Or, here is a man who has been afflicted with a sore bereavement. The light of his household has been darkened, and life is a burden. Suddenly the Gospel of Christ, with its abounding consolations, its exceeding great and precious promises, awakens a new hope within his soul, and lifts the burden that had weighed so heavily upon him. Filled with gratitude that he feels he must express, he builds a memorial church; and, that it may fitly express his love to the God who has brought him out of the darkness, he spares no expenditure in its adornment. It is the natural and spontaneous expression of the man's gratefulness.

Now, this being so, what shall we say of the spirit which blinds the eye alike to the beauty of the monumental church, and to the beauty of the grace which reared it, and says: "Why was not this ointment sold and given to the poor?" Whatever we may say of it, we know what Christ says of it from the words of the text. He rebukes it in his words, "Judge not, that ye be not judged."

We must regard this eulogy, first of all, as our Lord's appeal to us for charity in our estimate of our fellow Christians' lives. The eulogy is not: "She has done the absolute best that could have been done in the circumstances," or "the best that you could have done;" but "she hath done what she could." Perhaps the disciples were right; perhaps it is true, that the money would have been better expended in relieving the wants of the poverty-stricken in Bethany. Our Lord does not enter upon the discussion of that question. If Mary's conduct was mistaken, her love and devotion sanctified the mistake, and called forth the most gracious words that were ever spoken by the Master to a disciple.

I do not like to dwell upon this part of the subject, because my speaking of it may seem to suggest that those whom I address are prone to censoriousness. I do speak of it, let me say, because all of us are tempted to it; and most of us yield to the temptation oftener than we imagine. I speak of it to warn you and myself against it. It would not be strange if, in yielding to it, we should prevent a sincere disciple from offering the only natural and self-sacrificing homage of his soul to Christ.

II. But returning to the eulogy pronounced by Christ, I remark again, that it was spoken because the anointing was done out of love to Himself.

It seems that He selected for special praise an act that could not immediately bless the world, in order to show to the Church, throughout all time, what are the distinguishing traits of Christian labor. Had Mary, in the fullness of her grateful love, done what the disciples urged that she should have done; had she, in order to show her love to Christ, sold the ointment and distributed the proceeds to the poor, she would have deserved the eulogy quite as much as she did. The singularity of the incident is that Christ selects her for praise, in view of an act which did not help the poor or immediately advance the interests of his Kingdom? Why was this? I answer, to show to you and me what trait it is that must characterize all Christian labor; what trait it is that makes it Christian. What is this trait? We know that it is not relief of the distressed. For the inspired Apostle teaches, that though we give all our goods to feed the poor and have not love, it profiteth us nothing. Not the giving to the poor, but the love makes our labor Christian. And just this is what Christ's words teach us. Mary exhibited the spirit of discipleship, although she fed no poor, because what she did, she did impelled by her burning love of Christ.

It is only when the love of Christ impels us to labor that our labor becomes Christian. The term Christian does not describe any particular kind of labor. It describes a spirit in which the labor is performed. If that spirit be present, the work is Christian whether it is preaching the Gospel or purchasing goods. If the spirit be absent, it is not Christian whether it is giving one's goods to feed the poor or giving one's body to be burned. This spirit is nothing else than the spirit of love and devotion to Christ, born of gratitude for what He has done and suffered for us. Nothing else than his love will meet with his approval or call down this benediction. If, however, you possess this love and seek to manifest it in labor for Him, He will readily excuse your mistakes in the methods you adopt to show it. I am speaking to fathers. You are a father, and your affection for your little child it is that makes your labor pleasant all the day long. Business worries you and tires your brain, and you would be tempted to give it up altogether, but that you remember your young growing boy at home, who, you feel, must himself one day be well started in life; and for him you put off the day of your retirement from the many cares of your business life. As you go home from your counting-room in the evening, this boy of yours meets you, and in some awkward, grotesque, blundering and most useless way, but still honestly, and out of the depth of his heart reveals his sincere affection for you. What do you do? Do you rebuke him for his blundering and awkwardness? Not at all. You thank God for the love that wells up from his heart. And during all his young and inexperienced life, you are quite willing to endure the grotesqueness and inappropriateness of its manifestation, if you can only be sure of his love.

Just this was the feeling of our Lord towards Mary, and just this is his feeling towards us. Let it be admitted that the outpouring of the ointment was useless. Christ did not need it. But what does He need? Our labors for the poor? Could not He, who spake and it was done, speak food into existence at once from the elements? Christ needs nothing that we can do. He values, more highly than all that we can do, the love which our labors reveal. It is this affection that sanctifies and ennobles and calls down his blessing on even our errors. It is because of the love of his people for Him, that He makes their weakness conquer the might of the world, and their things which are not bring to naught things that are.

Love to our Saviour is the first abiding trait of Christian labor. It is better in his sight than wisdom in devising means, or power in applying them. It is nobler than the eloquence of the preacher of his Gospel, and richer than the benefactions of the wealthy in his Church. He, who loved us and gave Himself for us, expects our affection in return. That affection is the source of his highest joy in heaven, as the hope of it was the motive which sustained Him in Gethsemane and Calvary. It were better for each of us, it were better for this Church, that all our conduct were marked by the wildest folly in men's esteem, than that we should lose the vision of a personal Redeemer, and lose this love of Him as the constraining motive of our lives. We can not do much for Him; we can not do much for the world. Our gifts and labors to be effective at all in spreading the Gospel, must all be followed by his Spirit. In our ignorance and weakness and short-sightedness, it must be that we shall do much that is useless, and much that in itself would be positively harmful. There is but one trait that can set right all our errors, and render harmless all our ignorance; and that is this affection for Him, in return for a love that passeth knowledge, and a redemption whose cost we can not fathom and whose glory we can not conceive.

III. I remark again, that this eulogy was pronounced, because the reality of the love was revealed by the self-sacrifice of Mary. The ointment was a costly gift; so costly, indeed, as to call forth remark from the disciples. This was the basis of their expostulation; that Mary should, for the time, have impoverished herself for so useless a purpose. But it was just this costliness that made the anointing appear to Mary appropriate; and it was the self-sacrifice which it involved, that made it acceptable to Christ himself. For the self-sacrifice was the sufficient evidence of the reality and depth of her love.

We profess to be disciples of Christ. As his disciples, we profess to love Him. If this discipleship is true discipleship, and our love is real love, it will be manifest in sacrifice of self. And when I speak of the sacrifice of self, I mean the costly outgiving of ourselves in some way for the honor of Christ. I do not mean that it shall be shown in some conspicuous way before the world. It is given to few so to sacrifice themselves, that men as well as the Master shall award them titles to martyrs' crowns. The place for Christian living, the place for the revelation of love to Christ in sacrifice of self, is the lot in which God has placed you. Do not fear that your lot is wanting in opportunities for its display. There is not a day, not an hour, in which, unobserved, you may not lay upon the altar and sacrifice, for Christ's sake, some impulse of your nature, which, if permitted to go unsacrificed, would dishonor Him. There is not a relation in which you stand to men, in which you may not find opportunity to deny yourself in love for Him who loved you and gave Himself for you. There is not a child whom God has given you, in connection with whom you may not deny your desires of worldly honor, in order to show your love to the Redeemer.

Opportunities for self-sacrifice! They are as abundant as the temptations of your life; they are as large as the wealth which God has intrusted to your care; they are as costly as the most precious objects of your earthly affection; they recur with every day of your life on earth; for every day, and every talent, and every possession are to be laid upon the altar for his sake. It is only when we thus sacrifice the whole of self, that we reveal a love worthy our discipleship; and it is only such consecration, that will call down upon us from Him praise like that which He bestowed upon Mary, when He said: "She hath done what she could." Love and self-sacrifice then are the great distinguishing traits of Christian labor. These must always be included in its definition. Not this work, not that work, not even giving to the poor as the disciples thought, not even giving our body to be burned constitutes Christian work, but any toil, however secular or however useless, which is the genuine outflow of self-sacrificing love to Christ.

So that the great question, that we are called to ask ourselves constantly, is not what great things we are accomplishing, not how wisely we are proceeding, important as these questions are, but: Is the impelling motive of all we do, a self-sacrificing love of our Lord? And that such a love may be ours, let us not fail to sit like Mary, often at his feet, and listen to his gracious words. "Let us often be found in the deep shades of Gethsemane, and at the foot of the cross on Calvary. There let us linger, meditate and pray." There shall we learn to love Him more deeply than we have ever loved Him. There alone shall we imbibe a spirit, which will make our whole life a sacrifice of a sweet odor, and well pleasing in his sight.

IV. But the eulogy thus spoken by our Lord not only reveals the two abiding traits of Christian labor. It also serves to show the limit of our responsibility. Our responsibility is limited only by our ability. "She hath done what she could." Mary exhausted her resources, and acted according to her light when she anointed Christ. It was because such an anointing seemed most appropriate, that she chose it as the mark of her affection. It was her best. And what we do for Christ must be our best, if we would earn his praise.

But—and this is the truth to which I wish to call your attention now—it is *our* best, and not the best that some one else could have done, which secures for us our Lord's approval. The disciples believed that they could have expended the money to better purpose than Mary. Well, suppose that they could. The Lord did not judge Mary by the disciples' wisdom. He did not expect the man with two talents to accomplish as much as the man with five. You may make grave mistakes in the gifts that you bestow upon objects of charity. But if, in self-denying love of your Lord, you make the bestowal, the Lord will reward you not according to your mistakes, but according to your love. In the parable of the talents, is the wicked servant denounced simply because he hid the talent in a napkin? I do not so read it. If he had loved his Lord, and had supposed that the hiding was the best use that he could make of his Lord's money, and so returned it—doubt not that his generous master would have praised his love if not his wisdom. But instead of loving he hates his master, and reveals his hatred in the words: "I knew thee that thou art a hard man, reaping where thou hast not sown, and gathering where thou hast not strewed, and so I hid thy talent." And it was because of not his want of wisdom, but his want of love that his Lord denounced him. Mother, do your best with your children for Christ's sake, and do not fear that you will lose your reward because of your want of wisdom. Man of business, work for Christ everywhere and every way you can, and doubt not that even your mistakes, if they are committed in love for the Lord, will receive, not a rebuke, but a reward from Him, and not only so, but they will be made to bless mankind.

V. For—and this is the last truth to which I advert—the Lord takes good care of the results of all loving and self-sacrificing, though it seem mistaken, work for him. Suppose that we call Mary's anointing a mistake; suppose that we say it was useless; suppose that we go further and say that it was indelicate to obtrude herself on the Saviour in the circumstances. What then? This at least is obvious: her conduct sprang from her love to the Saviour, and, therefore, Christ took care, not only that Mary should be rewarded, but also that her love should bless the world. For, first, He made it a blessing to the very disciples who rebuked her. It became the occasion of teaching them a lesson, which, as the founders of the Christian Church, they needed clearly to understand. And He also made its influence beneficent for all time and throughout the whole world. "Verily I say unto you, wherever this Gospel shall be preached, this also which this woman hath done shall be told for a memorial of her." And from that day to this, it has enkindled the love and nerved the arms of his people; and it will continue to do so until He shall come again. And it will be so with us. The labor is ours; but it is his to make it sufficient. None of our

Christian labor, if it be born of self-sacrificing love, can fail. Let us remember and believe this; let us give more, and do more, laboring with encouraged hearts, and battling with new inspiration. For the gifts of our charity are in his remembrance, and the seed of our planting is in his nurture; and the reward of our toil is in his keeping, and the victory of our conflict is his to vouchsafe, who esteems as infinitely more valuable than all human might or wisdom, his people's self-denying love.

Brethren, let us thank God that we are the disciples of such a Teacher, the servants of a Lord so charitable in judgment, so generous in reward. He sends us into the world as the Father sent Him. He honors us in calling us to complete the work which by his death He made possible. If we give our lives to Him in love and devotion like those of Mary, our most secular labors will be labors for his Kingdom and our seeming errors will be made to bless mankind. For He is Head over all things to his Church; and, since He makes the wrath of man to praise Him, doubt not that He will take care that the living sacrifices of his people shall magnify his love and hasten the world's redemption. Amazing and infinite grace is this of Jesus Christ our Lord! It were enough to awaken eternal gratitude to know that He freely blesses sinners with salvation. Yet this is but the first of his bestowments. Once redeemed, they become his representatives in the world; and when, as such, they labor in his love, their reward can not fail, or their work be in vain. If but the love of Christ pervades our lives and constrain our sacrifice, the Spirit of Christ must follow our doing and bearing in his name. We may not, indeed, see now the fruit of our planting;

for the harvest of the Church is the consummation of all things. But the Master's word is pledged. The sun of his grace, and the rain of his Spirit now nourishes the seed we sow; and the ripened grain will be gathered and garnered at the last. O, doubting, despairing Christian laborer, father, mother, teacher, friend, wherever or however undergoing or overcoming in Christ's love for men; in view of these blessed truths, why should you despair? Of work for Christ at least, it is true, that in due season you shall reap if you faint not.

There may be those before me who are giving their lives to other masters than the Lord we profess to serve. My friends, we are not ashamed to have you set side by side yours and ours. Nay, we beg you to make the comparison. Think of the Head of the Church—Jesus Christ, the object of our love and hope and endeavor, as He is presented in the incident from which my text is taken—and then think of the object of your endeavors. I care not what it is, however low or lofty; wealth, power, social position, art, knowledge, earthly pleasure. You are never sure of your reward. If you obtain it, it can not meet the wants of your highest being while it lasts; and it can last only with this brittle life, which at best is soon rounded with the sleep of death. Your Master bestows his highest rewards on those with special aptitudes. If ever you labor mistakenly, you pay the full penalty of your mistake; and your very masters are themselves the sport of time and change. Wonder not, then, that they who give themselves to this world grow cynical and bitter as years increase, and cry out, like the wisest of them, "Vanity of vanities." Our Lord alone demands no special aptitude but love. Our Lord alone says:

"Well done!" to all his faithful servants. He alone is the Lord of time, and above all change. His rewards alone are satisfying and enduring. Therefore, we bid you come to Jesus Christ in faith. Young man or woman beginning life, and you who already have tasted the bitterness of disappointment, Christ calls you lovingly to his service, with two talents, or with five, or with but one. Make Him your Lord; and if you can but give a cup of cold water to man in love of Him, your reward can not fail; and that reward will be incorruptible, and undefiled, and will never fade away.

XXV.

THE JUDGMENT OF THE SPIRITUAL MAN.

"But he that is spiritual, judgeth all things."—I. CORINTHIANS ii, 15.

If you will read carefully the beginning of this letter of the Apostle to the Church at Corinth, you will observe that it is taken up with a defense of his conduct, as a preacher of the Gospel of Christ. With a great deal of care, he argues the wisdom of the course adopted by him, when he first visited their city as an Apostle of the new religion; the course, namely, of knowing nothing among them, save Jesus Christ and Him crucified. Instead of appearing among them—as we may suppose a missionary of the old dispensation would have done—appealing to their hearts and consciences by means of ritual and tradition, or instead of appearing as a philosopher, appealing to their reason with the wisdom of this world, he came declaring in simplicity, as neither Jew nor Greek would have done, the spiritual Gospel of the Son of God.

For a reason, which it is not necessary to dwell upon at this time, Paul, when he wrote this epistle, felt called upon to justify his conduct in coming to them, not with the wisdom of this world— which undoubtedly in this connection means a system of philosophy—nor with signs like those for which a Jew would seek, but with the simple truths and revelations, which constitute the faith of Calvary. In the course of this argument in his own defense, he states some of the most important truths in regard to spiritual things, contained in the New Testament, such as the following: "Eye hath not seen, nor ear heard, neither have entered into the heart of man the things which God hath prepared for them that love Him. But God hath revealed them unto us by his Spirit." And again: "What man knoweth the things of a man, save the spirit of man which is in him? Even so the things of God knoweth no man, but the Spirit of God." And again: "The natural man receiveth not the things of the spirit of God, for they are foolishness unto him, neither can he know them, for they are spiritually discerned." And again, in the words of the text: "He that is spiritual, judgeth all things." I wish this morning to separate this statement of the Apostle: "He that is spiritual, judgeth all things," from the context, and from the circumstances which led to its utterance, and to consider it as a distinct and general proposition. I wish to show in what senses it is true, that a spiritual man judgeth all things; and to set forth, as distinctly as I may be able, the very practical and important lessons that it is designed to teach.

I need not take the time required to discuss the meaning of the word spiritual, either as the Apostle uses it or as I intend to employ it. We all understand it to express both the character to be affirmed of a man, and the source of the character itself. A spiritual man is more than a moral man, as we usually employ the term moral; because he is moral on spiritual grounds, for spiritual reasons; because the fountain and origin of his morality lies in his spiritual and heavenly mindedness. He, who is spiritual, communes with God, loves prayer, dwells with delight on the things unseen and eternal which God has revealed by his Spirit. He has tasted the powers of the world to come; his faith has pierced the veil which conceals from the merely earthly minded those sublime, eternal certainties which eye hath not seen, nor ear heard, nor heart conceived. The light of eternity shines upon earthly things, and He beholds and judges them in that celestial light. The power of an endless life rests upon the life that now is. "The life that he lives in the flesh, he lives by the faith of the Son of God." I confidently assume that there exists no power on earth, other than the Gospel of Jesus Christ, adequate to bestow this spiritual character on man; and, therefore, I use the terms, Christian man and spiritual, as interchangeable; only asking you to remember that he alone is truly a Christian who is also truly spiritual.

I. Now with this brief explanation of terms in our minds, I ask you to notice first, an *unconscious*, or at least an *involuntary judgment* pronounced by the Christian on character. I say involuntary, because there is to be affirmed of it no active exercise of the faculty of judgment. The Christian, by being a Christian, the spiritual man by reason simply of the fact of his spirituality, judgeth all things. To illustrate what I am endeavoring to make clear, we all have heard of, and are familiar through its copies with the face of that Madonna, painted by the master whose name has given title to our modern art. So satisfying, so answering to the unformed image whose separate elements we had been unable to combine, is it, that it has become the Christian world's ideal of the woman who was so highly favored of the Most High. As often as we think of the Virgin, this face stands before us with its wondrous love and awe and rapture. Now suppose this well-nigh perfect symbol placed side by side with some lower and defective representation. Do you not see that the very contact of the two compels the judgment of the one by the other? The defects of the lower symbol appear with greater distinctness, and its more positive faults impress you as they never did before; until that which before the comparison may have seemed completely to embody your ideal of the mother of Jesus of Nazareth, is rejected as entirely unworthy. The clear outshining of the beauty of the one judges the defects and faults of the other, and so condemns it. In all this process the picture, of course, plays no conscious or voluntary part. Its simple existence is a judgment and condemnation of the other when placed by its side. Just such an involuntary and, perhaps, unconscious judgment of character by the Christian, the really spiritual man, is, doubtless, the most effective work that he does in the world. His purity, his spiritual and heavenly mindedness, his earnestness in labor for the good of men, the breadth of his love, the depth of his devotion, the voluntariness and cheerfulness of his sacrifices—as these traits of character are manifested, who does not understand me when I say, that such a man, though he does it involuntarily, though he may even be unconscious of the fact, judges and condemns those around him in whom these traits are wanting.

The more I study the life and character of Jesus Christ as a man among men, the more deeply does this power of his life impress me. If I were asked, what more than any thing else awoke that enmity, which finally led to his crucifixion, I should answer, that it was not his words, condemning wickedness and wicked men; for, though these were sometimes terrible, they were not often spoken, and when they were, it was with a tenderness and solicitude, which must, for the time at least, have disarmed all hostility. Neither was it any real fear on the part of those in power that He would destroy their authority with Rome or with the people, and grasp the power that they possessed. This He never sought to do, and they were well aware of it. But the simple presence of a life like his—so pure, so holy, so loving, so beneficent, so devoted to God and to the best interests of man—the mere outflow of his perfect spirituality judged them and their spurious religionism, their hypocrisy; and judging, condemned them. And so it was, that those of them, who did not repent and turn to God in prayer and faith, were led to cry: "Away with him, let him be crucified!" This was the condemnation; that the light shone, and by its very shining condemned their deeds of darkness. No wonder that they hated Him. No wonder that they shunned and would not come to Him. Not that his heart was not full of love and pity for them as for all other sinful men; but they would not come to Him, because they knew that his contact with themselves would be like the shining of the sun on a stagnant pool; revealing the seeds of disease which the darkness had served to conceal. So Christ, not as the Lawgiver or the Judge, but as the holy and perfect Man, unconsciously, certainly involuntarily, judged all things, all men, all systems, all teachers, all morality, all characters. He shone in Palestine, as the sun shines on the earth; revealing and so commending moral beauty where it had been concealed; and revealing and therefore *judging* and condemning evil, in men and methods, which, before he rose above the horizon, men had reverenced as holy and from God.

It is important, Christian friends, that we remember, that we are in the world, just as Christ was in the world. We are the light of the world; and we are not only by the profession of faith, and by more active labors to startle men into activity in the religious life; but, as the more important part of our mission, we are to let our light shine; so that without our knowledge, and certainly without our positive efforts, men will feel themselves judged and condemned, and thus will begin the work of preparation to enter the Kingdom of God. "It is universally conceded that the argument of a holy and beautiful life is unanswerable;" and it is this argument more than any other which Christ would have all his people urge. We call men, who are Christians, to confess Christ publicly with their lips, because we believe, as Christ himself has taught us, that the weight of such public confession can not but add greatly to the force of Christian statement from the pulpit. But what is the weight of a formal confession to the solid worth of the confession of a consistent life? The one is made once for all, or as opportunity is given; the other is permanent, unvarying, from day to day the same; the ceaseless shining of the sun from year to year around the world, revealing and judging, commending or condemning all things on which his light may fall.

We are accustomed to pray, that our lives may be consistent with our Christian profession; that we may walk worthy of the vocation wherewith we are called. I wish that we might always, when offering this prayer, have a due sense of the necessity of consistency; a necessity growing out of the fact, that so alone can we judge others in a way that will condemn them, and bring them humbled to Him who alone can make them holy. O brethren, let us remember our vocation and our vow to let the light, which Christ gives us, shine along the pathway of our lives. Would that we might realize this power of judgment that belongs to spiritual living! If they are not here to reproduce the life of Jesus Himself, and so to become lights that shall reveal men to themselves, standards by which men may learn both their need and the source of their supply; I know no reason why Christians are called to remain on earth, away from their Father's presence and his home. Even supposing no positively vicious influence to flow from the inconsistency of a Christian man or woman, it is enough to awaken a wholesome fear of it to remember, that by it we are neglecting to judge the multitudes, with whom in our daily lives we come in contact. This sin of permitting men to remain in darkness—so far as the failure to let our light shine permits them to do so—is not the consciousness of it enough, if that were all, to arouse us to the strong agony of prayer and effort, that our lives may be so spiritual, that their outshining will judge the lives of men, and, by judging, show to them the one source of eternal life?

II. Quite a different truth is the second, that I

notice as contained in this statement of the Apostle: "He that is spiritual judgeth all things." It teaches us wherein lies the safety of permitting so much *liberty* to the Christian in the New Dispensation. It teaches us also the condition upon which this liberty is enjoyed. Both the safety and the condition of the liberty lie in the fact that the Christian is *spiritual*. We are very fond of referring to our liberty as the disciples of Christ; we rejoice and give thanks, that we are relieved from the bondage to which our spiritual fathers under the Mosaic law were subjected. We love to contrast the system of minute regulations, which constituted the Hebrew law of religious living, with the freedom which breathes from every page of the New Testament. We place the law of ordinances side by side with the law of love, the self-denials commanded by God side by side with the voluntary self-denials practiced by the Christian, the old rites and ceremonies with the present entire absence of them; and we are filled no doubt with sincere gratitude, that our religious lives are developed under the influence of a system, whose great characteristic is the liberty of the individual disciple. Now all this joy and congratulation and thanksgiving are very well, if we are careful to remember two things: first, what exactly this liberty is, and secondly, the condition on which we may safely exercise it. But these, I fear, we are all liable to either mistake or forget.

What then is this liberty enjoyed by the Christian disciple? It is certainly not freedom of action. The moral distinctions, so clearly set forth in the Old Testament, are neither abrogated nor ignored in the New. Indeed, this liberty is not even freedom of action in respect to things morally indifferent. A Christian does not possess the right to do or leave undone any act, just because in itself it is neither right nor wrong. The liberty of the New Testament is a liberty not of action, but of judgment. It is well expressed in the text, and the words which immediately follow it: "He that is spiritual judgeth all things, and is judged of no man." In no particular are the Old and New Testaments to be more forcibly contrasted, than in the absence of the rules of conduct in the latter, of which there are such a number and such a variety in the former. The Hebrew found himself shut up on every side by a system of precepts so minute and so varied, that he could with difficulty be placed in any position for which he could not find a definite behest. And his religion, the practical and active side of it at least, consisted largely in his obedience to these precepts, the reason of many of which, it is fair to presume, he was unable to understand. It is not difficult to perceive the wisdom of God in ordaining a system so complex and comprehensive as the Mosaic Law is, when the condition of the people for whose government it was intended, is remembered. Brought out of Egypt, where they had lived in the most degrading servitude, with little knowledge of the true God, they were the veriest children in spiritual things, and, like all children, they needed to be directed by very severe and specific laws. A clearer revelation, a less burdened ritual, a freer and more spiritual religion would have been of little use to them. It was only after men had been educated by the dispensation of rule, and been raised to a higher plane of spiritual living, that they were ready for its abrogation. The fullness of time at last came, the types and shadows of the law were fulfilled in the Gospel. The religion, whose characteristic was rule and ritual, gave way to the new religion, whose greatest glory is that it is spiritual, therefore free. It requires no extended discussion to convince us, that while detailed rules and precepts were eminently appropriate in the preparatory and ceremonial age of our religion, they could with propriety find no place in the final dispensation: just because the latter is spiritual, because of its clearer and more direct revelation of God and our relations to Him, because of the more enlarged intelligence of the New Testament disciple.

The theory of the New Testament, if I may use the word theory in connection with such a subject, is that the Christian, because of the new revelation which God has made, because of the close relations that subsist between him and his Saviour, and because of his own spiritual character, is able himself to answer the questions of duty which inevitably arise in his life. Thus he is at liberty, no longer a bondsman to laws and precepts and ordinances. Being spiritual, "he judgeth all things, and is judged of no man."

You will observe then, Christian friends, and this is the practical truth which we ought to remember, that, while as Christians we enjoy perfect liberty of judgment in regard to all courses of conduct, all the acts and habits of our lives; the ground and reason of this liberty is our *spirituality*. It is because we are so near to Christ; because his revelation is so clear; because the means of grace are so plentiful and powerful; because communion with God is so free; because we have knowledge and power which the saints of old did not possess, that we are free to judge for ourselves. And therefore it becomes us to remember, that while our judgment is free, the judgment, in every case that comes before us, must be rendered on high *spiritual grounds.* If it is not so rendered, we forfeit the right because we ignore the condition of our liberty.

For freedom, whether in political society, or in religion, is not a blessing to be bestowed on all alike. No parent thinks of permitting a child to exercise it. There are nations which have recently shown themselves utterly unprepared for it. There was a time also, when it could not safely be given to the Church of God. Now it is bestowed. But he who receives and exercises freedom, does so at his peril. Men have been wrecked by it, because they have forgotten the prime condition, that it must have at its foundation this spirituality which Christ in his Gospel alone bestows. He alone that is spiritual; he alone, who like Paul in judging, remembers his relations to God, to Christ and to his fellow men; he alone who has learned to say, "if meat make my brother to offend, I will eat no flesh while the world standeth;" he alone, whose conduct is determined by faith and hope and love in the Lord Jesus Christ, is spiritual, and may therefore judge all things and be judged by no man.

III. I should like to dwell on this truth at greater length, because I regard it as one of the most important subjects that can engage the attention of Christian men, in these days especially, when relations are so complex and cases of conscience are so many. I pass on, however, to notice in conclusion one other truth taught in the text, namely; the mode of the soul's growth in the knowledge of religious and spiritual truth. And here I shall be very brief.

It would have been one thing if the Apostle had said: "He that judgeth all things is spiritual." He would in such a statement have taught that the way to divine knowledge and to holiness lies through the intellect. In saying, on the other hand, that he that is spiritual judgeth all things, he teaches that *the path to divine knowledge lies through the heart.* The truth, thus stated, is the truth taught by Jesus himself in the words so often quoted: "If any man will do the will of God, he shall know the doctrine." I can not stop to unfold it. I can only reiterate the truth, that the path to divine knowledge is the path of obedience; that the growth in the knowledge of the Lord Jesus Christ is the result rather than the cause of growth in grace; that the Gospel addresses itself primarily to the heart and conscience, rather than to the understanding of man. It is only when man's spiritual, man's religious nature is awakened from the lethargy in which it is sunk by the pressure of earthly cares and by sin—it is only when the spiritual nature is aroused, that man can begin to know God or spiritual truth.

This statement might be applied in many directions. Let me only say to Christians, that it should impel them to seek in their hearts the source of their ignorance of God. It is in the coldness, may I not say the deadness of our spiritual sensibilities, that we shall find the reason why we can not appreciate the higher revelations of the New Testament. All of us doubtless find many of the statements of the New Testament dark sayings; but their darkness may all be resolved into our spiritual inertness. Only he that is spiritual can judge all things. Only he that is spiritual can discern the mind of the Spirit in the Word and the Providence of God. "Sin in the heart is the most fruitful source of error in the head," in respect to God's truth. No disciple will learn God's mind, until he shall come with ear and eye and heart all opened, and his spirit docile to the teachings of the Most High. This Bible, with its sublime unfoldings of the ways of God to men, will be a sealed book to every one who does not come to it quickened in the spirit. There is a sense, in which we must read it on our knees, if we would understand it in its relations to our own souls. For only on our knees, in communion with the Most High, can we gain that power of spiritual vision, which will enable us to read aright and judge aright the truths and facts, the promises and prophecies which it contains. He alone that is spiritual judgeth all things.

In view of this truth last announced, I speak to all before me, in announcing the Gospel of the Son of God. He that believeth hath life; he that believeth not hath not life. I hold up Christ to you, and on the authority of this revelation of the living God affirm, that the only path to that divine knowledge which is itself eternal life — the only method of growth in holiness — is through that spiritual quickening which comes through faith in the Son of God. This we declare to be the last hope at once of the world and of the single soul. He alone that is spiritual can judge all things — duty, truth, or eternal safety; and the one source of this spirituality is He who is the way to duty, the truth, and the life. Therefore, let us believe in Him, learn of Him, live in Him. Through Him alone can we obtain power to judge all things that God has already revealed; and through Him alone can we be prepared for that clearer revelation of God, when we shall see Him face to face, and know Him as we are known.

XXVI.
HOPE AND PURITY.

"And every man that hath this hope in him purifieth himself, even as he is pure."—I. John iii, 3.

The verse which immediately precedes the text is as follows: "Beloved, now are we the sons of God, and it doth not yet appear what we shall be: but we know that, when Christ shall appear, we shall be like Him; for we shall see Him as He is." In this verse, you will observe, there is a very clear statement of the relations which the Christian now sustains to God. "Beloved, now are we the sons of God." I wish that all of us, who have accepted Christ as our Saviour, might oftener reflect on the intimacy of the relation thus brought to view. Could we interpret all the dealings of God's providence in the light of it; could we not only believe, but feel that every thing is as it is, and comes just when and how it comes to us, because we have received not the spirit of bondage again to fear, but the spirit of adoption whereby we cry, "Abba, Father,"—how far more easy would it be for us, in times of disaster, to accept submissively what is ordered!

All, whom I am addressing, know that upon the

source from which they come, depends the spirit in which we accept both what is enjoyable and what is full of pain. It is hard for one to receive even favors from another whom he dislikes or has reason to distrust; but faithful are the wounds of a friend. A child easily forgives the chastisement of a loving parent, but will long cherish resentment against a stranger who has wronged him. And could we, who have heard it so often, and who have so earnestly professed our faith in its truth, feel in the hour of calamity, as we should feel it, the truth of these inspired words, "Beloved, now are we the sons of God," how easy it would be to respond to all affliction: "Father, thy will be done"!

The Apostle adds to the statement of our present relations, a statement concerning what is and what is not known of our future condition. This much is known: that when Christ shall appear, we shall be like Him; for we shall see Him as He is. All that the Word of God reveals of heaven may be resolved into this likeness of Christ. To attain the stature of the perfect man—this is the end, so far as we are concerned, of all labor, endurance, and worship. But there is much that is not revealed in regard to our future state. There are honors and pleasures which it was not possible to make known. The great Apostle, caught up to the third heavens, beheld in vision a glory which he might not reveal. "It doth not yet appear what we shall be." The prospect of this unspeakably blessed state constitutes the hope of the Christian, of which the beloved Apostle states the influence in the text: "And every man that hath this hope in Him purifieth himself, even as He is pure."

As thus understood, the text suggests for our meditation the purifying influence of the hope of the Gospel. The subject is a large one; and I can not hope to do more, in the course of a morning's sermon, than indicate a few thoughts, which I trust will not at once be dismissed from the mind, but will be cherished by all who hear me as subjects of future and earnest contemplation. Let me begin then, by calling your attention to a well-known general truth; namely, that so far as its influence on conduct is concerned, hope is always more powerful than its opposite, despair, or even than fear. Indeed, we may put despair out of the calculation. No statement of the kind is more nearly self-evident, than that melancholy is the parent of indolence; and the truth of no statement of the kind is better attested by observation. The comparison would better be made between hope and fear. And the superior power of the former is seen at once in the fact, that of the two it is the more positive. In addition to this, hope—that is, the expectation of some desired object—never paralyzes the powers, as does fear. The soul is often stunned by the anticipation of misery; but it is invigorated by the prospect of better things. And further than this, though fear may lead to violent and spasmodic effort, it seems to be lacking in power to call forth effort that will be sustained for a long period; the energy which it inspires soon dies away. On this account the Gospel seeks more often to excite hope than to awaken fear. It holds out to man more promises than threatenings. Its language is more often that of encouragement than that of foreboding. So, the Apostle Paul writes to the Church at Rome: "We are saved by hope." And so the Apostle John writes in the text: "And every man which hath this hope in Him, purifieth himself even as He is pure." This is the general ground of the Apostles' statement, that purity is the fruit of the hope of purity in Christ.

Perhaps we shall best make the statement practical, by endeavoring to answer three questions suggested by, and, as we shall see, answered in the text. What is this "purity," which it is the object of the Gospel to bestow? What are the sources of the "hope" that it will be ours? And what we are called to do, in order to make the hope effective in our lives? For that we are called to do something, is evident from the words of the text: "Every one that hath this hope in Him, purifieth *himself.*"

I. First, then, how shall we define or describe this purity of man? This is not so easy a question to answer, as at first sight it may seem to be. For in this world, at least, purity or holiness is conceived of as negative merely, as the absence of positive qualities. When we endeavor to image a perfect man, we instinctively think of him, not as possessing certain traits, but as wanting others. The positive, palpable thing in this world is sin. It has such thorough possession of us, that it has not only blunted our moral perceptions and dulled our moral sensibilities, and to some extent perverted our moral judgments, but it has also modified our prevailing moral conceptions. Living in a sinful atmosphere, ourselves weakened by the presence of sin within us, beholding its effects about us on every side, our first conception of holiness is negative; we think of it simply as the absence of sin. It is interesting to observe that this is the way in which the Old Testament most often portrays holiness. Take, for example, the Ten Commandments. The Ten Commandments are the best description of holiness that the Hebrews possessed. All of these, except two, are negative commandments; and this negative form was adopted just because the positive moral image before the minds of the Hebrew people was the image of sin.

I need not stop to show that this negative conception of purity must fail in power to invite and move men. The human soul has never been affected powerfully by mere negations. If holiness were only the absence of sin, it could not command the powers of the soul. Only positive beauties and happinesses command them. It is not enough, in order to woo the victim of poverty from his wretched abode, to dwell on the miseries and dangers of remaining in it. But once place before his senses, or before his imagination, another home abounding in sources of enjoyment, and then offer it to him; the positive picture will do what the negative picture was unable to do. It possesses what a great preacher calls, "The expulsive power of a new affection." Man will always be moved by a prospect of positive happiness as he can never be moved by a presentation, however eloquent, of his present miseries. For this reason, God gave to the world a positive ideal of moral purity; and that it might be more positive, He made the ideal real, in the Son whom He gave not only to die for, but also to live before men. We do not exhaust the meaning of the incarnation of the Son of God, therefore, when we say that He came to bear the iniquity of the world. Not at all. The world needed, quite as much as it needed an atonement, One who, by his life, would illustrate and make known the positive beauties of holiness.

There are two ways of thinking of light. We

may think of it simply as the absence of darkness. This is the negative view of it. Such a conception does not imply a knowledge of its positive beauties and glories. But this is not the only way of conceiving of it. We may think of it as shining in the midst of the refracting mists and clouds of the world; and, conceiving of it thus, we think of it as possessing the many and varied hues of the bow, that spans the earth after the storm. This will serve to illustrate the difference between the conception of purity which he has, who obtains it from the world around him, and the conception which he has, whose views of holiness are derived from a devout contemplation of Christ himself. The one does not discern its positive and many-hued beauties. The other seeing the Light of the world refracted by the storms in the midst of which the Light shines, discerns that purity is far more than the absence of sin; that there are beauties belonging to it, positive graces of character, faith, virtue, hope, meekness, patience, love; and these call forth the powers of the soul to secure them. You see, then, the vantage ground that we occupy who learn what purity is, through Christ. You see why the Apostles make so much of the life and example of the Lord; why it is that the New Testament is so full of statements like: "For me to live is Christ," and "If any man have not the spirit of Christ he is none of his;" and of exhortations like: "Let this mind be in you which was also in Christ," and "Let us run the race which is set before us, looking unto Jesus."

We often thank God for the gift of his Son. We call Him the most precious gift of the Father, the One above all others. We thank God for Him, because He is the one without whom atonement were impossible. No doubt these thanksgivings come from our hearts. But how much deeper would our gratitude be, if we could realize how much to us the person of Jesus is, as the embodiment of purity. We "purify ourselves as Christ is pure." Try for one moment to conceive what our views of holiness would have been, had He not lived on earth. How negative, how powerless to move the soul of man! We know, indeed, what the image of goodness was. We know what holiness meant to those, who, in the days of Rome's degeneracy, strove to attain it, not having known Christ. How full of despair were the lives of those devout men, whose only conception of purity was derived from surrounding corruption! How severe and unattractive their goodness! Brethren, the one adequate image of purity is Christ Jesus our Lord. And, therefore, all who would transform their deformed lives must live near to Him. In every view of Him, and in every sense of the words: "Without Him we can do nothing." When the perfect Christ is beyond the Christian's gaze, the appreciation of the beauty of holiness is lost, and the desire for holiness dies. It is an old and common-place exhortation, but one which you need often to hear: "Live as seeing Him who is invisible:" "Run the race set before you, looking unto Jesus."

II. Christ, then, is the image of purity that the disciple must keep constantly before him, if he would himself become so pure in heart as to enjoy the vision of God. But God not only gives us in Christ an *image* of purity, but a *hope* of purity as well. "Every man that hath this hope in Christ purifieth himself even as He is pure." What, let us ask, in the second place, is this hope?

I have already spoken of the power of hope as a

motive, especially of its superiority to fear; and I have called your attention to the fact that God who knew what is in man, in order to enable him to attain purity, gave to him a hope in Christ. It requires no words to convince us that Christ, as the example of purity, would do us little good, if we but beheld Him at an unattainable distance; if, when He was made known to us, it was also revealed that we could never become like Him. In that case, the revelation of the perfect Christ would be a torture and a curse. Whoever shall be finally lost, will endure no worse torment than the vision of that perfect holiness which he can never attain. Accordingly, it was not enough to give to man an adequate image of purity; it was necessary also to give him a good hope, that he could attain it. This God gives us in Christ. Every man that hath this *hope* in Him purifieth himself, even as He is pure.

One element of this hope is to be found in the *humanity* of Christ; in the fact that Christ was the Son of Mary as well as the Son of God, that He had a true body and a reasonable soul. The question of the divinity of Christ is not a more important question than that of his humanity. I am more often tempted to doubt the latter than the former. In every age of the Church, there have been earnest men, who, while taking the strongest possible ground with regard to his Godhood, have yet denied his real manhood; who believe Him to have been human only so far as his body was human. I believe the view to be not only radically wrong, but more than this, thoroughly destructive of man's hope of holiness in Christ. The very first element of that hope is that Christ, a man of like passions with ourselves, yet living a perfectly holy life, has shown us that holiness is not an impossibility to man. If Christ had no human soul, I can not understand wherein lies the hope that his life of perfect purity gives human souls. It is no encouragement to me to be told that an angel may maintain his purity. I derive no hope of holiness from the fact that a God dwelling in human flesh has maintained his perfection against the temptations which He in his sovereignty permitted to assail Him. My hope of holiness lies in the fact that our Lord took upon Him not the nature of angels, but the seed of Abraham; that He became our brother; and that, as our brother, with wants and passions responding to temptations from without, He overcame all temptation, and continued holy, harmless, undefiled, and separate from sinners. My hope of purity is based on his human life.

Another element of this hope of purity in Christ is to be found in his revelation of the *forgiving God*. Despair of attaining purity of soul often arises from the supposed distance of Christ from us, but oftener from the fear of God. The sense of justice in man, as well as the revelation which God has made of Himself in the world around us, leads man to despair. The question, "How shall man be just with a holy God?" he has been unable to answer. Despair of purity has been the result; and the result of despair, in its turn, has been deeper sin. Christ came to answer this question of questions. He revealed God's willingness to forgive; and explained his own life and death as the ground of God's pardon of man's sin. He revealed the great truth, that it was possible for the holy God to remember men's sins no more against them. He said to men, "Ask, and ye shall receive," and then taught them to ask for the forgiveness of sins. We have heard this so often, that we think of it as little as we do of the rising of the sun. But suppose that these words of Christ were blotted out; suppose that we were relegated to nature for an answer to the question: "Can man be just with God?" what would be the response of the heavens or the deep? Would it be such as to awaken in man a hope of holiness? No, friends. It is because Christ has revealed the great truths of God's fatherhood and of forgiveness through the death of his Son, that we dare to cherish any hope of purity whatever. So, again, the hope that purifies is a hope in Christ.

There is one other element of this hope. It is Christ's promise of *divine aid;* his promise of the indwelling of God. Christ not only gives us an example of purity in his human life, and the assurance of God's love for us; but, in order to make this hope in Him full assurance, He promises to every one who trusts in Him, the aid of God himself in becoming pure even as He is pure. We do not know much about the indwelling of the Holy Ghost. We can not explain it. We may not say that we can recognize his presence. But the fact is certain as the truth of the words of Christ. No promise is more clear and definite than Christ's promise of the Holy Ghost: "And I will pray the Father and He shall send you another Comforter, He shall guide you into all truth." "The Spirit helpeth our infirmities;" "He maketh intercession within us."

These then are the great elements of the hope in Christ, which, when we possess it, both enables and leads us to purify ourselves, as Christ is pure. The humanity of our example, his revelation of God's forgiveness, and his promise of the Holy Ghost. Without the hope thus constituted, holiness were an absolute impossibility. God help us not only to rejoice in the hope given us, but day by day to grow more grateful for the love which has bestowed it.

III. But finally, what, let us ask, are we to do in order to secure the blessing of purity, which the hope is intended to confer? To answer this question, let us turn to the text. "And every one that hath this hope in Him purifieth himself even as He is pure." He purifieth *himself*. The responsibility for our holiness is at last our own. The hope and the help are given of God, and given freely. Without this hope we must die. All the struggles and spasms of humanity, without divine aid, must prove in vain. But even with this aid the struggle is not to be given up. There is a time for sitting down and waiting patiently on God. But it is not so that we achieve holiness; this demands continued, earnest, unremitting warfare. God says to us, by his Apostle: "I have given you a perfect example. I promise you forgiveness of your sins. My power is ever at your call. Fear not; I am with you alway. But having given you this hope, the struggle must be waged by your own soul. Every man that hath this hope purifieth himself." Brethren, if, without this help and hope in Christ, we can do nothing, it is not less true that unless we co-work with God, it is impossible even for Him to endow us with the purity of Christ. Would that all of us might feel this truth! We have a great hope. We have every encouragement in this struggle for goodness. We are the heirs of exceeding great and precious promises. But the struggle is ours. "Every man purifieth himself." There is a dependence on God which springs from spiritual indolence. Let us pray against it, as we struggle against sin. For the struggle for purity is no short or easy conflict. The enemies are many and mighty. The field on which we war is one whose inequalities are all against us; and we ourselves are weak. Do we not all know how true this is—how terribly true each one of us shall find it to-morrow, in business, in our homes, in every place and in every circumstance? Against all these, we have this hope in Christ. Brethren, let us hold fast by the hope, knowing that without it we must remain forever in captivity to sin.

Every man that hath this hope in Christ purifieth himself. Hope is the inspiring motive. If we have no hope we shall faint in our exertions. But where is there ground for hope of purity out of Christ? Take this question with you, and ponder and answer it. Ask yourself: "What hope have I, apart from Him, that I shall conquer sin?" You will be compelled to confess that no other power can break the chains of your captivity to sin.

XXVII.

CHRIST A GIFT, NOT A DEBT.

"Thanks be unto God for his unspeakable gift."—II. Corinthians ix, 15.

Commentators differ as to the exact relation, sustained by the verse, which I have chosen for my text, to the passage which it concludes. In the passage, the Apostle Paul refers to a collection which he wishes taken in the Church of Corinth, for the poor Christians of Jerusalem. He had boasted at Philippi, of the readiness of the Corinthian Church to make this contribution. He now expresses the hope, that the result of the visit of Titus among them will prove that his boast was not vain. He asks them to remember both that "God loveth a cheerful giver," and that God is able to make all grace abound toward them; that they, having all-sufficiency in all things, may abound in every good work. Some commentators, among whom is Calvin, suppose that the "unspeakable gift," for which Paul here gives thanks, is that grace of giving, wrought in them by the Holy Ghost, by which Gentile Christians in Greece were led—or would be led, as he hoped—to sympathize with and make sacrifices for Jewish Christians in

Jerusalem; separated, though they were, by both difference of race and the broad expanse of the Mediterranean Sea. And certainly, this grace of giving was an "unspeakable gift;" a gift past the understanding of the times in which it was first manifested. What possible interest could Gentiles have in Jews, except the interest of enmity; or, if Gentiles could sympathize with Jews attached to them by ties of neighborhood, what possible ground could be imagined for the sympathy of Gentiles in Greece with Jews so far removed in space and circumstance, as were those who lived in Jerusalem. Such giving was a new thing in the world. It was a product of the new religion. Roman civilization had never produced it. The heathen intelligence could not understand the motives that impelled to it. It was, as I have said, a distinctly Christian grace; and the great Apostle to the Gentiles—accustomed to make large generalizations, seeing in the exercise of this grace of giving the prophecy of the coming day, when neither national nor racial distinctions would prove barriers to the outflow of human sympathy, seeing in it the harbinger of the day when " man to man would brother be "— could not restrain his " running pen," from writing the grateful exclamation: " Thanks be to God for his unspeakable gift."

Other commentators take a somewhat different view. They point to the fact that Paul was not unaccustomed to give vent to his active religious emotions in outbursts of thanksgiving, even during the process of exact and subtle argumentation. And this, they say, is an instance of his general habit. "This," says Dr. Charles Hodge, " is the more natural interpretation; because it is Paul's custom, when speaking either of the feeble love, or of the trivial gifts of believers to one another, to refer in contrast to the infinite love and unspeakable gift of God in Christ to us. The passage, therefore, ought to stand, as I have no doubt the vast majority of the readers of the Bible understand it, as an outburst of gratitude to God for the gift of his Son."

For the purposes of this discourse, it is not necessary to make choice between the two interpretations, which differ formally rather than really. For, if we suppose that Paul referred immediately to the grace of beneficence, he referred to it as one of the results of the gift of Christ to man. And if he had immediately in mind, the bestowment on man of the Son of God as a Redeemer, he was led to the expression of his gratitude, by the thought that among his benedictions is this; that He has wrought the new grace of benevolence in the heart of his disciples. Whichever interpretation, therefore, we adopt, the text is the expression of Paul's gratitude to God for the gift of his Son. With this understanding of its meaning, I have chosen it, as bringing before us a subject of meditation appropriate to the week during which our thoughts will dwell on the Sacrament of the Lord's Supper. In that ordinance, we shall remove from our minds all subordinate religious themes; and in our hearts all other emotions will yield to that of gratitude. And the subject alike of our meditations and of our thanksgiving will be the gift of God's Son; the gift in whom all others meet and from whom all others flow.

That Jesus Christ is a gift; that He is an unspeakable gift; and that we should give thanks for Him; these are the three simple but profound thoughts, on which the text invites us to dwell.

I. And, first, Jesus Christ, and, therefore, his redemption is a *gift*.

If Christ did not stand in the mind of the Apostle as a bestowment, why did He give thanks to God? If He was sent as something owed to man; if He came in obedience to the impulse of the divine justice, gratitude to God was not the appropriate emotion with which to meet and receive Him. Justice may call forth our adoration, as every moral quality must, when revealed in the perfection in which it exists in the divine mind. It may awaken our awe; for all moral qualities possess sublimity. But we do not thank God for his justice; for it is of the nature of justice that it is owed. Your heart does not really overflow with gratitude, when a debtor discharges his obligation to you, or when a judge endeavors fairly, that is, justly, to determine a controversy to which you are a party. Justice is your right; this you may demand; this nothing can take from you. You may be the creature of a day; you may be the most incorrigible of sinners; your heart may be deceitful above all things, and desperately wicked; and your hands may have been active in violating every commandment of the decalogue; still you have a right to demand that the Almighty will be just in all his dealings with you; you have a right to demand that not a flaw of unrighteousness shall characterize them; and when this has been done you owe Him no thanks; because justice with Him, or any being, is not a matter that lies properly within the province of the choice.

This fact, theologians have sometimes expressed by the statement, that justice is an attribute of God's moral nature, while mercy is a trait of his moral character. That is to say, if there is a moral being on the throne of the universe, He must be just. We can not doubt it. The constitution of the universe reveals it and our own consciences affirm it. There is, indeed, not a physical, but a moral imperative, binding God not to do unrighteousness. But there is no such moral imperative, binding God to go beyond justice, and to do all that mercy suggests. If there were such an imperative, mercy would no longer be mercy, but something else. Hence the moral law does not command mercy. We are commanded to give God his due, and to give their dues to our fellow-men. But mercy, we are not commanded but besought to exhibit and to exercise. Thus, as a living theologian has pointed out,* the great dramatist was right, when, in the comedy of the "Merchant of Venice," he represented the Court as powerless to compel Shylock to be merciful to Antonio, and to forego the exact forfeiture nominated in the bond; and right also when he made Portia, the lawyer, say—

> "The quality of mercy is not *strained:*
> It droppeth as the gentle dew from heaven
> Upon the place beneath."

It is for this reason, also, that while one may confidently predict that the Moral Being, governing the Universe, will be just, no one may confidently predict that He will be merciful. I read, during my summer vacation, translations of all the plays of the greatest of the Greek dramatic poets. Throughout all of them is the awful thought, not so much expressed, as implied, that the Fate above the Deities will be just; following holiness with reward, but

---

* Shedd: "Sermons to the Natural Man." See the sermon, "The exercise of mercy optional with God."

pursuing sin with slow, it may be, but with certain vengeance. But in the pages of the lofty and profound Æschylus I find no hint that Fate is merciful. And what are the great false religions of the world—the religions that have lasted for ages—but religions of fear? And why are they religions of fear, but that, along with the consciousness of sin, there has always been the confident expectation that God will be remorselessly and inexorably just?

Attempts there have been, to prove that mercy and justice may be resolved into one attribute; to prove that however different they may be in their manifestations, at bottom they are one. But the attempt has never been made elsewhere than in a Christian land. The mistake has never taken possession of minds, except those prepared for it by their knowledge that God has revealed himself to be merciful. And the theory, even in a Christian land, was never widely influential. Justice and mercy can not be resolved into one attribute, until it can be shown, and it never can be shown, that the condemnation of a criminal, and the pardon of the same criminal, are the offspring of the same intuition. Therefore, though no special revelation was needed to show God to be just, a special revelation was needed to show God to be merciful. Men know Him to be just; the physical laws of the universe, the idea of moral government, and their own hearts all proclaim it. But how could men know that He is merciful, unless the heavens had been opened, and a revelation, such as we possess in Jesus Christ, had been made to the sinful and despairing race?

It is at this point that we grasp the exact significance of the word "gift," as applied to our Lord

Jesus Christ. "Thanks be to God for his unspeakable *gift.*" He is at once the revelation and the embodiment of the mercy of God; of that trait of character which leads the Most High to do more, unspeakably more for man than He owes. And, therefore, Jesus Christ must be accepted as a gift, or he is not accepted at all. You and I must come to the cross of Christ confessing that our redemption is not a debt owed to us. This is the first condition of salvation. This is the meaning of conviction of sin. There is no such thing as conviction of sin, if God owes forgiveness to the sinner. How can the soul be bowed down before the Most High God, if, on any ground and in any sense, it is true that God owes salvation to him? The same truth is involved in the exercise of repentance. Repentance would be utterly out of place, were any obligation laid on God to bestow redemption on man. And so with prayer; for prayer is not a demand for that which is ours of right; it is a supplication for favors that are beyond our right. Thus redemption stands or falls, and the Christian life stands or falls, as Christ is accepted as a gift or as a debt. Thus does this truth take its proper place at the very forefront of Christian experience. It is the vestibule which we must enter, in order to pass into the Holy of Holies, where God reveals Himself as our Redeemer.

I am aware that doctrinal discussion is, by some, regarded as entirely inappropriate to a season, so tender as that which this day we begin. But religious emotion is grounded on religious truth; and religious truth must be accepted; and to be accepted it must be understood. And I know no point on which, in these days especially, we are so apt to be mistaken or confused, as we are on this very point, that our blessed Lord as a Redeemer was not owed to the race, and is not now owed to a single soul. From the incarnation to the redemption of the last soul received into glory, salvation is of grace. And the anthem most appropriate, both to earth and to heaven, is one composed in the spirit of the great Apostle's devout exclamation: "Thanks be to God for his unspeakable gift."

II. The Apostle characterizes this great gift of God by an adjective that may well employ for a time our thoughts. Christ is not only a gift of God; He is the *unspeakable* gift.

But if He is unspeakable, how am I, by employing *speech*, to describe what He is, and what He has done and will do for man? How, in other words, is a preacher to go about describing that of which the chief trait is that it is indescribable. Of course, words must fail here, and not words only, but thought. Time is too short, eternity alone will suffice for us adequately to learn and adequately to express the blessedness that is in Him, in whom are hid all the treasures of power and wisdom; who is Himself the fullness of the Godhead bodily. The most that we can hope to do, is to say certain things which will deepen our impression of the truth, that He is indeed an unspeakable gift.

And, I ask you, first, to endeavor to imagine the state of the world without Christ. Suppose that He had never been given to man. This seems an easy thing to do, and yet I suppose no harder task was ever proposed to the imagination. It is as hard to form a picture of the world as it would have been had Christ not come, as it would be to imagine the physical earth without the shining of the sun. For the earth owes not more, certainly, to the light and heat of the centre of our system, than man does to the incarnation of the Son of God. If you can imagine the confusion worse confounded, the utter wreck of the planet on which we live if the sun were utterly removed, you can begin to appreciate what the race would have been, had God not bestowed upon us the unspeakable gift of his Son.

Or if this method seems too barren, because negative, let us try one more positive. Let us recall the great truth, that the gift is divine, and that his sacrifice was a real sacrifice of divinity. I say that Jesus of Nazareth was divine. I mean by this, that He is God, co-equal with the Father and the Spirit. If this is not true, the Bible is not true. If this is not taught, nothing is taught in the word of God. Had the writers of the New Testament used the utmost care to select words that would express their belief that the Son of Mary is God over all, blessed forever more; what more could they have done, than has been done by them? Is there any attribute of Deity that they withhold from Him? Is there any work competent to Deity alone, that He does not perform? Is there any honor worthy to be paid alone to the Supreme Ruler of the universe, that they do not assert should be paid to Him equally with the Father and the Holy Ghost? I know of none. In all the great creeds and confessions of the Church, this truth stands out like a mountain against the evening sky. Christ is God; the gift is an unspeakable gift, because Jesus of Nazareth is equal with the Father.

And now, how is this divinity given to man?—for it is as a gift that we are to regard Christ. I answer, that when the Word became flesh and dwelt among us, the divinity that was his, though used for man, was never used for Himself. Being equal with God, the Son of Man never employed his divinity in his own behalf, but always for the world He came to save. This is a remarkable fact. It is not only that Jesus was divine, but that his divinity, during his whole earthly life, was wholly given to man. Read the Gospels and see how true this is. There were displays enough of his divine power, when on earth, to satisfy every earnest searcher after truth that He was all that He claimed to be. He raised the dead, He stilled the tempest, He healed the sick, the deaf, the blind. All this He did, not by a power that came and went, but that was his inherently. But He never employed it for Himself. Divine though He was, He accepted our limitations. He was born of a woman—born under the law. He was subject to his parents, and worked at his father's trade—supporting Himself, not by miracles, but by hard labor. Thus He lived for thirty-three years; and though tempted again and again to exert his divinity for himself, He never did. He emptied Himself; He gave Himself utterly for you and me. Take up the crises of his life—like the temptation. Do you doubt his divine power, who took five loaves and two small fishes and with them fed five thousand? But He refuses to command the stones to be made bread for Himself. Hear the shouts of the people: "Hosanna to the Son of David!" Do you doubt his power to seize Jerusalem, who, a few days before, called Lazarus back from the under-world to his earthly life? And yet He does not seize Jerusalem; but is led as a lamb to the slaughter. The Roman soldiers mock Him with reed and purple, and bind about his aching brow a crown of thorns; and He knows that legions of angelic hosts are at his command. But He submits, until he cries "It is finished." Jesus was God, and had the power of God; but that power being given to man, it was never used for Himself. And if the power that belongs alone to the Almighty is unspeakable,—our Redeemer, because He used it for man alone, is an unspeakable gift.

We must add to the gift of his divinity the gift of his human nature also. If He did not employ his divine power for Himself, neither did He, as a man, live or die for Himself. I do not make this statement, at this time, as a theological truth. It is true, that Christ's life and death constitute the one perfect sacrifice to the holiness of God for the sins of men. He, who knew no sin, was made sin for us, that we might be made the righteousness of God in Him. This relation of the life and death of Christ to the law of God, announced and elaborated in the inspired epistles of the New Testament, can not be too often or too deeply pondered. But this is not the aspect of the truth on which just now I insist. Not only from the epistles in which Christ's life is explained, but from the Gospels also in which Christ's life is narrated, it is clear that every hour and act and thought of his human life were given to man. It is, indeed, a difficult thing to separate the divinity from the humanity of our Lord in our thoughts of them, blent as they are in a single personality. Great is the mystery of godliness, God manifest in the flesh. But this much is clear; that we do not include all the elements of this great gift, when we say that Christ never used his divinity for Himself. It is also true, that He never employed his *humanity* for Himself. All his human acts, as well as all his miracles, were performed under the sovereign control of a single aim; and that aim was the redemption of men. All that He did as a man, He did in order that men might not perish, but might have everlasting life.

One aspect of this truth, as I have said, is brought out in the Epistles; another is presented in the Gospels. It is the Gospel view of it, on which I wish now to speak. Christ, as there represented, was devoted to this single aim, as never mother was devoted to her child. For this He prayed and wept and besought both God and man; for this He had not where to lay his head; for this He endured the contradiction of enemies, the misinterpretation of friends, and the hidings of his Father's face; for this He trod the wine-press alone. This redemption of men, as the ruling motive of his life, was never suffered to fall below consciousness. It attended Him on every journey; it determined every conversation; it was the theme of every address; it led Him into the company of scribes and Pharisees, and of publicans and sinners; it made Him many-sided, as it made Him a man of one idea. The idea that men might not perish but might have everlasting life, ruled Him as no other idea ever ruled another man. It subordinated to itself all other purposes and loves and aims, and determined the life of his true body and reasonable soul, more thoroughly even than ambition moved Satan, when he made war in heaven. Brethren, it is as we thus unite Christ's divinity and Christ's humanity, and recall how utterly each was given to man, that we begin to appreciate the Apostle's words: "Thanks be to God for his unspeakable gift."

But there are other methods by which the propriety of this great adjective "unspeakable" may be made evident. Consider, again, that the gift of

Christ is the gift not only of his divinity and humanity, but of every other gift of God. Because He has given Christ, He gives all the rest. We are accustomed, in our ordinary conversation, to make a distinction between the blessings of the providence and the blessings of the grace of God. The latter we speak of as coming to us through Christ. But, brethren, through whom do the others come? Are they not ours because Christ is ours? Why, do you suppose, is this world upheld in existence? Why do day and night return with ceaseless fidelity? Why has God not left Himself without a witness in the world in giving us fruitful seasons, and filling our hearts with food and gladness? If I read the Word of God aright, we are taught to pray for daily bread in the name of Christ, as really as for the forgiveness of sin and the indwelling of the Holy Ghost. And if I understand the doctrine of providence, there is a beneficent providence, just because God has given Christ to be the Redeemer of the world.

Or again, in illustrating the propriety of this great word "unspeakable," consider the fullness of the spiritual blessings that are ours in Christ. I mean by fullness, the rounded, full-orbed character of the salvation that is ours in Him. Christ is a Redeemer, because He saves the whole man. We are apt to attach a very narrow meaning to the word salvation. The fact that strikes us most forcibly, is our guilt before God; and we call Christ a Saviour, chiefly because He saves us from the immediate consequences of our guilt; because "there is no more condemnation to them that are in Christ Jesus." But this is a very inadequate view of salvation. There is not a faculty of mind that He does not reinvigorate; there is not a power of our bodies that He will not endow with perpetual youth; there is not a want for which He does not provide; there is not a sorrow that He does not meet with everlasting consolation; there is not a capacity of our being for good and for happiness, for whose satisfaction throughout eternity, He has not made most certain and abundant provision. How are we to describe such a Redeemer? What adjective in our vocabulary will positively qualify Him? We can only do what Paul did; we must content ourselves with mere negation. We can only say: "Thanks be to God for his unspeakable gift."

I know that I have not exhausted the subject, for it is inexhaustible. I know that I have been very inadequate in my method; but what method would be adequate? It is just this inadequacy of speech and thought, that Paul means to assert when he employs the word. I have tried to show that Christ's divinity was given to us, and that his human life was a thorough sacrifice for us; that He not only gives us Himself, but is the source of every other gift of God; and that the gifts that flow to us through Him meet us at every point, and provide for our highest possible happiness throughout eternity. And yet, how poor, how feeble, how inadequate a presentation! And, brethren, it would be poor and inadequate were an angel to take up the theme, and chant Christ's praises in celestial strains. For a finite being can not grasp the infinite; a created mind can not fathom the love that passeth knowledge. At last, he, like Paul, could say no more than you can say, than I have tried to say to-day: "Thanks be to God for his unspeakable gift."

III. And thus confessing our inability, and that of all created intelligence, I pass to the last thought suggested by the text: "*Thanks* be to God for his unspeakable gift."

As Paul can not describe the gift, so he does not attempt to measure the gratitude due to God for its bestowment. It does, indeed, seem a lame and impotent conclusion to the treatment, however poor, of such a theme, that we should close with a term so ordinary, so often and so carelessly employed as this term "thanks." Is it not a striking commentary on the impossibility of our doing anything for God, that with the whole sweep of Christ's redemption in view, we can only employ a word, which, more perhaps than any other, we use as meaning almost nothing at all? How often we repeat this word "thanks" without discrimination, without meaning! It leaps to our lips, as a matter of course. Most often we forget that we said it. But this is all that we can say to God for his unspeakable gift. And yet, poor through constant and unmeaning employment as the word is, the thing that it expresses is the best and the costliest offering we can make. For gratitude is protean in its expressions. It includes all that we are. It involves the bestowment of ourselves on God. And so, in view of our subject, let each of us ask himself: Am I grateful? Does my heart beat with real gratitude to God for the bestowment of a benediction I had no right and no reason, other than his mercy, to expect? Brethren, let us ask this question on our knees, in the solitude of our places of secret prayer. And having asked this question, let us not dare to shrink from another, still more searching: "How am I manifesting my gratitude?" When you shall ask that question sincerely, doubt not that there will rise before you the painful vision of opportunities neglected, and work unfinished, and souls uncared for, and time moving swiftly on.

Christ is a gift, an unspeakable gift; but just because He is a gift, He must be accepted before He can be a blessing. He may be rejected. He may, if not positively rejected, be neglected. To reject or to neglect Him, is to place one's self under the Law: and the declaration of the Law is this: "The soul that sinneth, it shall die."

www.ingramcontent.com/pod-product-compliance
Lightning Source LLC
Chambersburg PA
CBHW022106290426
44112CB00008B/566